SIXGUNS
AND
BULLSEYES

and

AUTOMATIC PISTOL
MARKSMANSHIP

BY WILLIAM REICHENBACH

SIXGUNS

AND

BULLSEYES

and

AUTOMATIC PISTOL MARKSMANSHIP

BY WILLIAM REICHENBACH

Skyhorse Publishing

Skyhorse Publishing books may be purchased in bulk at special
discounts for sales promotion, corporate gifts, fund-raising, or
educational purposes. Special editions can also be created to
specifications. For details, contact the Special Sales Department,
Skyhorse Publishing, 307 West 36th Street, 11th Floor, New
York, NY 10018 or info@skyhorsepublishing.com.

Skyhorse® and Skyhorse Publishing® are registered trademarks
of Skyhorse Publishing, Inc., a Delaware corporation.

Visit our website at www.skyhorsepublishing.com.

10 9 8 7 6 5 4 3 2 1

Library of Congress Cataloging-in-Publication Data is available
on file.
ISBN: 978-1-62087-372-4

Printed in the United States of America

SIXGUNS

AND

BULLSEYES

**"COME ON, RICKEY. GET HOT!
Make this last one a 'Ten' too!"**

EDITOR'S NOTE

William Reichenbach's

SIXGUNS AND BULLSEYES

AND

AUTOMATIC PISTOL MARKSMANSHIP

by Dr. Jim Casada

This volume of classic firearms titles brings together what
were, in their original format, two distinct works. Their inclusion within the confines of the covers of a single book is
eminently sensible. For starters, both efforts were written
by the same author, William Reichenbach. Moreover, each
of the treatments deals with handguns, and each was intended to complement the other. Indeed, when the two
works were published by Thomas Samworth under the imprint of his Small-Arms Technical Publishing Company,
Automatic Pistol Marksmanship was described, in the promo-
tional literature printed on the dust jacket and issued sepa-
rately, as "a companion volume and continuation . . . of
Sixguns and Bullseyes." Together these "small Sams," as
they are sometimes called in the out-of-print book trade,
have long been cherished by handgun enthusiasts. Now, after many decades out of print, they are again available in
what is literally a "two for the price of one" situation.

It is somewhat surprising that these two slender volumes
have remained out of print—and largely unavailable even
in the used sporting and gun book trade—for so long. Certainly the works were positively received when first pub-

lished, and they have subsequently been accorded positive evaluations by gun bibliophiles. For example, Brian R. Smith, in his important reference work *Samworth Books: A Descriptive Bibliography* (1990), offers insight on the enduring intrinsic and material values of the duo. Referring to *Sixguns and Bullseyes,* he writes, "The methods [of shooting] expounded by the author are of merit and interest," and he finds *Automatic Pistol Marksmanship* to be an interesting little volume, recommending it as "a worthwhile . . . addition to the handgun enthusiast's library." Smith further notes that most of the subsequent works in the general subject area "borrowed heavily from the methods and techniques Reichenbach presented."

Another noted student and bibliophile specializing in the shooting sports, Ray Riling, also has praise for the two volumes. In *Guns and Shooting: A Bibliography* (1982), he describes *Sixguns and Bullseyes* as a "brief but satisfactory coverage of the art of handgun shooting." Riling rates *Automatic Pistol Marksmanship* as a solid primer for those interested in "practical" shooting with handguns.

The passage of some threescore years since these books initially appeared under the editorial and publishing genius of "Mr. Sam," as Thomas Samworth was known to his close associates, has done nothing to dull their luster. But it should also be quickly noted that Reichenbach's "small Sams" have always been something of bibliographical redheaded stepchildren in comparison with some of the larger, more popular Small-Arms Technical Publishing Company imprints, such as Roy F. Dunlap's *Gunsmithing* or John "Pondoro" Taylor's *African Rifles & Cartridges.* Unquestionably this circumstance is due in part to the fact that both works appeared when the United States was in the depths of the Great Depression. Many folks were far too busy trying to keep the wolf from the door to think about books that focused on recreational shooting. Therein, too, lies at least one reason the books so seldom appear in listings from the out-of-print trade.

Indeed, neither of Reichenbach's efforts makes an appearance in one of the most commonly consulted guides to prices for books in this field, Richard A. Hand's *A Bookman's Guide to Hunting, Shooting, Angling and Related Subjects: A Compilation of Over 13,450 Catalog Entries with Prices and Annotations, both Bibliographical and Descriptive* (1991). Given that Hand compiled the list from catalogs by booksellers, this is a sound indication of just how seldom the books are offered. I have seen *Sixguns and Bullseyes* listed for sale only twice, both times in 1989, the price in each case being $100 for a decent but by no means pristine copy. I acquired one of these copies, in very good condition but with a tatty dust jacket, and felt I had done reasonably well; but the fact remains that the price tag is quite a leap from the cost of $1.50, at which the book originally sold. Another indication that both Reichenbachs are not readily available is found in the pages of the *National Union Catalog of Pre-1956 Imprints*. Only a handful of copies of each book are located in major American libraries.

These considerations do not, however, suggest that original copies of the two Reichenbachs are extraordinarily valuable. According to Brian Smith, foremost authority on Samworth books, later printings of *Sixguns and Bullseyes* "are relatively common, and often seen in the dust jacket. First impressions are not all that rare, if one is persistent." He considers *Automatic Pistol Marksmanship* to be somewhat more difficult to locate. My opinion is that Smith understates their rarity, and certainly there is no denying the fact that both books are choice collector's items. With some luck and, as Smith says, persistence, you can probably locate and acquire copies of both books, dust jackets intact, for a total of $250 to $300.

The printing history of *Sixguns and Bullseyes* is an interesting one. An earlier version of the book appeared in 1935, under the intriguing if somewhat misleading title *The Elusive Ten: A New Deal in Revolver Shooting* (the "new deal" comes from the phrase President Franklin D. Roosevelt used to describe his program to get the United States out of the grips of the Depression). It was published by an obscure operation, and in all likelihood the author underwrote the publishing costs. Be that as it may, reviewers praised it as "the best handgun manual ever written," and that likely explains why Samworth said that "its excellence and general application were such that the edition was soon exhausted." The new version, published in 1936, was, as Ray Riling says, "virtually a new edition," and in his preface to the new edition Reichenbach indicates that the book was completely rewritten. Perhaps more important, it also benefited from the keen, experienced editorial eye of Thomas Samworth, so much so that the author suggested that Samworth had "taken great pains to 'make the first edition look sick.'" It might be added that the changed title was also an improvement in that it provided a better clue to the book's contents. As mentioned above, there were several printings (or impressions) of this book — in 1936 (in addition to the initial printing) and 1943, distinguishable from the first impression by the ad page dates and the fact that the place of publication is given as Plantersville, South Carolina, rather than Onslow County, North Carolina.

There was but a single edition of *Automatic Pistol Marksmanship* (published in 1937), and to my knowledge this is the first time the book has been reprinted. There were, however, several printings of the first edition. Like *Sixguns and Bullseyes*, the first printing is readily distinguishable from subsequent impressions by the place of publication listed on the title page, the first impression having been made in Onslow County, North Carolina, the later impressions in Plantersville, South Carolina. The book is also quite fragile because of the thin, embossed cover (present in *Sixguns and Bullseyes* as well), and Smith recommends acquisition of "a second copy for reading purposes."

Little in the way of personal information is available on William Reichenbach. He does not appear in any of the standard biographical directories. We can determine he was married because he dedicates *Sixguns and Bullseyes* to his wife, Agnes. In truth, though, the dedication to *Automatic Pistol Marksmanship* is more revealing, for it is redolent of an author who almost certainly deserves description as an eccentric if not an out-and-out curmudgeon. It reads: "Dedicated to 'The Left Wing' of Our Pistol Shooting Fraternity." That can be interpreted in various ways, from political leanings to (as I suspect was the case) the fact that the author was a left-handed shooter.

Reichenbach wrote in a chatty, almost conversational fashion, and some critics have condemned him for this. On the other hand, his down-to-earth style makes for easy reading and easy understanding, two key characteristics of manuals or primers, as these two books were intended to be. Reichenbach actually took considerable delight in flaunting his "common man" approach and said, "It was not in me to talk highfalutingly to my brothers," and he reveled in "blissfully ignoring all literary precepts." That may be overstating matters a bit, because whatever the author's views, those of Samworth were indelibly imprinted on the published works. Samworth knew the gun fraternity backwards and forwards, and what he did was to make Reichenbach a readable author without robbing his books of their peculiar flair and homely appeal. Those hallmarks, along with the enduring value of the books' contents, explain why the two works reprinted here have weathered so well the demanding test of time. Intensely practical, easily read, and retaining their timeliness to a surprising degree, *Sixguns and Bullseyes* and *Automatic Pistol Marksmanship* are now united in a single volume.

Jim Casada

ROCK HILL, SOUTH CAROLINA

SIXGUNS
AND
BULLSEYES

By

WILLIAM REICHENBACH

Illustrations by Philip Plaistridge

Skyhorse Publishing

Dedicated
to my wife
AGNES REICHENBACH

CONTENTS

Part 1

Part 2

PREFACE TO THE NEW EDITION

We are in a position now to judge whether my idea of a Revolver Manual deserves a place in the market—The first edition of "THE ELUSIVE TEN" was sold out within a few months.

The original manual seemed quite a bold undertaking. The critics—the big shots, you know—stared at each other in sheer amazement at the effrontery of the unknown amateur.

"What the h—?" they muttered and—However, their fairness was above reproach! They gave the book a break!

After reading it, they were actually pleased over "THE ELUSIVE TEN" and they did not withhold their praise. But then, could they possibly have been Experts in our sport and be unfair at the same time? Our sport isn't made that way!

There was one aesthetically minded bloke who, although quite taken with the matter treated, criticised my writing style—as being too conversational, as being too much at variance with academic concepts.

Nevertheless, the enthusiastic approval of all the many readers (from as far away as New Zealand) who took the trouble to send in their reactions,

(Among them many ambitious police officers—bless their hearts) made me wonder who in h— could have been right?

No! It was not in me to talk highfalutingly to my brothers.

In this, the second edition which I *rewrote entirely*, I thought it best to go on pleasing the "SHOOTER" and not the professional Aesthet— since I do not seem to be able to please both at the same time!

Blissfully ignoring all literary precepts, therefore, I shall release this edition. Old friends will not recognize the manual in its present new form since it not only has been remodeled from the ground up, but it also has been considerably enlarged, in response to numerous requests. (Double its former number of pages). I have, among others, added several chapters on the "dope" hinted at in the first edition and have cut loose generally. The first-edition-readers should get a whole lot more out of this book and, doubtlessly, they will chuckle when they now find a more or less friendly "dig" here and there.

My publisher, to use his own words, has taken great pains to "make the first edition look sick" and I think that he has succeeded.

May this "Sixguns and Bullseyes" make me as many (and more) friends as the original one did!

WILLIAM REICHENBACH
Wantagh, L. I.
New York.

MY ALIBI

Ah—Life sometimes takes unexpected turns!—Permit me to tell how the first "Elusive Ten" came into being.

If some irresponsible companion had not induced me, after many years of estrangement from our sport, to take up handgun-shooting again, the idea of the manual might, forever, have stayed hidden in the folds of my brain.

As if I had been waiting for just such a slight impulse, I fell to shooting with considerable zest.

Being sort of thorough-going, I shot and studied at the same time. Although I shot well, I was not happy. The fact that many of my associates did not seem to catch on to the art was extremely disturbing to me. They assured me that they had studied all available literature on the subject. That they were trying, pains-takingly and untiringly, was obvious. I proceeded to give them some pointers. And lo and behold! (what it means I don't know, but lo and behold!) they progressed.

And an idea was born.

Maybe, (I said to myself) there are other shooters who have tried and have never succeeded? Maybe I have a message to convey? Maybe I have stumbled onto something too valuable to be allowed to perish in obscurity? Maybe I can satisfy a demand for an illuminating treatise? Just try and stop me.

I was certain, almost from the very beginning, that the cause for the poor performances generally seen in revolver shooting, was to be found in inadequate knowledge of the true technique. Coaching, with rare exceptions, was done along antiquated lines, wholly lacking in results. My studies had convinced me that only a radical departure from the trodden paths of outdated teaching would provide the solution to the difficulty.

Should I let it rest at that?

No, the trouble with me was that I was so serious about this thing that I could not keep it for myself. I felt that I *must* relate my own experience so that others may benefit. If the reader should suffer my book in silence, and if I could not stir him out of his lethargy and force him to take the matter just as seriously as I do, then my writing technique must be blamed. The matter itself, I know, was worth any one's while.

The question, therefore, seemed to be less one of justification for the conception of this book than one of finding apologies for its style, or lack of style. Although old-timers might shoot me on sight, I had to gamble on being useful to you, my dear reader. You alone were to be the judge.

I prided myself in calling my brain-child a "manual." It probably is one. It sounds rather nice. To start with, I had made a firm resolution to let the manual deal solely with the technique of holding, aiming and firing a revolver. I did *not* want to talk about loading and unloading a gun nor about the procedure for inspection. Furthermore, if the reader were to seek information on internal and external ballistics, I felt that I could safely advise him to ask one of the gun-cranks down the block. They are more numerous than wild rabbits. The bit of technical stuff which might be found in my manual was just thrown in to impress the student.

As for the title, I believed it should have reference to the exasperating goddess of the confirmed target shooter, namely, "The Elusive Ten." The "Ten" referring, of course, to the "Ten-Ring" of the target. But why should the "Ten" be described as elusive? If the reader did not already know the answer, he soon would.

Satisfaction at having realized a latent propensity for writing, can be complete only when the driving factor is the honest urge to submit knowledge gained in study, knowledge which we know is lacking in many quarters.

It seems simply unbearable to know that with the excellent material we have in our country, we should have so few successful revolver shots.

The irony of it!

The revolver was invented and perfected right here and it actually played an important role in the building of our vast empire and yet we are essentially *not* a nation of revolver shots.

Europe has been much more consistent. There the modern automatic was perfected and the actual percentage of fine marksmen over there brings home, quite forcibly, how really sad the picture looks in our country. What is the cause of that? It cannot be blundering legislation alone, controlling the distribution of hand-arms, because Europe too has legislation of various kinds. Am I to believe that it is nothing but lethargy, pure and simple? Indifference toward a sport which imposes so much control over one's self? Are we Americans really steeped so much in nervous haste, in impatiently tackling the more vivacious sports only, sports which demand feverish action? Football, baseball, boxing, etc.? Not quite! Take fishing, or its more scientific branch: Bait Casting. We have there many thousands of really good performers. Why should that sport which surely demands skill, patience, knowledge, nerve control to a high degree, produce so many experts? The answer is simple: The equipment and the technique have been developed methodically and logically. Cannot we say this about Revolver Shooting also? I am afraid that the answer must be partly in the negative. Without a logically developed technique we discourage too many aspirants. It appears as if only sporadic efforts have ever been made on the part of those that *should* have been leaders, namely the experts in our sport. It is true that we have had and still have some remarkable shots, but they either tackled the job of distributing their knowledge in quite an unsuitable or dispirited, way, or not at all.

I have made an effort in this manual to fill the gap and do hope that interest will be stirred up among the "coming experts" to cause them to take a leading roll in the development and the distribution of the true technique of Revolver Shooting.

We in America still cling to the revolver, as witness our vast police forces, guards, most clubs, etc. How vitally important then is it to provide them with revolver "technique" something which up to now they evidently do not possess.

This new Manual contains much controversial matter. There may be criticism galore. At least, I hope so. That would be fine! Anything should be better than the present indifference on the part of our should-be-leaders.

We *need* new blood!

New ideas!

PART I

VENERABLES OF THE OLYMP

Webster will concur that I imply no slur.

Neither is the title meant as a compliment for the old-timer! Or as Homer used to wail:

> *Oh, you silly stick-in-the-mud,*
> *Why keep your nose so high,*
> *When weary feet are shuffling the rut*
> *Of oblivion?   Oh, tell me why?*
>
> *Why, if you are good with the six-gun,*
> *Guard your knowledge with concern?*
> *Why not grant the youngsters fun,*
> *Give them a chance to learn*
>
> *The art of target-revolver shooting?*
> *Are you afraid they might start hooting*
> *The highpriest of a simple art,*
> *If the "mystery" should depart?*

Maestro, dear Old-Timer, where, oh where, is the crop of successful shooters which your ability should have developed?

I wish to say here that I admire nothing more than an expert revolver shot, and, naturally, my deep admiration includes you Old-Timers. However, I must ask now: "How much of your experience have you divulged, you rascals? Were not most of you satisfied to play cock of the walk, soaking up the dumb admiration of the small fry?" Facile princeps.

It is true that some of you have written books, but because of their high prices, they were inaccessible to the army of revolver enthusiasts. Some of you have approached the matter in a scientific way, which is so much Greek to us dubs.

Were we beginners not left more or less to our own devices?

What we *wanted* and *needed* were precise instructions, available to every one—directions guiding us step by step, not the agony of having to find out things by our lone selves, by the trial and error method. How else were it possible that we still have so many thousands of enthusiasts who have never achieved even the mediocre?

Take the vast number of army men, police officers, guards etc., the majority of whom handle their guns in such a desultory fashion, that, to break their necks, they cannot even hit the proverbial barndoor.

Will my little book be a good mentor?

I aim to address only men and women of intelligence, thereby reducing the number of possible failures by a great percentage.

I believe that the group which proves to be intelligent enough to digest my treatise will get somewhere. They may not all turn out to be champions, but they will give good accounts of themselves.

I plan to use a suggestive method, cloaked in conversational language, hoping it will prove to be helpful. It has been, where I have instructed personally.

The written word, naturally, cannot fully replace actual demonstration. We all know that. But, for intelligent people, great elaborations or endless repetitions will not be necessary.

Although I trust that I am offering a concise system of my own, there is no issue at stake between you Old-Timers and me. I ask no indulgence from you. Things such as preponderance of hold over squeeze, or vice versa, are only matters of opinion and should not be subjects of dispute.

I could point out the fact that systems, any systems, are debatable but their only criterion must be their success or their failure.

And, my dear Old-Timers, we do really have too many, entirely too many dubs—shall I say, in spite of you?

But: let's get on!

FIRST OFF

You newcomers to our circle—Let's get acquainted!

We will get on faster if we understand each other!

Whether you are the city-editor on some paper, or perchance, a mechanic in a garage, or a millionaire with callouses on your hands from cutting coupons, in one respect you are all alike. All of you have tinkered with guns—or have thought about them.

There is a fascination about hand-guns which, I believe, is entirely sentimental. Maybe, one of your forefathers rode a cavalry horse and scared the poor animal with some great, big and frightfully heavy horsepistol—Or, he might have been embroiled in some elegant duel about this sweet thing or the other—Or again, he may have emptied his six-shooter over his shoulder while urging along a purloined pinto.

We all like to think these things and talk about them. And say: Haven't we all read those exciting Wild West and Detective stories? Oh, what those fellows couldn't do with their guns—And, although we know now that the weak-hearted authors laid it on a bit, now and then, just hand us a story with some good shooting in it—and we will read it even now, doddering as we are. The writers have become a little more careful nowadays—And our modern guns are different and they are being improved constantly. Yes, the pot is boiling!

True, we may have become a little more practical, a little less easily moved, a little skeptical, but we still cherish deep in our hearts a desire to be deadly marksmen with a six-gun and to be known as such.

But we dismiss the thought as just a little foolish. What would be the use? And, anyhow, it would be too difficult.

Dear Readers, young and old, why should such a desire be foolish? True, we would not want to reinstate the rather wild and lawless times of the gold rushes, of the border towns, of Indian warfare. But, why should we not indulge in revolver shooting as a *sport?* Do you know that many, many thousands of us have been shooting with a six-shooter for years? That there existed all along a fully organized sport of target-shooting? Well, it is the truth. Every year, as the sport becomes more popular, many thousands more become interested and are converted into Target-Addicts.

And one of the objects of this manual is to make our sport more popular!

Still, you believe, that it would be too difficult to take up. Let me tell you, and I really know what I am talking about, practically anybody can become an expert at our game. *You too.*

It is admitted that so far, the systems of teaching have been rather desultory. It was more or

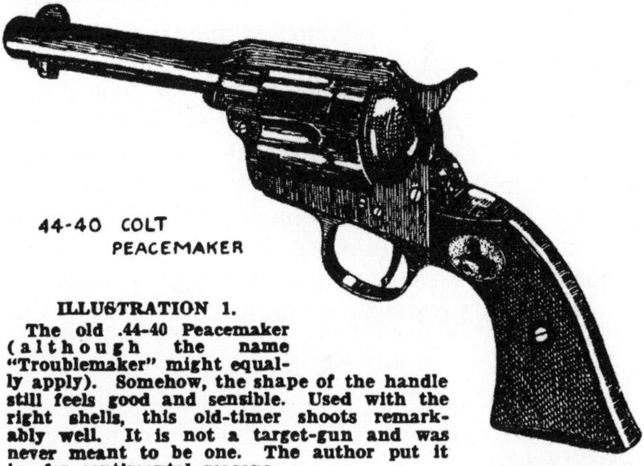

44-40 COLT
PEACEMAKER

ILLUSTRATION 1.
The old .44-40 Peacemaker (although the name "Troublemaker" might equally apply). Somehow, the shape of the handle still feels good and sensible. Used with the right shells, this old-timer shoots remarkably well. It is not a target-gun and was never meant to be one. The author put it in, for sentimental reasons.

less a matter of one shooter giving the other little hints here and there. In spite of the fact that there has been altogether too much mystery around good marksmanship, the sport has grown by leaps and bounds.

There need be no mystery any more. This manual has been written to initiate you along easy and logical lines. Read it and get interested.

Our sport, although noble, is not expensive at all, but what you get out of it, will be priceless! Your whole bearing will exude confidence. Your nervous system will improve. Your attitude to-

ward the world in general will become more tolerant, with the knowledge that the richest man in
the world cannot buy, with all his money and
power, your ability to shoot well with a six-gun.

Study the manual carefully and practice as outlined and I promise you that, within a very short
time, you will be able to astonish your friends with
your good marksmanship and thus realize a long
cherished dream.

(And you get something for nothing, namely
mastery of the rifle. A good revolver shot will
always shoot a rifle equally well, although the re-
verse does not hold true.)

You must provide the initial interest, the co-
operation, the perseverance while *I* shall peddle the
"technique." *Together,* we will master the subject!

That is why I need to make your acquaintance.
Let me introduce my credo: Although the Revolver Enthusiast and those whom we hope to con-
vert into such, may come from all walks of life,
they must have one thing in common: They must
be intelligent!

Ours is a sport which does not condone dumb-
bells—Sorry!

Ah—and you, my friend—?

Intelligence! We won't bother why—Let's just
divide the sheep from the —err—whatever it was—
and tell the others to better take up "Ping Pong"
or "Schafskopf."

You and I will sit over in this corner and shake
hands! Even, if you don't learn anything from
me, you will find entertainment and, moreover, you
will be reasonably sure that you are "intelligent,"
what?

And we can proceed to the next chapter.

TAKING STOCK

Some of us are afflicted with what the ladies are prone to call "Fickleness." They claim that when we find an interesting hobby, we play around with it for a while—Sooner or later, we grow tired of it and look around for something else. Our fancies. (they say) are like dainty butterflies that land timidly on a bud, nip a little honey and flutter away to the next flower—That's why (they claim) we have so many duffers in Golf, in Tennis, in—oh, in all kinds of sports. Maybe, they are right. Of course, we know that we shall be more consistent than the portly gentleman of fifty who suddenly gets a yearning to flit over the two hundred yard hurdles, and losing his interest after a few trials, goes back to collecting stamps. Shall we have it said about us that we may have the physical equipment alright, but that we haven't got the tenacity —call it "thickheadedness," to learn a thing properly and stick it out, till we have mastered it?

Ah, about this, you have to be sure! If you take up handgun-shooting, brother, you are going to be married to the thing and stick! Otherwise, it will be a waste of your money and time.

On the whole, there is nothing so terribly hard about handgun-shooting.

Take my word for it! The wonderful thing we can say of our sport is that everybody can become an expert in it.

You doubt that?

Alright, I'll even amplify my statement: Experts are not born! They are made! By themselves! And anybody can do it!

Nobody with enough intelligence and the wish to start properly and to stick, will fail. If you are reasonably healthy and have fair use of your limbs and eyes, that is all the physical equipment you need.

Sure! Some get there faster because their physical faculties make things easier. Naturals? Why, "Naturals" are found in every sport. They are as common as dimes. "Naturals" don't always become Experts, though. It depends entirely on what idea the individual has of where to stop. If you make up your mind to try and become an expert, you are bound to be one! And it won't take so long either.

This is not just talk, my friend! I know!

But, will you ask, why in so and so do we have so few experts?

Ah me—I don't want to hurt anybody, but have you ever heard of "the wrong way to start?"

Let me make a statement: 99% of all the non-expert shooters don't even know how to "hold" a revolver. And, if they don't know how to hold it, how can they expect to hit anything? There are other things—Whose fault is it? Let's forget the past!

To succeed in revolver shooting (and by that I mean to score consistently well above the average) will require something of you.

Unlimited patience, constructive self-analysis, and non-flagging enthusiam are some of the absolute essentials. You must learn to wage a winning battle against the perils of discouragement. You must deny yourself the luxury of emotional outbursts of temper.

Indeed, the matter of consistent high scoring is dependent on far more than just the eye, the hand, and the trigger finger. You must go behind the obvious exterior, to the nervous system, the centre of your physical control. Before you start, you must gauge the extent of the importance of control. Approach the sport with the determination that your foundation shall rest on solid, substantial, bed-rock *control* rather than on the treacherous sands of shifting emotion. In short: Keep cool. Be willing to try again. And always, always keep your chin up!

You must have a real, intense desire to improve constantly. You must find yourself looking forward with enthusiastic anticipation to the next time your club shoots. You must have that insatiable urge to do better. And when you don't do better, as will sometimes be the case (for, after all, this is not an easy sport), do not permit that overwhelming urge to lessen. A casual interest cannot carry you to the heights.

We will assume that the author of this manual knows what he is talking about.

Just deliver yourself into his hands! I have outshot some good shooters with their long-barreled target weapons, using just a little, short-barreled defense gun. Why could I outshoot them? Because I started right! And I stuck! Not because I am a child wonder.

ENTHUSIASM

Let's get some fresh air into the house. Out with all the ingrown ideas which we may have fostered up to now! Let's start afresh! And let's be enthusiastic!

Do you know that many consider our "Target Sport" to be the finest of all? Something to be proud to belong to? Listen! I have fenced and rowed—I have done practically everything in the way of sports, and I was fairly good; don't fool yourself. But "Target-Shooting with Handguns," brother, is the king of them all.

First off: Look at the people you meet in our sport. You won't find any cheaters and chisellers. They don't last long. The innate honesty of the target is too uncomfortable for them. "Braggards" are weeded out almost at once. Give them a pistol. The way they pick it up and aim it, spills the story—Braggards are good only for one laugh—a horse laugh.

We shooters have to be, innately, good sportsmen. We are forced to command intelligent patience, a gentlemanly indulgence—It doesn't make any difference whether we are "Captains of Industry" or "Strugglers at the lowest rung," our sport makes us all equal—We must, of necessity, be gentlemen!

Ah, is it not a pleasure to associate with gentlemen?

There are infinitely more inducements—

You know how it takes every ounce of strength for a tennis-player to drive his ball.

You have seen how exhausted the oarsmen are when they step out of the racing shell.

Have you not observed the twisted features of the runner, denoting the tremendous outpouring of physical energy?

Well, in our sport, there is no such physical exertion. We are bent upon positive "in-action." We must control the urge to expend physical energy. We must begin and stay "inactive," through mental control. Are we able to do that? (Hush, Dear, keep out of this!)

What a challenge!

And, as we go on we will have little relapses in our progress and we must screw up our courage and call upon our reserve of enthusiasm. And we overcome the little set-backs and replenish our well of enthusiasm—and, before long: We are there!

To continue: We own a gun! We own a real gun! We own what we have always hoped to have, although our desire never went beyond a vague romantic wish. But now, it has become a reality! We fondle the thing and admire its strong lines, its heft, its balance and we exult at the thought of the potential power which lies sheathed in its mechanism. We accept with awed mind its silent challenge: to attempt to master its death-dealing faculties, to accomplish the feat of hitting small objects at a great distance, just by pointing its short iron tube and squeezing a small trigger. If this were easy to do, the challenge would not have much appeal. If all that were necessary for success, were great physical strength, then we might as well stop feeling intrigued.

But, we know, it is a task of "Mind over Strength" and that, my friend, is where we meet on an equal plane. You have the same chance as the next fellow, in our select group of intelligent students, if—yes, *if* you are enthusiastic.

I see you champing at the bit!

I don't blame you.

Come on, then!

WHAT DO WE FACE?

Don't grind your teeth and mumble: "Why doesn't the geezer get down to brass-tacks?"

A little patience, my friend.

I intend to present a definite method! Not just a hodge-podge of tricks and hints. This method is

designed to lead you on, in easy, logical stages.
You will find a certain sequence, which I want you
to follow. Don't hop and skip around, looking for
shortcuts! Take each chapter and "digest" it, before you go on to the next one. If you trust me, it
should be easy. I am more interested in making
an expert out of you and to prove my theory, than
to hear myself talk.

But, I need your co-operation!

You must want to "understand" and "work." By
"work" I do not so much mean endless practice, but
rather: constant and intelligent thinking. You
must keep in mind that you must "start" right.
Start with the beginning and not with the end.

After I have told you how to "hold" the gun, I
shall have to say something important about "how
to stand." Then you will be told the importance
of "relaxation," how nonchalance will inspire confidence. Fourth: How to "move" the gun from
your shoulder toward the target in sighting position. (All this you have to *absorb* and still you will
not be ready to do what every simpleton does
when he first picks up a gun, namely, to sight and
snap the trigger.)

You have to realize that as future expert you
have to *know* things, not guess at them, that you
have to *master* things before you can attempt to
sight your gun. Heck, anybody can sight a gun
some way, but can he also hit things?

After that, we go on and *soak* in what will be
said about "aiming." There is the mastereye to be
determined and you must know what a "bead" is.

Finally, you will hear about "squeezing" and firing the shot and you will be surprised to know that
a chapter is devoted to "breathing." There you
have no less than seven distinct fundamental re-

quirements. These you must impress upon your mind until they become second nature. Let's run over them again: Hold, Stance, Relaxation, Moving the gun, Aiming, Squeeze and Breathing. Seven little things to master and your cherished goal is reached.

Have I scared you?

Or are you still interested? Then look me in the eye and promise that you will strictly adhere to the instructions in the forthcoming chapters. Promise that you will regularly follow the suggested easy practice exercises, and, dammit, you must succeed!

GUNS AND HEADACHES

Now comes the difficult part of the whole thing. Picking suitable guns for my friends is a thankless task, indeed. I shall try to be as impartial as I can. There is quite a flock of handguns on the market, but for the most part they are absolutely unsuitable for our purposes. If this were a compendium on fire-arms, I would have to delve into each and every piece of machinery offered. But, being confined here to a Manual on Target-Shooting, I am forced to make a careful choice of just a few outstanding guns and let it go at that.

Those of you who want information on more guns, I shall have to refer to Colonel Hatcher's excellent book.

You will notice that I show two kinds of calibres —namely the .22-calibre, which fires a rim-fire shell, and the .38-cal. using a centre-fire cartridge.

In taking your choice, you should keep in mind what kind of work or competition you intend to take up. In many competitions, for instance, rim-

fire weapons are not permissible against centre-
fire guns, the contention being that the heavier
recoil of the latter would impose an undue dis-
advantage.

The rim-fire shells are very economical, and in
view of the lack of noticeable recoil and muzzle
blast, this calibre is a great favorite. The centre-
fire 38-calibre revolver, on the other hand, is a
real he-man's weapon, and although a little harder
to conquer, many experts swear by it and look
with disdain upon the smaller calibres.

In a way, it is a toss-up which calibre would give
better results in target work. While the smaller
calibres are easier to handle, the bullet holes made
by the larger calibres cover more territory.

There is one category of target guns which
I shall, intentionally, leave out. I refer to the so-
called "Free Pistols". These are very extreme
single-shot models, on which science and ingenuity have expended their help to an almost uncanny degree. Short of leather-upholstered resting
facilities and melodious musical accompaniment,
they are the last word in hand guns. They are,
however, frisky and unwieldy, besides being very
expensive, and for our purpose we can forget them
without regret. They are barred from most
matches.

In this revision of "The Elusive Ten" I cannot
resist the temptation to treat this chapter more
fully than formerly.

There are, principally, the products of three
American makers which are worthy of serious consideration by the prospective target shooter, namely
those of Colts, Smith & Wesson and, last but not
least, Harrington & Richardson.

Right here, I like to comment on the sort of

fanaticism which owners often practice. Take, for instance, the Automobile field. The Packard owner praises his car to the skies and finds fault with everything else. Talk with ten people owning different cars and, by Golly, you won't find one car with which there isn't something wrong! One

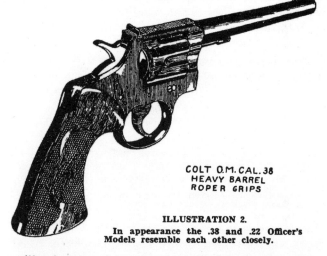

COLT O.M. CAL. 38
HEAVY BARREL
ROPER GRIPS

ILLUSTRATION 2.
In appearance the .38 and .22 Officer's
Models resemble each other closely.

will observe the same peculiarity among gun-owners. We are talking here of only three leading makes, but we might as well make up our minds right now that the Colt, the Smith & Wesson, and the Harrington & Richardson-guns are not only the best guns in the world, but also the worst!

Well, I aim to keep out of this! Although I shall give you my honest views, remember: They will be only one man's opinion.

Let's start with COLT: We have their Officer's model, both in .38 and in .22 calibres. The latter is generally called the "sister" to the larger calibre and, probably, it is. I have no objection to the sobriquet, since sisters needn't necessarily be twins. The small sister differs from the bigger one in that it has more heft around the waist and balances differently. A matter, by the way, which could easily have been adjusted by the factory. The cylinder, although of the same circumference, has smaller shell-seats and therefore considerably more steel weight. The same condition exists for the barrel. For some mysterious reason, the sights on

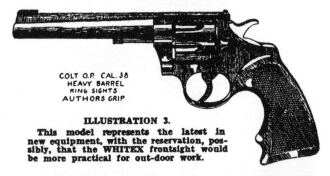

COLT O.P. CAL.38
HEAVY BARREL
KING SIGHTS
AUTHORS GRIP

ILLUSTRATION 3.
This model represents the latest in new equipment, with the reservation, possibly, that the WHITEX frontsight would be more practical for out-door work.

the two models have been made to look differently too. I agree that, if the guns were absolutely equal in weight, balance and looks, one would have to go through the annoyance of inspecting the muzzle hole, to tell them apart.

These are two fine guns! The .38 calibre has been a favorite in important matches for years and has bagged many fine records. The newly introduced heavier barrel is a decided improvement.

Before one plays around with the Officer's models seriously, one should make sure that the working parts of the action are carefully polished and honed, and the trigger pull adjusted to no more than a smooth three pounds.

I have always objected to the archaic sights that the Colt boys persist in pasting on these fine guns. They, the sights, are truly the shooter's despair, in a pinch. I advise the ambitious student to look at Ill. 3, which shows this model equipped with King's ribsight. The definition is excellent and, when making windage or elevation adjustments, all that is necessary is to "click" the respective screws. Every click represents a change of impact of ½ inch at 75 feet. This same picture shows the gun fitted with a special walnut grip developed by the Author.

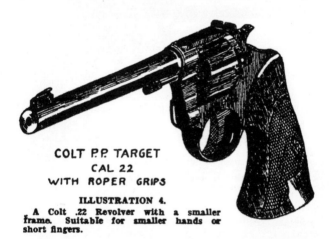

COLT P.P. TARGET
CAL 22
WITH ROPER GRIPS

ILLUSTRATION 4.

A Colt .22 Revolver with a smaller frame. Suitable for smaller hands or short fingers.

Walter Roper of Springfield makes excellent stocks for this model as can be seen from Ill. 2. I warmly and strongly endorse his grips.

With smoothed action, King's rib-job and Roper-stock, you have about the finest that can be had and you better be careful with your alibis.

It isn't the Officer's model that will be at fault! For Shooters with small hands, the .22 COLT

Positive Police is the gun to choose, because of
its smaller frame and lighter weight. The action,
if polished and properly honed, will be found to
be very agreeable. All other suggestions for Target Guns given above, apply equally to this model,
of course.

SMITH & WESSON K.22.
ROPER GRIP

ILLUSTRATION 5.
This sketch represents the S & W "K-
Model" which is made in both, .38 and .22
calibres. While the latter is named the
"K-22," the former is conveniently, called the "Smith and
Wesson Military and Police."

Next we pass on to SMITH & WESSON. Boys,
I really don't know to whom to hand the laurel
wreath for excellent guns. I am in a tough spot!
Right in the middle of the fire, what? But patience, my dear Doug! Presently I am going to
sing about your K-models, the Military and Police
in the .38 calibre and the "K .22". I am flabber-
gasted how the S & W boys do it, but their actions
are velvety smooth, as they come from the factory.
No additional honing necessary. I almost suspect
them to do this careful honing secretly on their
premises.

And the two jiggers mentioned shoot as agreeably as is humanly possible. Their sights show a whole lot more sense too! Yet, King's rib job is more modern, particularly with a 1/10th inch red patridge post and chromium mirror. The grips are just as oppressive as those of the competition. Those coffee-pot handles must be patented, the way they hang on to them! Again, Roper has to step in to furnish something sensible. Well, you factory boys, you persist in staying thickheaded and, therefore, your uncle has to take you to the wood shed!

The really fine actions that one finds in the K-models, make shooting an outright pleasure!

Score "50" for Colt and "50" for S. & W.

Oh, wait! S. & W. used to make a singleshot Tip-up model, both in double and single actions. As if the tremendous success of these models, last-

SMITH & WESSON   22 CAL. PISTOL WITH
WEIGHTED BARREL & SPECIAL WAX GRIP

ILLUSTRATION 6.
The manufacture of this Tip-Up model, single or double action, has been discontinued, more the pity.

ing for years, had gone to the heads of the S & W boys, they decided one fine day to drop them. Whatever still floats around in the market, is eagerly sought by those in the "know". Master, forgive me, but your divine ways are inscrutable! Don't bring up the "Straightline". Why the hell didn't you consult your betters, instead of going off half-cocked like that?

Of late years, HARRINGTON & RICHARD-SON, who used to putter around with cheap guns, have gone to the fore with their new double-and single action Revolvers, not to forget their Single Action Single-shot USRA-model, all in the .22 calibre.

I don't know what it is, but these damn pistols, despite their faults, group amazingly well. I have to be awful rotten to stay out of the "90s." People

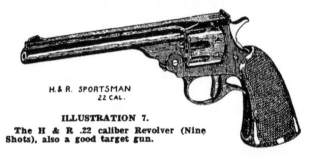

H. & R. SPORTSMAN
22 CAL.

ILLUSTRATION 7.
The H & R .22 caliber Revolver (Nine Shots), also a good target gun.

tell me that it must be the barrels. But, I had it drilled into me, ever since I was a baby, that no shooter could hold better than the lousiest barrel would shoot in the machine rest.

Can it be the action? Or the balance?

Whatever it is: It's there!

I hold no brief with things that do not show the best quality throughout and, if one buys qual-ity, one has to pay for it. Since the prices of the H & R stuff are way below those of other makes, H & R must have skimped somewhere. Miracles are not supposed to happen anymore! Or, maybe, H & R are philantropists—?

They surely are boys that know how to think "modern." They furnish a battery of five or six different grips for each gun to choose from. You can accommodate yourself, your neighbor and even your in-laws. If you want a grip with a thumb-rest, however, (And I think it is a necessity) you have to seek refuge with friend Walter Roper of Springfield. The USRA-model, singleshot, I rank with the best European Free Pistols, as far as performance is concerned. Objection: The trigger-pull, although short and crisp, seems too heavy and free. In order not to violate manufacturers' precedents, the H & R boys have some thickheaded ideas of their own about trigger action and, of course, they are wrong! Despite the good target results! However, it is a matter of a few shekels to have an intelligent gunsmith take off a few licks here and there. Then you will have something to brag about! Personally, I favor the 10″ barrel, although some people who really can shoot, show preference to the 7″ and 8″ barrels. Just get a

H. & R. 22 CAL. 10″ BARREL PISTOL

ILLUSTRATION 8.
The "United States Revolver Association Model," .22 caliber, Single Shot, described in the text at greater length.

few wags together and have them discuss the merits of different barrel lengths and "they're off!", as the nigger said when he got his fingers in the lawnmower.

Before I ramble on, I should make mention of a few revolvers that, to my way of thinking, are just on the border of being target guns, namely the Colt "Shooting Master," the S & W ".357 Magnum" and a "Colt Magnum," of which I have not shot the latter.

If you are a big and strapping specimen with extremities big enough to strangle your favorite In-Law with one hand, take the "Shooting Master," by all means. It's a .38 gun on a .45 frame, fine action and performance, but hefty, brother, hefty!

I hear that the big bruisers from Los Angeles, the Cop-Champions, like the Shooting-Master and do very well with it. That California climate, what?

Now, if you want to get the thrill of your life, put yourself behind the S & W .357 Magnum, 6½" barrel. That Magnum shell has a muzzle velocity of 40000 feet and goes through three oxen, provided they stand in line. Maybe, it's only 10000 feet and one ox, but it feels like the former. When it goes off, a feeling of "He-Man-ship" surges through your breast. The damn bullet seems to defy gravitational influences—It has such a flat trajectory. Take this same gun and put some ordinary .38 Midrange shells in the cylinder and that rather powerful cartridge sounds and feels like a .22 Long Rifle. Potentialities there, brother! But, better put on some muscle first. If you discard the silly grip and displace it by a Roper handle, you have a fine target *and* hunting gun in one. All you need is a horse.

But, we have something here, Boys! What I mean: something to admire!

Through the dreary stagnancy of Handgun manufacture there breaks a ray of aggressiveness, the beginning of a show of willingness to experiment. Mind you, the advent of a new gun costs money and the returns are in the hands of the Gods. But S & W went ahead and put that .357 Magnum on the table. If the shooting world had evinced any desire for such a gun, it had kept quiet about it. Everybody just went on using the available guns and grumbled about the lack of pioneer spirit on the part of the manufacturers.

That's just the trouble with us sportsmen! We are not satisfied, yet we trundle dumbly in our rut. Instead of studying the thing and demand, in clear terms, that this and that be improved, we just squawk in undertones. Now, if a manufacturer goes out of his way and offers an egg which he

SMITH & WESSON 357 MAGNUM
ROPER GRIP

ILLUSTRATION 9.
The much discussed .357 Magnum Hyper-Super-Revolver, fitted with Roper stocks. See text.

himself has laid, that's "NEWS!" Good News! It is immaterial whether the new product meets *all* the secret wishes of the shooting nuts. The very birth of something different gives the perplexing and hopeful angle. Maybe, a fresh wind will blow after all and brush away the cobwebs that hang over the brains of the placid manufacturing genii? The .357 Magnum has possibilities, I tell you!

With the equipment paraded before you, there might arise some confusion in your mind as to what gun to pick. I might advise you right here that you should buy a .22 calibre gun first! Your progress will be very much faster and surer. The bigger calibres can wait! The time will come when

the "seeker after revolver technique" will crave
for a larger calibre; but, in the beginning, take
the .22 gun. You'll thank me for it!

HOLD

A baby, as we know, has little trouble finding
the place where the milk grows. To find the proper
hold for a Revolver is equally easy. Nobody but
a perfect moron will pick the barrel-end as being
just as convenient as the other extremity. But
right there is where most people stop thinking
and that's why we have so many people that can't
shoot. There are 14 different ways of holding a
soup-spoon, 6 ways of gripping a tomahawk and
431 ways of getting the goat of your mother-in-
law, but there is only *one way* to hold the stock
of a Revolver.

"Why be so fussy?" will you say. My dear
fellow, telling somebody what the correct hold is,
is like an initiation into a Hindu-temple. I always
get jittery when I undertake it and I shall go
into my grave long before it is time. I have had
more than one intelligent pupil who, getting along
in jig-time, will suddenly neglect his hold. They
all have a way of compressing their lips and putting
the glint of stubbornness in their iris. Here I am,
trying to convince the thickhead that his progress
will stop at "80" or thereabouts. (Mind you, I
am doing it for nothing.) And he had promised
so faithfully not to branch out on his own until
he got to his goal.

Well, in this Manual the pupil can't talk back!
So listen brother: There is only *one* correct hold!
Get it? Thank you!

First off, we must realize that holding the stock
of a Revolver should entail no physical strain—

the gun should feel natural. We have some apostles who jeer about "ladylike grip" and so on. Those birds, probably, never have shown anything in the way of fine shooting. Just don't pay any attention! You can please only one master and listening to a number of "know-it-alls" will only set you back. Alright, we place the stock between the middlefinger and the ball of the thumb. Then we drape the other fingers lightly wherever they feel comfortable. Got that? Now place your thumb on the latch—and presto!

Mind you, just drape the fingers around the stock, and do *not* touch the stock with your fingertips at all.

The lower part of the trigger finger touches the frame and should steady it. The little finger, also with its lower portion, does the same further down the stock.

The action of the first two digits of the trigger-finger is being dealt with under the chapter entitled Squeeze.

No pressure in any part of your hand, mind you! That seems to be the whole secret of HOLD. However, it may not be amiss to amplify this statement. There is a reason for everything, as you will see presently.

Suppose, we practice the thing a little——

Just a minute! Don't pick up the Revolver like that—Take your hand off the gun! Are you a right-hander? Alright, pick the gun up with your *left* hand and *fit* it into your right. Look at illustration 10. The idea is to give your shooting hand every possible help. You need it!

After you have "fitted" the gun into your shooting hand, study illustration 11. You will notice that the picture gives the impression of effortless

FITTING THE GUN

ILLUSTRATION 10.
The five fingers of the left hand (if you are a right-hander) support the weight of the gun while you "fit" it snugly into the shooting hand. With a cocked gun, the left thumb rests under the hammer, thus preventing any accidental discharge. The left hand is removed only after the "fitting" of the gun is completed.

relaxation. A handgun is not a blackjack or a club that must be gripped tensely. Violence or notice-able pressures are oriented in the cylinder and barrel, not in your hand.

Let's analyze the situation! Not only for the sake of correct learning, but also as an aid in ac-quiring consistency. Your middle-finger has the function to support the weight of the gun. It is placed where the trigger-guard meets the grip.

You recall that the other fingers were placed below, first the ring-and then the little finger. Only if you were very stubborn would you wish to change this order.

Alright! Now, these fingers touching the *front* of the grip, would tend to make the gun tilt down-ward. We don't want that! Here is where na-ture comes to our assistance. As you will observe, the ball of the thumb is still unemployed. How about it? Right! Place that against the back-strap (The rear-edge of the grip) and—there we are. No more tilting, what?

But, we can't have the thumb floating around idly. Lay it on the latch. Now, look again at pic-ture 11.

Contrary to the beginner's usual conception, the gun must be held lightly! Just firmly enough to take care of a little bit of recoil. This light hold is beneficial in many ways. It tires you less. The gun remains steadier. Your motions and reactions are less acute— If you can bring yourself to re-gard the Revolver as a delicate instrument, you have gained much.

How does it feel?

We agree that the weapon is supported by the middle-finger; in fact, it literally hangs on it. Close to the second joint and on the side of the middlefinger (i. e. the side nearer the thumb) is the point of support. On the revolver, the corresponding point is directly in the rear of the trigger guard. This point serves also as a fulcrum. The pressure exerted by the middle, ring-and little finger towards the rear is opposed by the ball of the thumb. The *vertical* movement of the muzzle, caused by the working of the mechanism and recoil, is checked by the thumb resting on the cylinder latch and by the ball of the thumb. The *horizontal* movement of the muzzle is governed by the palm and the sides of the trigger-and little fingers, as mentioned before and again the thumb, by its strategic position on the cylinder latch, comes into passive function.

By now you will readily appreciate the importance of what I said previously. *Do not touch* the revolver grip *with your finger tips!* The slight pressure they exert against the left side of the stock, the amount of which you cannot control, will destroy the delicate state of balanced forces (opposing pressures) which you are seeking to establish and maintain until after the weapon is discharged.

Now, try to memorize the procedure and practice holding the gun in the *same* way *every* time. Get into the habit!

I might as well whisper a secret in your ear. It is all-important that, once you have found the correct hold, you must take and maintain it in exactly the same manner, with every shot—today —tomorrow—next week—all your life. Don't shift around! You should have invisible callouses in certain places in your hand and the stock should have invisible grooves and bumps, through your method of taking the same hold all the time. I

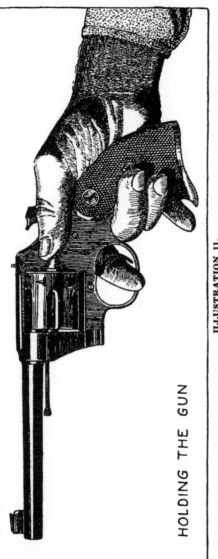

HOLDING THE GUN

ILLUSTRATION 11.

The impression which the hold should give, should be one of utter ease, of the complete absence of strain or effort.

The hand should appear as if holding a musical instrument. Observe the shadows which middle-and ring fingers throw on the stock of the gun, illustrating that the tips are kept away from the stock altogether. The thumb rests on the cylinder latch. One can distinctly see the little finger supporting the right side of the stock, while its tip is also kept away from wood. No furious clamping of a "fist around a club."

said "invisible." You don't apply any pressures and therefore should not get callouses and wear grooves into the stock. I just used a sort of metaphor.

Another, and probably better, way of expressing what I mean would be to imagine the stock covered with a delicate film which, upon first correct contact with your hand, would show the impression of all the little skin wrinkles and folds of your hand. This impression, we go on imagining, must not be disturbed and, each time we resume our hold, all these skin wrinkles and folds should match the first imprint.

Start slowly and pedantically—Do it right! Practice it! And by and by, the gun will slip into the same place automatically—and that's what we want!

STANCE

Ah me, you will sigh, what do we want with "stance?" We don't aim to shoot with our feet. Do you know that one of our foremost revolver-experts who read my exposition on stance in the first "Elusive Ten," wrote me that he thought it important enough to apply it in practice? Well Sir, we deal with this thing called "stance" because it is imperative to our success, not because we want to fill valuable printing space.

Did you ever observe a man slightly under the weather giving a speech to the world at large? We are not concerned here with what he may have been blubbering, but didn't you see that his body was swaying back and forth?—There we have it! *His body swayed!* Now, if the man had only had three legs, he would have presented a steadier picture, regardless of how much friend alcohol were

urging him to sway in the breeze. We, of course,
are more dignified. We don't hold speeches—not
at street corners. We are busy drinking in knowledge, not alcohol, knowledge about "Swaying."

We can begin by making a little experiment.
Alright! Stand in the middle of the room and
close your eyes. After a short while you will have
the feeling as if you were swaying—You *are* swaying! You are *falling!* You feel that, if nature had
only provided you with another leg, things would
be much steadier. Right? That's the trouble with
having only two legs. A horse can *sleep* on its
feet. We humans can't even stand steadily when
fully awake. This is not a philippica against nature's shortsightedness; it is an endeavor to impress upon you the fact of "body sway." The best
shooter, be he as steady with his arm as possible,
will sway. His gunmuzzle is carried across the
bullseye, in unison with the sway of his body.
He has acknowledged that and he has taken steps
to minimize the evil by assuming a correct stance.

Suppose, you were to acknowledge this fact now,
instead of later? It would save a lot of time.

Alright then: The body sways in the direction
of your chest. Just stand with your feet about 14"
apart, the toes facing the target. Raise your hand
and point with a finger at the bull. You will see
that the finger moves mostly up and down.

Now point your toes both to the left and have
your right shoulder face the target. Your finger
will now travel across the bull from left to right
and vice versa.

This kind of sway would interfere with your
shooting, what?

Your shot-groups would be distorted. Swaying
in the direction of the line of fire, your groups

WRONG POSITION

ILLUSTRATION 12

Here, the artist–chappie went "whole hog." In order to enter
into the spirit of "swaying" properly, he went and got hisself
tight. His model looked like a Chinaman to him; however, he
still maintains that the execution of the "spats" is faultless.

The sway of the body is toward and away from the target and
will cause the muzzle to bob up and down, vertically across
the target.

WRONG POSITION

ILLUSTRATION 13.

The gentleman shown, obviously, is conscious of being in a tight spot. His position is the "duelling position." The idea is to offer as little as possible to shoot at. His body is swaying toward and away from the reader and the gun, consequently, will oscillate horizontally across the target.

Since he has forgotten what the fuss was all about, he will feel relieved if he should miss his opponent entirely.

would tend to spread unduly in a vertical line, and horizontally, of course, if your torso were swaying across the line of fire.

Obviously since we cannot eliminate swaying altogether, we must try to minimize it. If we were to take a position somewhere between the two extremes just mentioned, it would be evident that our finger could not travel as much in one direction as before. You would find, in fact, that your finger—or, if you were holding a gun, the gun-muzzle—moves within a very restricted area, vertically and horizontally, but not enough to do much damage.

Following up our reasoning logically, we will now consciously apply the principle of correct stance:

(1) Stand with feet close together, facing in a direction of about 45 degrees to the left of the line of fire.

(2) Move left foot straight to the left, a distance of 10 to 14", more or less, to find a comfortable position.

(3) Now raise the heel of your right foot, turn on the ball of your foot to the left, until you reach a position of comfort.

As agreed before, even now the body will sway, namely in the direction which your chest is facing. But since—for right-handers—your target is over to the right, your gunarm has to be swung in the direction of the target, also to the right, in a line between your chest and your shoulder. In other words, we introduce a sort of half twist in your torso and that is why the muzzle travel is so greatly shortened.

We can further reduce the disturbance by placing our body-weight correctly on both feet. We

ILLUSTRATION 14.

Although in this fashion plate the Expert is absorbed in serious concentration on his task at hand, his whole body, from the little toes (which are hidden here by expensive shoes) up to the gun-muzzle, suggests complete relaxation and bodily ease.

In this position, the body sway is toward and away from the lower left corner of the picture. The muzzle will waive vertically, horizontally and diagonally across the target, but its travels either way are greatly diminished.

"toe-in," until we can feel pressure on the outer margin of each foot. We also distribute the weight equally on both feet and on each foot evenly between the ball and the outer edge and the heel. In short: We were born with full soles and we should use as much of the sole surface as possible. This should be a boon to people with flat feet, what?

A study of the pictures 12, 13 and 14 will assist you in getting the idea.

I hope, I don't have to implore you not to dismiss the matter of stance as trivial. "Stance" is one of the seven fundamentals (See page 13). Get into the spirit and practice "stancing." See that you spread your legs so that you feel comfortable. The spread is individual—There is no hard and fast rule about the matter of inches. The stance must be comfortable and theoretically correct. You see, the thing you want to avoid is: having any tension in any part of your anatomy and that includes your shoulders, arms, body, legs and feet.

Your left hand which you find to be hanging rather helplessly, should not be cause for giving it any thought. It is best if you just put it in your pocket and forget it while your pistol is up.

RELAXATION

We are coming along fine, my friend.

In the first "Elusive Ten" I made a rather sweeping statement when I said: "You have one of the most deadly and manly weapons in your hand that science has developed; yet the handling of it is to be of the most delicate nature imaginable. Brute strength and ferocious desire are only handicaps." Since then I have received numerous endorsements of this viewpoint. Yes! A handgun is *not* a cocobolo club! It is more like a sensitive apparatus. You don't want to tense your body up as soon as you step on the firing line. You are not a cave-man ready to tackle a bear. No, you are the musi-cian who wants to coax a tune out of your in-strument.

Forget that your pistol may be something war-like, something aggressive—You do not intend to smash or break things—Your's is a game of nerve against muscle, of intelligence against brawn.

It makes me grin to think of those bar-flies of the pioneer days who, with an oath, jerked their shooting iron out of the holster and lammed a fusillade across the table, missing their opponent! At five feet—Hell, unless they *threw* their revolver, they couldn't have hit the mirror behind the bottles. "Blue eyes chilled to the color of steel—" My, My —How vastly more true that bleary eyes should chill at the thought of plain water—

Brawn, brother—

One can't hit the ten-ring, a little over an inch in diameter, at 60 feet, while gritting one's teeth and scowling.

Relaxation, my friend! Relaxation!

Take the darn tenseness entirely out of mind and body.

Just relax! Shooting does not require muscular exertion. (We are still talking about handguns and not about dice). It's positively asinine to tense your muscles when there is no call for it. You are not wrestling or lifting heavy pianos—You are just relaxing—

I surmise that, although you are reading my ad-monition to "relax" when shooting, with avid in-terest, you won't do it. Not right away! You have been filled with the wrong ideas too long and it takes some time to get rid of your old conceptions.

Nevertheless, for complete success, you will *have* to do it eventually! What's that? Brother, you surprise me. You *would* be "the" exception. You really meant it?—Thank God, one sensible man! Here is something for the wide world to hear: This reader has resolved to practice "relaxation" right from the *start* and he sees no sense in fooling around for ages until the wisdom finally breaks through.

Man, your *are* progressing!

For those who think that relaxation might imply a sort of "Step-an-Fetchit-attitude"—let me say that we are talking of *intelligent* relaxation, not of laziness or carelessness.

While we are at it, let's look up Webster for a definition of "Nonchalance" and "Complacence." We need a certain amount of these too. You don't want to try too hard! That would not be true relaxation. True, while we are about the process of shooting, we are serious, even pedantic, yet we should not act as if something enormously important were to take place on the outcome of which hinges a question of life and death.

No—No!

We are concentrated and will try to get every shot out according to Hoyle—We are not in the habit of wasting a single shot thoughtlessly, but we must remember that life will go on serenely even if we should not get a perfect target.

Get the idea?

Again! Don't try too hard!

On the other hand, we have stopped fooling and kidding. There are some people who never seem to grow up. They are like young pups, although not quite as droll. They have no dignity. They are smart, in their way—but, they will never amount to much. They need not be vicious, mind you, just bubbling in their empty way. That kind might interfere with your work. One finds these pests sometimes—I have!—If you cannot ignore them, if you cannot get them out of your hair, then it is time to get tough! After all, you have to think of yourself and of your sport. A swift kick in the pants seems to offer itself as the best remedy and, if you have to, let them have it!

There is no danger of making your sport too sombre. We will have enough fun of the intelligent kind, without these monkeys.

MOVING INTO POSITION

This chapter concerns itself with "rhythmic safety." We are handling a loaded gun! Even if we are only practicing, with empty shells, we have to acquire the safety habit. Our object is to bring our gun forward into shooting position in a manner which should look good and, more important, should be safe at all times. To that end, the muzzle when not actually pointing at the target, should *always* be directed forward and upward, at an angle of 45 degrees from the shoulder.

One single shot going wrong, perchance hitting somebody either directly or through ricochet, would be more eloquent. But, you and I are intelligent and thoughtful and we have made up our mind to learn by the experience of others who were less fortunate.

Let's put this movement into a formula: When bringing the gun forward into shooting position try to describe with your hand a harmonious oval, in any easy flowing continuous movement.

The intent is more in the nature of an auto-suggestion, namely through an easy continuous flow of movement to abolish any and all jerkiness.

Jerks, abrupt and angular movements, are detrimental to the creation of the perfect atmosphere, in which all fibres in the whole body, through absolute relaxation (with the exception of one little part of the trigger finger), work together in ideal coordination.

To be explicit:—With the cocked gun in your hand pointed upward and forward at an angle of 45 degrees, start a movement from your shoulder in the direction of the target (describing a flat arc) —aim—squeeze—hold the trigger—continue the arc flatly backwards—back to your shoulder—release the trigger *at the end* of the completed oval—relax! Relax mentally. Don't sag to your knees and lie on the floor. Just loosen up. Keep your gun muzzle up and forward, or put the gun on the shelf.

Again: Cock your gun. Start again from the shoulder (with the muzzle forward)—describe the first and upper part of the oval, in the direction of the target—aim—squeeze—hold trigger down— complete arc back to your body—release trigger —relax.

And the same with every shot.

This constant arc-movement, comprising, as it does, the follow-through (also found in golfing parlance), by keeping the trigger compressed after the shot, refers to Slow Fire only. In Time and Rapid Fire the gun is kept forward.

A deeply hidden precautionary measure is put into practice. *Never is the gun pointed carelessly at objects which are not meant to be aimed at.*

Cultivate this precaution until it becomes subconscious and *never violate* it.

SIGHTING

When I predicted that our sport demanded intelligence, I knew what I was talking about. I warned you!

We shall have ample proof when wrestling with the problem of sighting.

Not that sighting were difficult or hard to understand—Not at all! It is simple, amazingly simple, but—Yes, a "but"—

Oh, that I had the eloquence of a Bryant—The problem, I repeat, is not the intricacy of the subject—It is the stubbornness of the individual.

Proceed, my dear Watson, proceed!

Sighting is the task of keeping your sights (Those little jiggers on top of the handgun) horizontal, on a level plane—They must not be tilted

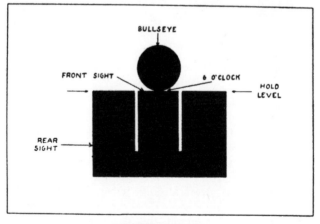

ILLUSTRATION 15.

or banked to either side—We would call that "canting." Your sights should not be canted! Ill. 15 will show what I mean. Secondly, we hold the gun so that the picture of the front-sight fills in the slot of the rear-sight—not too high, nor too low, not too much on either side, but right in the centre of the rear-sight-slot. The top of the front-sight is even with the top of the rear-sight and, the front-sight appearing thinner than the width of the slot, you should observe a fine line of light

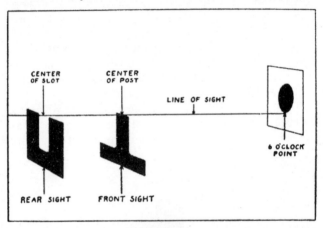

CENTER OF SLOT

CENTER OF POST

LINE OF SIGHT

6 O'CLOCK POINT

REAR SIGHT

FRONT SIGHT

ILLUSTRATION 16.

on both sides of the front-sight. Try it!—Everything level and centered? Fine—!

Your eyes have now performed the job of aligning the sights—You are holding your gun at arm's length, the barrel directed at the target.

To complete the thing, we manipulate this alignment (without disarranging it) under the bullseye, at the so-called "6 o'clock" point. An imaginary line should connect this 6 o'clock point with your eyes, passing over the middle of the front-sight which, as you know is centered in the rear-sight-slot. This imaginary line we call the "bead." I don't know why we call it that. But the "bead" it is. Look again at Ill. 16. Simple what? I'll say. But wait, my friend! We are not through yet. Now, the thing gets interesting—

Alright, try the "bead" again! I see, you are making the mistake common to all beginners. You have one eye screwed tightly together—What's the matter with you? Haven't you got *two* eyes? Then, why the hell don't you use them? First off, it would look much better. Secondly, when you screw up your face like that, you employ a series of face-muscles which should be at rest—relaxed. You remember, don't you? No muscles are used in shooting—everything should be untensed—? Alright, no harm in repeating: In shooting you must be completely relaxed and if you tighten up any part of your body—and that includes the face —you will detract from the intense concentration which should be directed solely toward the mechanics of shooting. Don't make it harder for yourself!

Come on: Both eyes open! We want to get you to make it a *habit* to shoot with "both eyes open" so that you may get a binocular and plastic view of both targets and sights! In serious shooting, for instance in police work or in war-fare, keeping "both eyes open" will enable the shooter to not only see his whole target but also what goes on around that target.

You will find it a lot of fun, this shooting with "both eyes open" and it is very valuable.

However even with both eyes open, only one eye will strike the "bead." The other eye sort of supplements this task—it is an accessory that rounds out the picture.

Which eye does the beading? That is individual. It might be your right eye or your left. That bead-

ing eye is appropriately called the "master-eye."
We determine it as follows:

Hold a pencil at an arm's length from your eyes
and line it up with some vertical line in the background—say a door jamb.

Now, close your left eye and observe whether
the pencil has moved away from the jamb-line.
If it has not moved, then your open eye (in this
case the right one) is your Master Eye.

If the pencil should move upon closing your left
eye, open both eyes and close the right eye. You
will then find that again the pencil remains stationary and (it being open) the left eye is your
Master Eye.

Ah—we got that down!

Let's assume that your right eye is the master-
eye.

O. K. now: Look straight at the target. Both
eyes are open! Now, let your gun-arm come *up*
slowly—Your eyes are trained on the target and
on *nothing but* the *target*. Slowly, your gun will
appear within your field of vision. Don't pay any
attention to the gun! Keep both eyes glued to the
target and—What do you observe? Although you
do *not* look at the gun, you will clearly see the
barrel and the sights. You can't help seeing them!
What has happened is that your field of vision
takes in more than just the small target and, as
soon as the sights appeared within this sphere,
you could not ignore them anymore. But, the precept upon which this happened is deeper than that.
The viewing lines from both of your eyes converged
upon the target at a certain angle. If you had
looked *through* the sights, this angle would have
been much more obtuse. With the acute target-
angle your eyes had to go into one focus only,

namely that of the target. Looking through the sights would force your eyes to change their focus constantly: from rear-to frontsight, to the target, back to the sights and so on, because you have to keep these points under observation all the time and at the same time.

Which of the two angles looks more logical and sensible to you?

Whew! I am talking myself hoarse, but I am glad that we agree!

It may be that, at first, you see two images of the sights, one distinct and the other less pronounced. Don't let that discourage you. After a short while, the secondary image will dim and finally disappear. Many pupils manage the trick at once. But, don't give up if the first attempt should not be successful.

The following birds-eye-sketches will help to explain the situation:

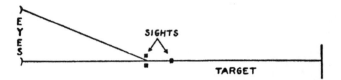

The lines converge upon the rear-sight, are then squeezed together into one line, which strained line then travels over the front-sight towards the target.

The effect is an unclear view of the target. You are "sight" conscious and your poor eyes are being kept busy changing their focus all the time.

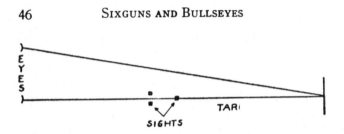

The viewing lines converge upon the *target* and
the sights are lined up behind in an effortless,
secondary operation. It is obvious that the effect
is a plastic or stereoscopic view of the target—
You are "target" conscious.

Of course, there may be a possibility of your eyesight being faulty. But your Oculist or Optome-
trist can generally correct the situation by the use
of suitable shooting glasses. In cases where a complete correction is not possible, the physician
should be asked to strike a medium by prescrib-
ing lenses which show the sights clearer than the
bullseye.

Assuming that everything were properly attended
to, we now come to the practical application of
what we have absorbed so far.

Oh no, my friend, we don't want to hit the "Ten-
ring!" Not yet! That would be too small for the
beginning. It occupies only a small part in the
centre of the bullseye.

Easy does it! Let me suggest that we try to
hit the bullseye only, I mean, any *part* of the
bullseye. Do you think that you can curb your
impatience that much? You have to—in the beginning.

Alright then, we are satisfied with hitting the
black only.

I have spoken of the "6 o'clock" point. Our
sights are adjusted so that when we aim at this point,

the bullet (If everything else is right) will strike the centre of the black.

But, we are modest by force of necessity: We don't want to hit the centre of the black. Not yet.

Therefore, I say: Don't aim at 6 o'clock! I want you to aim at the whole bull! Don't aim at the 6 o'clock point! Don't!

Here comes the supreme test of your intelligence. You must accept my statement that there are more important things than aiming at the 6 o'clock point, things such as "Hold"—"Stance"—"Relaxation"—

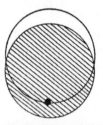

The upper circle represents the entire bullseye. The shaded circle is the permissible waving area. If the trigger is squeezed while the frontsight waves within the shaded area, a bullseye will be scored.

I repeat: Don't try to hold your bead at 6 o'clock. Why?—You remember, we have learned under the chapter "Stance" that our hand will be in constant motion. We cannot prevent this! The muzzle of our gun waves continually left and right and up and down—With a person of apathetic or sluggish temperament, such movements will be less pronounced and less jerky. Still, this uncontrollable motion of the muzzle persists and we shall have to accept it as normal. If a person claims that his hand is "steady as a rock," give him your best horselaugh. He is nuts!

Now, the bullseye is about three inches in diameter. You just let your muzzle wander in and under this bullseye (I refer again to the sketch on page 47) while you squeeze the trigger slowly. When the bullet leaves the barrel, it will speed on to the black and drill a hole in or near the bullseye. That's what we set out to do!

Instead of intensely arresting our bead at the tiny 6 o'clock point, we stroll within the ample confines of a three inch circle, which is very much easier. While leisurely doing that, we can pay better attention to the little thing which we shall describe in the next chapter.

SQUEEZE

Some people object to the word "Squeeze." They claim that "Pressing" sounds better. I don't know —Suppose, we stick to "Squeeze?" It's much more romantic.

You know, if it weren't that I am so allfired up about handgun shooting and its intricacies, I would really shy away from writing this chapter.

The topic is a very important one, but it surely is a hard one to put on paper.

It is not just a matter of jotting down the essentials. Verily not! Having usurped the position of mentor, I have to put my entire soul into the thing, to batter down the unintentional resistance which you are sure to put up. I said "unintentional resistance" and I meant it.

'The perplexing angle about "Squeeze" is that it is so infernally simple—and there lies the danger.

I admit and appreciate your co-operative willingness, yet—

Well, let's see—

The thing in a nut-shell would sound like this:

"Don't hastily *pull* your trigger, but 'squeeze' it slowly."

There!

Can you make anything out of that?

I thought so!

Just a second! I need a little bracer—there—that's better!

Alright then: Take your gun—See that it is *empty,* barrel and cylinder—

Sure about it?

Now lift the Revolver into shooting position and do exactly what I advise *while you read this.*

Slip your index-finger into the trigger guard—Not too far—not too 'little—Grip and gun feel comfortable?

Now: Find the trigger!

Barely touch it!

Fine!

Now crook your finger a little—Just about 1/1000th of an inch—not more—Got it?

Put on a little more pressure—slowly—slowly—another 1/1000th of an inch—Keep on adding one thousands after another—Not so fast! Another 1/1000th—

Hold it!

Release the trigger—Put the gun down and rest your hand!

Boy, I just sweat blood for fear that the hammer might strike. You see, I wanted the first demonstration to stop just before the hammer fell.

You did nobly—You were just a trifle too fast—

Restraint is what I am after—There must be no impulsiveness about working the trigger. We are trying to absorb the finesse of "squeezing." It is a matter of depressing the trigger in small instalments. Of course, the action is a continuous one—

There is no staccato—We just pile up 1/1000th of an inch after the other, smoothly and slowly. Alright now: Pick up the gun again—Crook your finger—Remember: 1/1000th of an inch at a time— A little more—again a little—another 1/1000th— another—Hold it! *Don't let go* of what you have! Just hold it there—You were too fast again—O.K., slower now—another tiny impulse—

B I N G . . . . . . !

(The hammer fell and struck into the empty chamber.)

Don't pay any attention—*Keep on squeezing*— squeezing, till the trigger won't go any further— Got it? Alright, release the trigger! Put the gun down and take a rest! After the click, I made you keep on squeezing because I wanted you to "follow through"—

The golfers use that expression very often. They complete the swing of their driver *after* the ball is hit—They "follow through." We will hear later what the advantage of "following through" is. My dear fellow, you do me proud! You must be an exception! I had no trouble at all with you—

You will be an expert in short order.

Upon reflection you will find that the hammer fell when you didn't expect it—On some point in your slow working of the trigger, the hammer struck. You didn't know when and where that would take place—

That's "squeezing."

Sure! That's *all* about "squeezing"—There's nothing more.

Simple?—Of course, it's simple!

But, I've had my troubles—with simple things —particularly with squeezing. If it hadn't been for the fact that you were so attentive, I would have had trouble with you too.

Naturally, the term "1/1000th of an inch" was just a pictorial one. It was my idea of how to express a "tiny impulse."

We don't need a micrometer to measure such impulses—The thing is that they be "tiny" enough.

Now, when you are alone, by yourself, practicing piling up *tiny impulses* on the trigger, you may need a little mental assistance.

Suppose, you use your imagination then—Invent a situation in which some unpleasant thing creates the desire in you to postpone and "draw out" a required decision, as much as possible—or some such thing. The following is very effective:

Imagine that your mother-in-law is staying at the house—has been staying for weeks—Naturally, you are a little on edge and not quite responsible. In your irritation, you have just called your wife a "Sucker"—She storms out of the room—You know what's coming—Right you were!—You hear the well-known firm steps of her mother outside of your door—You pick up your pistol—Then you start squeezing the trigger—The door pops open and—there is your nemesis—The lust of battle in her eyes, the old lady blows up her cheeks—Now, imagine that she "dasn't" speak until the hammer clicks—Get it? Naturally, you take your time about it—There is no undue curiosity in you, clamoring to know what she thinks about you— you already know! You just go on squeezing— No hasty pulling this time, what? Sure—All the time in the world—Another 1/10000000000th of an inch—Boy, am I fast—Say! This thing is getting serious—I don't believe that you are listening to your teacher—Please, wipe that expectant intensity off your map! After all, this is only a psychological experiment—Your gun is *empty* and not pointed at *anyone* in particular. —

Boy, oh Boy, that "squeeze" would have been the acme of perfection—

Need I say more?

If anything, I should add that the only muscle that did any work during the squeezing action, was the contractor muscle of your fore-finger.

Everything else stayed relaxed—your hand, wrist-arm, etc., etc.

You may take a drink, Hector. That's all for to-night!

BREATHING

I am not a doctor and I am not going to converse about inhalation and exhalation and what takes place inside of you—

I am a shooter and you want to be one!

If I were to say that "breathing" is important—but, why quibble?

Of course, we live and we must "breathe"!

But, we live and we must *not* "breathe"—err—I mean—

Let's start all over!

When the gun is up and the trigger is being squeezed, you must hold your breath!

There!

When you breathe in and out, your chest expands and contracts, moving and shifting a whole group of powerful muscles—But, have we not set out to shun the employment of muscles? Ergo: Breathing interferes! The movement of such muscle-groups as your shoulder-chest and neck-muscles would, indeed, seriously interfere with shooting—You could actually see the muzzle move in rhythm with these muscles.

Haven't we got enough trouble already and are we not trying, by various means, to quieten that muzzle?

Compromise? Sure!

How?

Inhale and exhale slowly and deeply a few times! Lift your gun! Are you ready? Now: Inhale normally! Let some of the air out and "lock" your throat!

You have now a comfortable amount of air in your lungs to last a short time—None of the muscles mentioned are strained—everything is loose—

And, while you squeeze the trigger, *you hold that breath!*

Don't hold it too long, though. The air in your lungs is soon used up, your body wants a fresh supply and will let you know it, too. Your Revolver will start to become heavy, your eyes will blur —Release the trigger and take the gun down! Lay it in your left (Ill. 10) and rest your gunhand!

It takes resolution to lower the gun when you are all set for the shot. But, it is better to do that than to waste a shell.

Deliberation, my friend! No "throwing" of shots with a gun too heavy or with blurry sights.

When you are ready again, "fit" the gun into your shooting hand (Ill. 10), lift it up—inhale normally—let some of the air out—lock your throat—the same cycle.

Yes, take the gun down if you are not sure of perfect conditions! It's absolutely safe as long as you let the trigger alone and keep the muzzle pointed forward.

DISCOURSE ON HABIT

You remember, I used the word "Habit" quite frequently—Of course, having an intelligent audience, I should not want to define the word and I am not going to be long about it.

It is just the fact that "Habit" and "Practice" are so very closely interrelated which makes me take up the topic at all.

We agreed on the necessity of "Practice." The word suggests, however, something physical, something drudgy, doggedly unintelligent—something unpleasant that one should try to get over with as quickly as possible—In short, "practicing" is considered as inevitable, below the bane of intelligence.

I agree with you (Conditionally, of course): Practice in itself, by itself, is senseless, stupid. It is what practice *does* to you *that* we are interested in.

Take the case of juggling three balls. We sometimes see performances which leave us spellbound. The artistic ease, the beautiful flow of movements, the amazing infallibility fill us with delight. Our admiration directed at the finished performance, makes us wish that we could do the same thing—

When we ponder, however, what an overwhelming amount of practice the artist must have gone through—and we are distinctly conscious of that —our brows wrinkle in uneasiness. We grant that part without discussion. We sense the stony path that leads to the heights. But we dismiss that thought hastily and give ourselves over to the enjoyment of watching the confusing skill. However, the artist cannot *possibly* control and direct the easy flow, the split-second timing, by hav-

ing his brain pull levers here and there, in bewild-
ering succession—It would be inhuman—It isn't
done that way either. Actively directional brainwork is dispensed with in the finished performance.
We might say that it is a matter of physical and
mental reflexes only. The conscious brainwork
was done during the practice-part.

You never thought about it quite that way,
what?

Let's nail it down: Directional intelligence is
required *not* in the finished performance, but in
the practice part. I can now qualify what I meant
by "conditional" when I spoke about "stupidity of
practice," in the opening of this paragraph. I had
no intention to fool you—I just wanted to develop
the thing logically.

"Practice" in unity with an orderly system of
learning is *not* senseless and stupid, not while all
of your intelligence is required for it—

But, we mustn't stop there—

Our first act of exercising our intelligence is the
realization that we must *learn* the *right* thing. Our
second resolution is to *practice* the *right* thing,
admitting the pedagogical benefit which will de-
rive.

Ah: There's the root! The "pedagogical benefit"—And, what is it?—"Habit" my friend: Habit.

Through practicing we call to work certain physical and mental reflexes, which we already pos-
sessed in a dormant, undeveloped sort of way. First,
these reflexes have to be called quite energetically
—But, by and by, they come with greater alacrity,
they come easier and, finally, they become so finely
attuned that no conscious brain-effort is needed.
We "feel" that we want them—and there they
are! We are not even conscious of "feeling" that.

(The procedure is the same whether we work on the right or the wrong thing. Good and bad habits follow the same force. But, could anyone see much sense in acquiring the wrong habits? Of course, not!)

Transposed into shooting: We don't have to make a conscious effort of wanting to "squeeze" the trigger—We just do it! Through our friend "Habit." We manipulate all the fine levers and valves of sighting, squeezing, timing, in an instinctive way—through habit. There is no short-cut around "practice." No amount of intelligence, no mass of wealth, no divine intuition will accomplish what only practice can do: Develop habits.

As a master of the handgun, you perform on the strength of habit, and habit only!

I don't know whether I succeeded in explaining myself fluently and clearly enough, not being a scientist, but, the importance of this chapter diminishes in the same ratio in which you admit the necessity of "practice."

It really doesn't matter whether you practice because you know the psychological or physiological reasons for doing so, as long as you do practice!

And *practice* you *must!*

RESOLVED THEREFORE

Come on! Let's look backstage! Let's see what kind of an impression we get, watching an expert We are now acquainted with the seven fundamentals and will see things with a critical eye and understand better.

There he is—He holds his Revolver in his left hand and steps leisurely up to the firing line—He faces the target and takes his stance. (Exactly like I told you) Now, he "fits" the gun into his right. He lifts his arm and beads the target—See, how deliberately he does everything? No jerky movements—His torso is relaxed—his face looks serene and both his eyes are steady on the target—(You remember what I said about "positive inaction"?) You wouldn't think that he is doing something extremely difficult—What a sight! A picture of absolute and tenseless inaction—What co-ordination!

What—extraord— BRRRRAMMMMM! Goodness gracious! Did it startle you? But see, he looks through the scope and nods his head. I bet he hit the "ten."

My God, don't you wish you were he?

I am impressed just like you. I get a definite esthetic pleasure out of watching an expert. It must be the apparent absence of the dramatic in his deadly inaction—We know what a terrific concentration lies behind this inactiveness—Relaxed, yet intensely concentrated and purposeful—And out of this studiedly relaxed poise flashes lightning—destructive—murderous—smashing a hole in the ten-ring. How you wish to be like him.

You *will*, my friend! He started out the same way! He was not born the master. He studied and practiced *just like you* will have to do.

Dammit, don't give me the impression that all my labor with you has been wasted—You don't want to become and stay "just average"! You want to be like him!

Practice as often as you can! Maybe, you do not have the facilities for shooting on a range each day—Not at all necessary! You don't need a range for your short daily work-out! Any room will do—You practice "dry"—with dummy shells!

Stick a little black paster up on the wall, at the height of your eyes, stand back and go through the motions—Keep constantly watching and correcting yourself! Remember the seven fundamentals! Just "squeezing" won't do if you forget about "Hold" and the other items. Of the seven functions some may seem less important than the others, but only in their entirety will they complete the scheme!

Aim at the little paster; aim the way you were told—hold your breath and squeeze slowly. Do it every day for a few minutes! Don't do anything hastily—When the hammer clicks keep your bead and *call* your imaginary shots just as honestly as the real target would. You'll get the hang quickly —you will know when the muzzle flickers with the hammerclick and when not—no fear.

Make a resolution to practice regularly! And stick to it!

All the top-notchers went through the same routine.

It isn't hard to do—It doesn't take much time; just a little determination—

Don't you feel how earnestly I am urging you? For *your* sake?

Hell man, it's *you* that wants to become an expert! I *am* already one! And *I* have to practice to *stay* one!

PART II

ASCENT TO THE OLYMP

We may imagine now the elapse of three months —a period given over to diligent practice along the lines suggested in the preceding chapters.

Slowly, our application of the principles has been "absorbed" by our system, and, what was, at first, uncomfortable labor to us, has now become an irrepressible force, necessary to our happiness. "Practice" has cultivated "habit" and, through habit, we approach the finished performance. And now is, perhaps, the time to enter into the second stage of this business of handgun-shooting.

What we have learned and practiced so far, my friend, were the rudiments, the fundamentals of the game.

You are now shooting around "80" on the Slow-Fire Standard American Target—with a bullseye of abt. three inches in diameter. The distance is 60 feet—! Just think of it: Three months ago you couldn't even hit the proverbial side of a house and now: Twenty yards away there is a little black circle and you are able to smash into that circle ten times out of every ten shots—

But, you are eagerly looking beyond that—You are not an "expert" as yet and you have set your heart on that goal—or bust!

"What?" the uninitiated will exclaim, "Isn't that good enough? Why, it's simply uncanny!"

But, you know better now! "Heck!" You will say condescendingly, "I want to be an 'expert!' I want to be able to hit the *center* of that black circle (The ten-ring, a scant inch in diameter), not only any old part of it! I will make it my business *never* to shoot *below* 85!"

Ah—I am sure of your soul now, my friend! You are imbibed with enthusiasm. You *couldn't* give up the thing even if you *wanted* to! You have been bitten! And badly bitten!—You are a "Gun Bug" now, waiting to be admitted into the inner circle, the circle of experts!

The things that I will say have added significance now, since you are not a rank beginner anymore. You are aware now why I said certain things in a certain way—I applied "suggestive education"—It enabled you to grasp matters much faster—Things "clung" with greater tenacity that way, than if some dry exposition had been employed.

And now that we have grown up, we can use different approaches—We can get to the bottom of things and call them by their right names—We can conscientiously adjust some parts of the structure which look incongruous, without endangering the project itself. Because you have a fuller understanding of things now—.

Listen then:

We started out as beginners and we have succeeded in erecting a structure. We find it sturdy and sensible—But, like in most other things thus begun, the touch of perfection is missing.

We will try to acquire that now!

On certain points we must re-adjust ourselves.

There is the material that we used which must be discussed more fully. And, we are compelled to add here and there, to complete the picture.

Take, for instance, the matter of "tenseless" hold. You remember how I stressed the importance of shooting without tension or muscular exertion. While that holds true, principally, the subject was intentionally not carried to its logical end, in the first part of this manual. You see, the error into which every beginner invariably falls, is his tendency to clamp his hand frantically around the stock of the gun. Where that habit originated, seems to be a mystery. Nobody corrects the beginner—Is not everybody else clutching the gun? The very fact that there are so many *dubs,* does not seem significant. The unfortunate beginner who starts thusly, following a silly tradition, is handicapped. He has to *unlearn*—and start all over again. How can one break this conception handed down from, God knows, where? By analyzing the thing right from the start and teaching the proper amount of tension? No, that would be doomed to failure. The beginner is not in a position to discriminate between various degrees of tension. His noodle knows only one thing: "This gun is a dangerous apparatus—One must grip it tightly."

Now, in order to divorce the pupil from this fixation, I tell him instead: "We don't want any tension *at all!*" I teach him to consider the gun as a delicate instrument that must be handled tenderly—The idea of frantic clutching never enters the pupil's mind—And, that is important. Because, gripping the stock tightly does not only involve certain sets of muscles—It means also: Tightening of the mind! And things such as "relaxation," "nonchalance" are automatically banned.

The pupil, physically speaking, may err in the other extreme—But, that will not be detrimental at all. He will find out soon enough that a certain application is necessary—But, he will increase such application with great reluctance, because he has been initiated into shunning "tension." He starts from the bottom and not from the top!

My dear fellow, you will be relieved to know that there *is* a way to hold the gun a little firmer, without having to exert yourself.

Take a playing card from a deck. Open your right hand and stretch it! Now, hook one long edge of the card in the flesh of the first digit of your middle-finger (The digit closest to the palm) and the other edge of the card in the fleshy portion of the ball of your thumb—Got it? Now, relax your hand! See, what happens? The card is held securely in your relaxed hand. It requires *effort* to hold your hand *open,* but, when the hand is *relaxed,* it *closes!* That's its natural way. We utilize that by hooking the gun-stock into our open hand in the same manner as the card, and, as we relax the hand it will bend itself around the stock and hold the gun. Skin-tension—Get the drift? Why didn't you think of that before?

But, we have to get on or we'll have a five-dollar tome, instead of a manual, on our hands!

As this treatise deals with the revolver and not with the automatic, the unscientific construction of the revolver must be recognized and, perforce, be overcome by several logical muscular applications.

The metacentre of the revolver is wrong, we should say, if there were an exact science of revolver-shooting. (Maybe there is, but we needn't bother). Such centre would be found to be com-

posed of the relation of centre of weight to the
mysterious action of the recoil, superimposed by the
mechanical action of levers, springs, friction, etc.
There is the fact that the centre of weight changes
with every shot.   The weight-load of the cylinder
gets lighter after every cartridge fired and thus
influences the action-coefficient.

I know this sounds semi-scientific.   However, I
defy anyone to prove that the revolver is really
the answer to the prayer, by the expert, for the
ideal target gun.

As I said, the inherent weaknesses of the weapon
will have to be counteracted by certain muscular
applications.   (The curious fact that most major
target records were made with revolvers is merely
a proof of my statement that its weaknesses
can be overcome through *correct* muscular applications.   Still, the automatic, in my humble opinion,
is going to take the place of the revolver, in time
to come.)

The directional actions of the trigger and hammer, to begin with, must be counteracted.

The backward squeeze on the trigger tends
to pull the muzzle down, while the fall of the hammer will jar the weapon out of countenance. We
can now, by using a downward hold with the
thumb on the cylinder-latch, in combination with
the position of the ball of the thumb, practically
counter-balance the directional actions mentioned.
If we support the gun further with a moderate side
pressure of the lower part of the little finger and
of that part of the trigger-finger which touches
the frame, we further minimize the evil forces.

The test is simple.   After cocking your gun,
place a ten-cent piece on the top of the round barrel near the muzzle, behind the front-sight and

squeeze. The coin should stay on the barrel. (Mucilage barred, of course). It is a matter of a little experimenting to find the right *minimum* amount of thumb and finger pressures necessary to prevent the coin from dropping off.

The proper squeeze, combined with the judicious use of thumb and little and trigger-finger for support of the gun action, has, you will remember, been mentioned in the first part.

I also advocated in a former chapter the absolute *relaxation* of the muscles of the shooting hand, although I spoke of opposing pressures. We must now readjust ourselves by accepting consciously a few minor muscular applications.

Mind you, I do not say even now that you must religiously do thus and so. I am simply again pointing out certain places where the gun should be supported. It is unique with every one how to achieve this support. If all our hands were alike and if we all were using the same gun with the same action, I might attempt an exhaustive elaboration. What should happen, as you know, is this:

The forepart of the trigger-finger applies a delicate, zephyr-like action on the trigger.

The lower portion of the trigger-finger exerts a fine steadying pressure against the gun's frame.

The thumb, resting on the cylinder latch, steadies the trigger action effect on the gun.

The ball of the thumb touches the back strap.

The middle finger supports the main weight of the gun and also acts as a sort of fulcrum in cocking.

The ring and little fingers complete the grip (although the ring finger does not call for any muscular action).

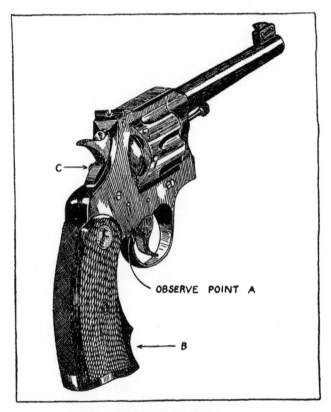

ILLUSTRATION 17.

Point "a" on frame against which lower portion of the trigger-finger exerts a slight steadying pressure.

Point "b" against which the lower portion of the little finger exerts a slight steadying pressure to the left.

Point "c" is the cylinder latch on which the thumb is placed.

The picture permits a view of the special inset which lowers the position of the middle finger. The stock has been length-ened correspondingly by the same inset, which is in one piece and can be easily detached.

Also the back-strap against which the ball of the thumb bears, can be clearly seen.

When looking at the Rear-and Front-sights one should also study the illustrations 15 and 16.

While the *tips* of middle-ring and little fingers must *not* touch the stock, the little finger where it touches the stock with its lower part, should exert a light steadying pressure to the left (Ill. 11, shown on page 29.)

There is no perceptible bend at the wrist. The whole arm, wrist, and hand point effortlessly forward. You find now, to your surprise, that the matter of grip, all at once, has become of major importance, and rightly so. If you now combine squeeze and perfect hold, you certainly do have a fine equipment.

Still, my friend, remember again: The main part of the hand should not be tensed; neither should wrist or forearm muscles.

UNITY OF HOLD AND SQUEEZE

Debates on the dominance of importance of Hold over Squeeze or vice versa, are as futile as the question on whether the hen or the egg came first. I shall let you form your own opinion!

Take: "Squeeze." What *is* "Squeeze?" Or rather: What is the difference between "Squeeze" and "Pull?" There is none, unless we were to define the "Squeeze" as a "retarded" pull. Why do we employ the "retarded pull?" Because, with a "retarded" pull we are enabled to *control* the maintenance of our pre-determined hold on the Revolver. It stands to reason that, if we were to just "pull" the trigger, we would create a more or less violent disturbance in our hold. We *squeeze* so as to have as little disturbance as possible—We *squeeze* so that, from the beginning to the end of the trigger action, the muzzle of our gun remains as steady as possible, without flip or flicker. Of course, we could achieve this steadiness of the muzzle even with a hard pull, *if* we assumed a hold which counteracted the resultant violent influence. It is easier and more natural, however, to hold the gun *lightly* and to avoid muzzle disturbances through careful *squeezing*. That is why we favor the "Squeeze" and condemn the "Pull." But mind you, "Squeeze" alone would not perform if you had a hold on your gun which did not counteract the slight disturbance which *even* the squeeze will exert. A correct and light hold will offset a careful squeeze—Hence, the importance of proper hold —Which is the hen and which the egg? It does not matter! As long as we try to assume a complete *unification* of both: Hold and squeeze.

Given the theoretical precept that your gun were sighted in for your eyes and you were to find that the shot-groups appear too much to one side, it is possible to shift the hand around the stock so that the trigger-finger reaches over further or less. If that finger reaches over too far, the gun would tend to shoot too much to the right—and vice versa. We experiment with this, until we find a hold which permits the recoil to throw the muzzle straight upward. And *that* is the hold which we memorize and practice.

As suggested before: If you take delight in teasing yourself, take your empty gun, place a ten-cent piece on top of the barrel (close to the front-sight) and squeeze the trigger. If your hold is right and you squeezed correctly, the coin should *stay* on the barrel—It is an excellent check-up! But it should not be tried while dinner is waiting.

While we are about it, we might as well dig a little deeper.

There are some prominent people who advocate

dispensing with the slow squeeze, after the beginner has grown up.

You are eligible and we shall therefore put this viewpoint under the microscope: What do they mean by "dispensing with the deliberate squeeze?" Well, they just *don't want* to squeeze slowly anymore! If your trigger were adjusted to a three pound pull, for instance, they say: "We take up 2 lbs. 15 ounces right away—These 2 lbs. 15 ounces don't release the hammer, so let's take them up quickly and, when the bead is right, we just have a puny one ounce to surmount and we are there— We are tired of never knowing when the damn shot goes off—"

Well, there is nothing wrong with that, what?

A little intricate though to pull just 2 lbs. and 15 ounces, not 2 lbs and 14 ounces or three pounds, but exactly 2 lbs. and 15 ounces—Maybe, I am a little prejudiced, but I really think that idea is rather dangerous, for us young hands. I shall not scoff at it—After all, the proponents are prominent persons—We shall not deny that, after many years of diligent practice, our bodily system may become so finely attuned that we could, instinctively, stop pulling just before the last ounce. I said *maybe!* We know that our bodily responses change from day to day and even from hour to hour—I mean, they are never constant. Emotional, physical, yes, even meteorological influences are constantly at work—We know that we feel more energetic, exhilarated, springy, when the morning sun shines in mild weather over a beautiful countryside, during our vacation.

Then take a gloomy, rainy Monday morning when we sit in the Suburban that hurries us back to the grind—

When it comes to courser reflexes we may find greater constancy, but when we talk of differentiating between 2 lbs. 15 ounces and 3 lbs, then we may find out just how unresponsive the human body can be—I have experienced times when I found a strange supreme sureness in my reflexes— Shooting high scores became an easy matter— These exalted conditions don't last long through —and they cannot be commanded. It is these periods in which we make those astounding records, that enable us to discard the careful squeeze and approach the ideal—In these moments we probably take up most of the latent pull *instinctively* and apply the last vestige at the proper time. Well, these states of mind and body need further thought and analysis and their embodiment in this manual would be dangerous. I just mentioned this topic casually so that you know what people mean—

But: Beware!

To revert to mechanics: There are really only two functions of the gun at the time of discharge which demand attention: We have (1) the actions of the trigger and hammer before the explosion and (2) a certain twisting effect made possible by the recoil. The first tend to pull the muzzle downwards and then partly upwards again, while the latter may throw the muzzle sideways if the hold is incorrect. What causes these movements and how can they be counteracted?

Let us consider the first series of motions: While you depress the trigger you work against a spring and lever arrangement inside the gun. This resistance, with the middle finger as a point of fulcrum, will naturally cause the front end of the gun to tilt downwards. The actual click of the hammer will, on the other hand, throw the muzzle

slightly upwards again.   The ball of your thumb
resting against the back-strap, in juxtaposition
to the middle finger, is fully able to offset the
downward motion, while the thumb itself, with a
slight but steady downward hold on the cylinder-
latch, neutralizes the upward flip of the muzzle
caused by the fall of the hammer.

We come now to the side-twisting in connection
with the recoil.   The recoil really should throw the
muzzle only straight upwards if it were not for
the inefficient way in which the novice holds his
gun.   (The   theoretically   straight   upward   jerk
caused by recoil is not sought to be corrected since
it has been compensated by the height of the front-
sight).   Usually, the novice clamps the tips of his
middle-ring and little fingers against the stock.
This, of course, will tend to direct the recoil-
motivated muzzle to the left.   To correct this,
the poor novice is taught to press with his thumb
sharply sidewise against the frame.   He is expected to actually work one side of his hand against
the other, instead of latently neutralizing expected
forces by strategic placement of support.

Now, suppose you take my advice and keep the
finger tips *away* from the stock.   You will find that
the recoil will be upwards only.   Refraining from
further theorizing, let me again make the statement that a revolver should be supported on five
points:

(1)   The function of the middle finger as a point
        of fulcrum and to carry the weight, is self-
        explanatory.

(2)   The ball of the thumb bears against the
        back-strap.

(3) The thumb acts downwards on the cylin-
     der-latch.

(4) The trigger-finger, where it touches the
     frame, exerts a steadying side-wise pres-
     sure and so does

(5) The little finger, with its lower portion.
     (See Illustrations 11 and 17.)

The gun is held quite effortlessly, and the tremors caused by rigid tension will be absent. The
argument that teaching the "Tenseless grip" might
lead the pupil to assume a "lady-like grip" is ir-
relevant. No normal human being in his right
mind, would think of toying with his gun. Nor is
the gun an instrument with which to "club" an
opponent. Tenseless shooting is a modern thought
and immensely important in the achievement of
mastery.

We said before that we shall have to experiment to find out how far the middle finger should
be pushed under the trigger-guard. If it goes in
too far, the gun will shoot too much to the right.
By shifting the hand forward or backward, you
will soon find a position which permits the recoil
to throw the muzzle straight upwards. And this
position, once found, should be memorized and
assumed every time you take the gun in your
hand. Once you find this position you are over
the hill and on your way to the expert medal.

Mention should be made of certain media which,
experience has developed, will facilitate the search
for the ideal hold. With few exceptions, the shape
of the grip of the revolver is such that, with the
middle finger supporting the weight of the gun,
the trigger-finger does not lie horizontally. In-

deed, the trigger finger is pointing very much downwards. Instead of just being crooked naturally when squeezing the trigger, the finger is forced to exercise the backward pull on the trigger in a way which is foreign to its anatomy. The trigger is easiest to work when pulled straight backwards. The trigger finger in its unnatural position will, perforce, pull upwards too. This fact has been recognized by experienced shooters, if not by some revolver manufacturers, and several remedies have been suggested. There are on the market certain inserts which can be attached to the stock. These attachments will place the middle finger lower and will, consequently, make the trigger finger assume a more horizontal and natural position. These attachments, however, have the common fault of shortening the available stock to such an extent that many shooters will not be able to place their little finger sidewise against the stock. I overcame this deficiency by having my dentist make a wax impression of my hand grip on the gun and then cast this impression in hard rubber. With my individual attachment, the cost of which was exactly $5.00, I now have a stock which is amply long for my hand and, at the same time my attachment gives me a very comfortable feel. (See Illustrations 11 and 17.) There are supplementary stocks to be had which will permit placing of all fingers and these are entirely practical. I have discussed this subject more fully elsewhere.

I find that this dissertation on hold has become rather involved and penetrating. I fear I may have overstepped the frame set for the manual, but I also believe that I could not have treated a difficult and important subject in a cursory way.

So much for that.

SYNCHRONIZED SIGHTING

Being out of the "duffer" class, we must now seek to cut down the tolerances which we permitted ourselves up to now—Our days of roaming with the bead within the generous borders of the three-inch circle, are over. Our goal is now to place our shots in the *center* of the bullseye and, our sights being adjusted correspondingly, we must direct our bead at the 6 o'clock point—We have acquired such fine control over the trigger that the squeezing process can be interrupted and resumed at will—We have not learned to hold our muzzle steadily at the 6 o'clock point—and we *never* will! No—the old muzzle wanders about in the wellknown manner—and the bead tags along. We now have to try to fool this unwelcome but inevitable waving—How? Well, in its travels across the bullseye, the bead must pass through the 6 o'clock point and, everytime it does that, we squeeze—As soon as the bead swings away, we *stop* squeezing—and resume it again as soon as 6 o'clock shows again. Everytime 6 o'clock registers we gain a little on the trigger—We never let *go* of what we have—By and by, there will come a point in our squeezing action where the hammer strikes and, since we have taken in our little gains only when 6 o'clock showed, the chances are that the hammer will fall when the bead momentarily rests at that point, or very near it. (What happens is that the impact of the bullet will be about 1½" above 6 o'clock, or in the center of the ten-ring. Our sights are set to get this result. The reason why the 6 o'clock point is made so important, is that the sights,—which present a black silhouette to our eyes show better against the white paper background, directly below the black bull. If held in the center of the bull, the black sight-picture would merge with the black bull and thus become obscured.)

Oh yes, this kind of synchronization between beading and squeezing is not easy—If it were, pistol shooting would not be the art it is! It's fine work and demands co-ordination of a high order.

You will notice now that I am not "easing" things off anymore—If something is hard to do, I tell you so. I couldn't frighten you anymore, because you are in a state now where obstacles only serve to spurn you on. Pistol-shooting has become an obsession with you now.

But, where there are shadows there is also bound to be light—Let's look for this light—No use, *making* things harder for yourself. Well, the light is close by: It is a peculiarity of the healthy human body that the vibrations, minute tremors, pulsations which result from the biological activity of the body, *vary* in their intensity. Ordinarily, we would not notice these signs of life, but when we extend our gun-arm and add a pistol at the end and watch the muzzle against a background such as the target, these signs become magnified in the manner in which the needle of the ammeter registers the otherwise invisible tiny electric impulses. The example is not quite relevant, but it will serve.

The vibrations and pulsations are distinctly visible at the muzzle-end and, observing them intently, we become aware of a constant change in their cycles. Sometimes, they seem to increase, but they always subside more or less—and, trained as we are, we actually see them entirely suspended for infinitesimal periods—We receive the fleeting impression as if all life had ceased and, our intense absorption and faultless co-ordination should respond if the atunement is fine enough. As I said, these moments are immeasurably small, but they are quite frequent. We have to find out how the rhythm of our intensity is tuned for the event of these "Oases" of apparent passiveness. Any shot that is released during these moments will unerringly puncture the centre of the ten, if the bead was close enough to the 6 o'clock point.

Well, Sir: We are not playing anymore with crude thumbrules, we are now working meticulously with micrometer gauges—We are craftsmen —We are artists—or hope to be!

In plain English: What we should strive for is: to squeeze only when (during one of the frequent periods of stillness at the muzzle) the 6 o'clock points rests over the bead.

Ah yes: Collecting stamps or playing pinochle is easier.

But, you and I, brother, know what we want, eh?

I have heard it seriously propounded that all a shooter can hope for, is to endeavor to stay in the black. If you were to resign yourself to such an attitude, you could score good targets only if Lady Luck were at your shoulder. It is entirely possible to stay in the black and score only an "80." If you are lucky, a few shots may slip into the "9" or even the "10." We shall dismiss such an attitude forthwith, since we are supposed to have graduated from the beginner's course in part 1. What kind of unintelligent shooting would that be? I had much rather see a close group of shots, even if such group should not happen to be all in the black. If you are able to shoot close groups (and that should be your aim), you are in a position to shift them by correcting your hold, sights, or stance. You are, at least doing conscientious shooting instead of having to trust to luck all the time.

Before this chapter's conclusion, I wish to relate an amazing experience. I know one of the instructors of a public institution who was considered quite a shooter and, who, quite possibly, landed his position on the strength of his achievements on the range. A most appalling school of thought found in him a vigorous proponent. The guiding idea seemed to be that since a beginner will always *pull* the trigger and since pulling will place the shot wildly below the paper of the target, he should be made to hold at the upper edge of the paper target. This, he said, would pull his shots somewhere near the black. Then, as the idea of squeeze is slowly hammered into the poor pupil's cranium, the bead is gradually lowered until the pupil can safely approach the 6 o'clock-hold. This process appears so unintelligent to me that comments are superfluous. The only merit of it seems to be that, even if disastrous, it is infinitely slow, and if interrupted early enough (before the pupil has lost all interest) it might not wreck the pupil's chances for all time.

We have here one of the reasons why the idea that the safest place is in front of an officer's gun is so prevalent. I have cited only one example, but it should be illustrative.

FLINCH-WOBBLE CO.

You surely recall the impressive advertisement on some tooth-paste, where a ravishing young lady sits innocently in repose, all by herself—and the caption says: "Beautiful as June, but—"? Ah, you see there is a "but." It furnishes the mystery and also the hook for the manufacturer's campaign. He takes pity on ravishing young ladies that will just sit—alone—without sprightly young knights fluttering about them. He has given the matter much thought and he knows what it is that keeps the knights away. He considers it his civic duty to do something about it. Knights should go afluttering and young ladies should perk up—That's the credo of vibrant humanity and no "halitosis" is going to undermine all that. No! No!

In shooting, we have "Flinch and Wobble" (Sounds like a vaudeville team, and really is). But these two are just terms like halitosis. They really mean more, because the owner *knows* that he has them.—He doesn't wait for other people to shun him—He goes right ahead and hates himself.

Ah—For the old uncle to step up and pat him on the shoulder:

"Come! Come now, my young, self-conscious lad—"

No, with you, dear Reader, I shall have to approach this thing a little differently.

Hark ye, then! Flinch and Wobble are affectations! They sound neurotic and, therefore, they have no place in our scheme of things! Alright! Let's take "Flinch" first.

You know how concentrated must be your efforts when lining up and squeezing—Heck, you simply haven't got *time* for foolishness!

Would you want to do the impossible? Your mind has a certain capacity only and that capacity is *all* taken up with your task of beading and squeezing—There is *no room* for any other thing! Just try to cram a little "Flinch" in—It can't be done! Unless, you take something *out* first—You don't want to do *that.*—Man, you need "beading" and "squeezing"—if you want to become an expert—Let other people court affectations—the hams, the no-amounts, the eternal flops—*You* can't *afford* affectations!

Think it out yourself! "Flinching" is an undesirable, distinctly muscular action—a muscular reflex-action, if you will—Isn't that something "alien?" Something that would clog up your scheme, nullify everything you learned a n d achieved so far? If you once admit the darn thing, it takes an effort to throw it out again—No!

You don't pay any attention if it should hover around—You concentrate upon what you *must* and, dammit, you simply haven't got *time* for other things—I'll be hornswoggled if I take time out to explain what "Flinch" is—I am not interested! It's unimportant!

Start with a .22 caliber Revolver and work up to the heavier calibers later. Let somebody (Do this on a safe *range* with a back-stop) manipulate your cylinder so that you don't know which chamber is loaded or not—And "squeeze"! Watch your muzzle and observe whether it flicks or not. If you held and squeezed carefully, your empty click (if you should have picked an empty chamber) will find your muzzle steady—

Flinch? Bah!

You know, teaching is often a wearisome game —because unimportant things occupy such a big space in the dome of people—

All right, let's get on with "Wobble" then—

Wobble; spelled: *Wobble*—That's all the importance it should have:

Know how to spell it!

It is a little more physical than Flinch—When you have shoveled snow all day, or after a strenuous day at breaking rocks for the government, or even after a certain time in the doghouse, your shooting may be influenced by "Wobble"—That happens to a violin-player too—The characteristics are a more or less pronounced tremor at the muzzle, sometimes accompanied by a surging up of nervous waves and a dimming or "fuzzing-up" of target or sights—

Of course, your intestinal disposal plant may be sluggish—you may have, what Doctors pronounce with an appreciative click of their tongue, a toxic colon—(Look it up, brother, look it up!) or your upper molar may scream for attention—

It is a sad fact that the biological functions of your body should be fairly normal. If the appendix bothers you: Out with it! It won't distress you half as much, if preserved in alcohol and exhibited on the radio-shelf.

But, given a fairly healthy body, and pestered by "Wobble," it is a good thing to indulge in a little rest, before you start shooting—Try to find complete relaxation by lying down—stretched out and every fibre loose—All disturbing or annoying thoughts should be dismissed—Breathe deeply and slowly—In short: Get some order into the seething carcass! Take your time about it! After you have settled down sufficiently, start snapping your Revolver *empty*—Observe the muzzle—A very good suggestion (only good on the range) is to prepare a few dummy shells. You know: No primer, no powder, but with bullet in it's accustomed place —When filling the cylinder, load one dummy, one sharp etc., etc. Whenever the dummy is hit by the firing pin, nothing will happen—A good chance for you to observe your muzzle—The next one will be sharp—and so on!

This is also good practice whenever you are too tensely keyed up, before a match or so—When the empty clicks show a steady muzzle, the re-assurance you feel, the returning confidence you experience, are the best remedy.

Here is something more: A good way to *spoil* your scores, is to fill your tummy to repletion—Or, if that should not prove powerful enough, take a few highballs. Give the stomach something to work on and kiss your scores "goodbye!". You know, of course, that your body cannot give you it's full co-operation in shooting, because part of it's attention is diverted toward the digestion pro-cess—And as far as alcohol, coffee, etc. are con-cerned: Haven't we made up our minds that com-plete "relaxation" opens the door to success? Well, why then play around with "stimulants?"

Stimulants and relaxation just don't agree!

And never mind the wonderful shooting which that and that fellow did there and there—and him being loaded to the gills—You *can* do **wonderful** shooting while tipsy, but how about "hitting" things? Most of the wonderful shooting done under the influence of alcohol was done "at the mouth."

Selah!

INHIBITIONS AND GHOSTS

Sometimes, I wonder if man is really the captain, of his soul—State of minds like "Happiness"—"Tranquil enjoyment of simple things" appear like chimera which eternally evade us—We wish them, but our impulse never leaves the stadium of "just wishing." The objects of our individual wishes seem desirous enough, but do we really go after them with all that we have? Does "wishing a thing" ever transcend into something more forceful? Do we *want* it badly enough so that we *must* have it, so that we *will* have it? What could it be that stops us from *willing* the object? Some say that "Fear" governs all our actions—Fear—But, let's stay practical!

Granted that "Fear" does stultify most of our desires, is not that realization in itself helpful? We have the name of the malady and we may look for a treatment.

At some time, in your early youth, somebody, in fun, may have unexpectedly switched off the light, plunging your room in darkness—You were genuinely frightened and you screamed in terror—The memory of that cruel joke has been buried in some deep brainfolds these many years—but, to this day you enter a dark room with a slight uneasiness—or you may have an inexplicable aversion against things electric—or you can't take practical jokes with grace. Something in your unconscious sphere always sets up defensive barriers which are called "Inhibitions." These "Inhibitions" often influence our behaviour when shooting. Let's assume that you have a range in your basement and that you are able to shoot a fairly consistent score of "85," *when you are alone.* As soon as you try to perform before other people, or in a competition, everything goes haywire and you find that your scores equal those of a beginner. Dirty work at hand! Some "Inhibition" drums in your ears and confuses you—The presence of other people makes you self-conscious—Silly, what? Now, without an extensive psycho-analysis, the underlying cause would be hard to find. It is entirely possible that, when a child, you were once mercilessly chided *in public* by some unthinking teacher. You knew that you had done your best and you felt that the public humiliation was unfair. The burning shame which you experienced at that time and which you have forgotten now, has etched its imprint upon your unconscious—And, whenever you are asked to perform in public, the fear of possibly muddling things and thus be again subjected to humiliation, governs you, although unacknowledged. An "Inhibition" at work! Possibly you are in that class! (I am afraid that most of us could shake hands—though the cause may have been different). If so, you can take counter-action! Oh, yes, you can! However, it seems imperative that, before one can administer the proper medicine, one must be sure of what ails one. Well, we have nailed down one inhibition and now for the medicine.

The remedy is "auto-suggestion." In plain English, one should find a formula which, if constantly and fervently dinned into our system, would break down habitual inhibitions. But, same as we have it in the medical practice, there are two kinds of medicine: one is allopathic and the other is homeopathic. The first one treats hot with cold (roughly speaking) and the latter treats hot with hot. This definition should suffice for our purposes. We now substitute "positive" for "hot" and instead of "cold" we apply the term "negative." Our two medicines are now called "positive" and "negative." It has been proven that in cases of a psychological order, the homeopathic treatment shows far more success than the other. That would mean, we should treat "positive" with "positive."

Our "Inhibition" is a *positive* one and the medicine should be a *positive* one—a positive auto-suggestion!

To show what I mean: Assume that you have the habit of getting up at 10 a. m. on Sunday mornings. (This is a positive habit and you are disgusted with it—You feel that the best part of the Sunday is wasted in bed) You have made up your mind to change that habit and to get up at 8 a.m. instead. You are now looking for the formula, for your auto-suggestion. You know that since you are combating a *positive* habit you must find a *positive* formula. It would, therefore, be *wrong* to say: "From now on I am *not* going to stay in bed until 10 a. m." You see that would be "negative." No! Your *positive* auto-suggestion should sound something like this: "From now on *I am going to* get up at 8 a. m. From now on *I am going to* jump out of bed at 8 a. m.! I *will* get up as soon as the clock strikes 8 a. m.!" That's *positive!* Get the idea? Applied to our shooting problem: We are hampered by a positive inhibition. Our auto-suggestion must be equally *positive*.

The following is an example of how an inhibition might work:

Yon are, of course, nervous and jittery—You don't feel at home on the strange range. Your name is called. You take your gun and your ammunition and walk up to the shooting line. Immediately, an ominous inner voice starts buzzing in your ears: "Here, here, fellow, you are not alone! Remember, there are people around—important people in whose minds you must establish that you are a shooter. See, how different the light is? Well, we are not at home, you know. Isn't it hot here? Why, your hands are moist. The stock feels sort of slippery, what? Don't you wish now that you had not entered? It's too late now!

You are in for it. I warned you. Don't tell me I didn't warn you. The bullseye doesn't show up half as well as in your basement and the sights look sort of fuzzy. For God's sake, see that you don't muff things. Have you forgotten that you should relax? How could one relax in this unfriendly crowd? Well, let's buckle down to work. You know, in order to make an "85," none of your shots must go out of the black. Well, I just wanted to remind you. Don't pull your shots. Gee, that bullseye surely looks pale. All right, make the best of it! There are 1001 things that are absolutely essential. Man, you *are* nervous! Hell, one fine shooter *you* are going to be. Ah, well, come on now! Everybody is waiting for you. Do you think you've got a full half hour for your lousy ten shots? Say, that's good! I just said "lousy." Maybe, I am right. Your shots may be lousy, at that. Hohoho. Up goes your gun. My, my, what a tremor—Who said that you should relax? Nonsense! Clamp your hand around the stock, it's slippery. Tighter! Tighter! O-O—you forgot to squeeze—Your own hard luck! Got an alibi? Don't make me laugh. Look again! Sure, look as much as you want. You can't change *that*. A "4"? Right! Well, nine more like that and your target will be exactly "40". You want to shoot an "85"? You and who else? It's no use! The target is already done for. There goes the second shot— What'd I tell you? A "6". Already "ten" down with two shots. What did you do now? A "9"? I saw you close your eyes when the shot went off. One of those lucky things, what? That's "eleven" down in three shots. Oh, what's the use? You might as well bang away. Ah—another "6"—that's "seventeen" down in four shots—That would be, let me see: an "83" and *six* more shots to go—Ah, go ahead and shoot your fool head off—You punk!"

Well, the above shows how the inhibition, the *positive* inhibition, may affect you.

All right! The medicine, Watson! You *don't* use a negative medicine by saying to yourself: "I am *not* going to listen to the voice of that inhibition again." That would not help! You say in-

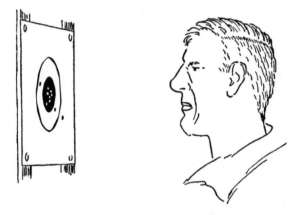

stead: "I *am going to* think along the following lines when I am up front: "Well, well, ol' boy, ol' sock! Here we are!" (Remember, you are nervous and jittery—the experience is new). "This range looks modern—the blast from your gun won't annoy you half as much here—In the basement, it *was* sort of awkward—And observe how well the bullseye stands out in the clever lighting —Nice people here—good friends all—See, how friendly they watch you, eager to oblige? There is no reason why you shouldn't do right well—Ah, over there are some of your competitors—My, how nervous they seem to be—I wonder what makes them so nervous? Oh well, everyone has his little troubles I suppose—Come to think of it: *You* didn't have any trouble today. Everything went along smoothly—like clockwork. Well, all I can say is that, if your competitors are *that* nervous, they will be playing right into your hand. But: Get set, my boy! It's your turn. Let's see: Didn't you shoot around "85" for the last few weeks? And yesterday, you reached a "90"—You don't

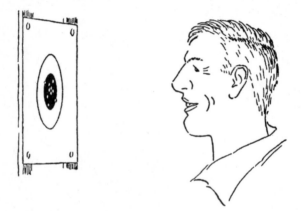

have to show anything extraordinary—Do exactly like you did in your basement—Maybe, you can show them something—Remember now: Hold-Squeeze—Oh heck, I forgot you do that automatically—Here goes: Hmmm! Not bad! You jerked it a little to the left? That's all right! You called it splendidly. Yes, the telescope says "7 o'clock in the nine-ring." Isn't that fine? All right, the next one! Man, you are doing wonderful. Well, life isn't so bad, what? See, how everybody smiles? Ah —another good one! Well, fellows, take the score! What does it say? "86?" "Hurray!"

In the latter example, we have applied our medicine and, it seemed as if it worked. We have "neutralized" our inhibition. That means, our remedy has proven just as strong as the sinister inhibition. Of course, the auto-suggestion need not be copied exactly. You can make your own medicine. Anything that is *positive* and purposeful, will serve as long as it restores the supreme deliberation that you need for good shooting. Why don't you try it?

Oh my, if a scientist were to see this, he might shake his head—Let him! I'll tell you a secret: Get three scientists together on one subject and, after they get through, they will have exactly three opinions. And all three of them are right!

And now: Let's leave this "inhibition-stuff"— Let it "stew" in your mind for a while. You'll be surprised!

There remains another little matter to be touched which, I am afraid, I shall not be able to elucidate fully—It concerns something intangible, something about which one cannot enlarge much: Ghosts!—What? Ghosts? Sure! At least: *One* Ghost—

Yes, we have a ghost in our shooting closet— Nothing aristocratic you know—nothing like the "White Lady of Pembrook" or the "Black Knight of Sagging Nees Manor"—Just a common, lowbreed ghost. The name of that ghost should indicate as much. Imagine a ghost called "Bug-a-boo" being anything but vulgar and lowclass? That's our ghost—Bug-a-boo—Whether we believe in ghosts or not, we've got to believe in this one! We may summon all our intelligence or logic and still we cannot explain this astral loafer away. What does he do? Oh, he just goes around and taps people on the shoulder. Anyone so touched immediately changes his behaviour. It is strange:

Where formerly we used to see a pleasant-man-
nered fellow-shooter, we observe that, under the
influence of Bug-a-boo's curse, this same fellow
takes to swearing. Not just swearing—I mean:
real cussing—He sours. Fits of blasphemy and
attacks of melancholia follow each other in quick
succession. This startling transfiguration has been
diagnosed as "slump." It is something for which
there is no remedy. When you have it, you just
have it! It's like having the Measles or the
Mumps which are, as we know, unpleasant, but
harmless and, thank God, they never last long. In
a similar manner, without treatment, Slumps pass
away. With some it takes longer, with others it
goes faster. Should we let the thing go at that?
No, we are too infernally inquisitive. We want to
know more! We just can't rest and accept things.
It so happens, luckily, that we can avail ourselves
of the experience of the eminent Professor Seminut, who has made a study of Slumps and their
symptoms and here is what he says: Quote: "Any
kind of endeavor which necessitates the utilization
of one's control over one's nervous system-mmmm
—mmmmm—mmmphh—Damn!" Unquote! Par-
don me a second. Have you recovered your
tooth, Professor? Well, my friends, I wasted a
perfectly good evening in the interest of science
and was able, 'finally, to elicit the following:

We cannot hope to be always in peak condition
in our sport. Success in handgun-shooting depends
too much upon the extent of our control over our
nervous system. Why should our nervous system
need such control? Well, life for most of us is
quite exacting—We don't live anymore the tranquil life of our forebears—simple—satisfied—un-
eventful—No, we are steeped in haste, in the ner-

vous pursuit of—of—err—*whatever* we are after. The world around us has stepped up the tempo and we have to step along—Naturally, there are conflicts and more or less violent emotions which will disturb the equilibrium of our nervous system— Now, (The good professor goes on to say), good shooting results can only be had when one's nerve machinery is purring smoothly—Just let an emotion or a succession of emotions *upset* the even beat of the machinery and you—you—have *upset* something. What I mean: you—have—*upset* something—or other—(Ooooh, that's terrible—It seems, writers have slumps too.) Persons with a sort of stoical temperament, I mean people like the Wooden Indians of yore, are less susceptible to this sort of thing—But, with us Moderns (Says Seminut) slight, often unimportant emotions act like— err—Plutowater, what? We just give in—and— slump.

You know, *I* have had slumps myself. Sure! Everybody has! I got over them! Everybody did!

Well, to begin with, it's unpleasant—Your scores are distinctly frigid—You cuss most shockingly— You don't know what in ever has come over you— It seems as if you had forgotten everything you ever learned. And, when you look at the target, bitterness wells up and you just know that the whole world is against you. In your calmer moments, you try to analyze the thing and you arrive at the conclusion that, coming a very poor second in the recent exchange of wit with your mother- in-law, has upset your whatyamacallit. You were subjected to "emotional stress," darn her hide, and, of course, as the professor says, control over your nervous machinery went to pot.

Your real mistake, my friend, was that you let

the thing *rankle!* You simply showed lack of "elasticity." Why don't you try to make it a habit to rob these things of the importance you are used to give them? If you meet up with things of an unpleasant nature, deal with them!—And then promptly forget them! If there are things that cannot be liquidated at once, lay them over—Bury them for a while—Don't think about them—If they creep up, make an effort to think of something else—You shall deal with them when you are ready! But in the meantime, you don't want to be reminded. To hell with them! If you can do that successfully, you have acquired "elasticity" and you will be a much happier man. Life is too damn short anyway! Then, when you step up on the firing-line, you are free! And that will show in your shooting—And these darn occasional slumps will pass away faster.

TIME- AND RAPID-FIRE

In this matter of time- and rapid firing in target work, I am, possibly, a lone soul roaming the ether. Think of it: One against the universe! Well, it's a unique position to be in, to say the least, and reminiscent of the one man in the regiment who believes that he alone has the correct step. The Colonel may put him in the cooler for his stubborness, but that does not settle the question, to my way of thinking. The Colonel and the Private just have a different viewpoint on affairs and, God knows, Colonels have been known to be wrong—Am I of the kind then that likes the accent on the *right* foot while all the others put their *left* foot forward first, out of pure cussedness? No Sir! I just care to be *shown* that I am wrong—that's all.

Will somebody in the whole wide world tell me, why the dickens we should have "Time-and Rapid Firing?"

One at a time, please—All you with long whiskers, stay away!—

Gentlemen, the line forms on the left!—Think hard now, me buckos—

Only logic will slay me!

Is there *one* among you who has seen actual combat, be it in war or police work, who will truthfully say that time-and rapid-fire with handguns, the way we do it at targets, is of practical value?

(Being able to draw your gun quickly, get in the *first* shot and a telling shot at that, is a horse of a different color. *That,* brother, is an art in itself. My good friend McGivern specializes in that stuff and you better read my second book when it comes out.)

Ah, Gentlemen—the silence is overwhelming—

Could it possibly be that time-and rapid-fire is justified only as a means to put variety into the sport?

I'll be generous! I'll even help you with a suggestion. Isn't there some *indirect* advantage in time-and rapid-fire in that it compels you to get going at a given signal?

Some of us may have become *too* deliberate, you know. We are entitled, in slow-fire, to fully ten minutes to get ten shots out and that may have caused us to drift into "freezing" at times; that is we can't get the shot off and have to lay our pistol down so often that the effort of shooting becomes hard mental labor—To just remonstrate with you would not help! You are entitled to ten minutes and, dammit, you want ten minutes. Ah, but in time-and rapid-firing they blow a nasty whistle and in twenty or ten seconds, you must dispose of five shots—like it or not. Well Sir, you are pretty competent in slow-fire and the little matter of speeding up the whole procedure should not feaze you—

Granted, therefore, that time-and rapid-fire have the pedagogical value of taking the pedantism out of our sport, teaching you to think faster and reach a determination faster, then these two kinds of firing can be accepted by us with equanimity. As for their practical use in war or encounter, they are of no general value. Well, our lenient attitude constitutes a compromise, what? The Colonel *and* the Private are both wrong and right!

That being settled, I would like to say that both: time-fire (five shots within twenty seconds) and rapid-fire (five shots within ten seconds), are not hard at all!

The first thing the shooter will do when first seeing a "rapid-fire" target, is to exclaim: "Oh bull, what large eyes you have.—" Right, brother, but let's tackle the thing with a bit less condescension. We have agreed that this new kind of shooting is to teach us to make up our mind faster.

Take "time-fire": There will be the blow of the starting whistle and, after 20 seconds (During which time we have to fire five shots) the whistle will blow again. Now, 20 seconds is a long time— but, just *how* long? We can't look at our watch with one eye and line up the gun with the other. There is nothing to audibly tick off the seconds with and if there were, we wouldn't want it—We would have no time to listen—Our attention is on the gun and the target. What then? We can attune our system to measure off 20 seconds, through habit! Obviously, a certain rhythm is required, say a beat of four seconds for each shot. How can we measure four seconds mentally? Well, in the beginning, we use a little sentence as a guide, for instance:

"Twenty-*one* and oodles of time."
"Twenty-*two* and oodles of time."
"Twenty-*three* and oodles of time."
"Twenty-*four* and oodles of time."
"Twenty-*five* and oodles of time."

If you have an electric clock at home, look at its large second-hand. Murmur the above slowly and evenly (Don't frighten the cat!) so that each sentence takes up four seconds—In a very short time you will manage perfectly. Put the emphasis on "one, two," etc.

Then change the routine. When the second hand just leaves 12 o'clock, start murmuring and *look away,* mumbling all the time, one sentence after the other, *without* a pause in between, until you have finished saying: "Twenty-*five* and oodles of time." Check with the second-hand and you will find that it just passes the 20 second mark. Try a few times more and you will be as accurate as the clock. If you are not too dizzy by now, we can go on!

You may say now that you have established a certain time-value in your mind and it must be put to practice.

All right then: Take your *empty* pistol and point it at your small black sticker on the wall, to one side of the clock. When the second hand passes 12 o'clock, start talking softly and immediately direct your sights and eyes at the small sticker— Everytime you get to the word "Oodles" you *squeeze* the trigger (Don't pull it—Watch the muzzle!)—Go on talking, without pause—There will be five "oodles" and five squeezes. As the word "time" leaves your fillings for the fifth time, look at the second hand and lo and behold, twenty seconds have passed, never to return again.

Try this every day for a few minutes and I guarantee that, within a week you will have the thing down pat. You are then ready for the range!

The first few times, old friend "recoil" may upset your rhythm a little, but, as you take care not to go after high scores in the beginning, but make an effort instead to let your shots fall within *evenly* spaced intervals, it won't take long to get used to the rhythm under fire, with the help of your little poem.

If you should have the good fortune of somebody else timing you, all the better. When his whistle sounds, start reciting and by the time "oodles" rolls from your tonsils, you are squeezing. Keep on talking softly without pause and squeezing softly—until the whistle blows again. Remember the first whistle is not a signal to fire away—It is merely an announcement to start mumbling—You have lots of time—No hurry—and your bull is sooooo large.

As time goes by, your aiming gets mechanized and your squeeze is accelerated—Habit is a great thing—With its help time-fire will appear very much easier than the painstaking slow-fire on the very much smaller bull.

In rapid-fire, the time allotted is ten seconds for five shots—and our rythm-poem is changed to "Twenty-*one* and," "Twenty-*two* and" etc., etc., each sentence to take two seconds—Check yourself with the clock-second-hand—Your shots fall on the syllables "one-two" etc.

Again, we do not look for good scores in the beginning, but watch the even beat of the rhythm—Our shots are evenly spaced, until friend "habit" takes the burden of counting from us.

That's *all* there is to the mechanics of time-and rapid-firing. Just a little attention, a bit of serious practice—and no haste at any time!

We have seen now that, having determined beforehand the point at which the shot is to fall, we *must* squeeze when that point comes—even if the sighting bead should not be perfect at first. The word "rhythm" was chosen advisedly—In a string of five shots, one should hear each shot follow the other rhythmically, with evenly spaced time intervals.

In time-fire you may take a fresh breath after each shot, but your pistol must be kept at arm's length. You would loose too much time lowering it after every shot.

In the ten-second rapid-fire string, it is best to train yourself to take in just sufficient air to last for the entire ten seconds. A little practice will quickly teach one the correct amount of air needed.

Upon going into practice with sharp shells, it will be found that the necessity of maintaining a more pronounced hold becomes apparent. Your mental and muscular reactions must be studied with a view to finding a hold which will cause the gun, after every shot, to find itself in *exactly* the same position *as before* the shot without having to grope for the original hold. The recoil throws the muzzle up, and it has to be brought down again quickly towards the aiming point *in a short straight line*. (Don't attempt any fancy sky-writing with the muzzle). However, you have to "cock" the gun before it can be brought back to the target and this cocking should be done *without* losing your pre-determined rapid-firing hold. In fact, the whole secret of the new hold is that you should not only be able to cock quickly, but it should also embrace all the favorable elements of the slow-fire hold, so that you can get the proper supporting and squeezing actions for accuracy's sake. Use the recoil to facilitate rapid cocking, but find the universal hold. Constant practice and watchful experimenting cannot be dispensed with. One will find that the lighter recoil of the smaller calibres offers less of a problem than the heavier ones.

There is a hold to fit any caliber, but it is entirely up to the shooter alone to find his own. Personally, I follow the practice of clamping my finger-tips against the stock when cocking the hammer (but only then) and releasing the finger-tips for the shooting. In other words, I *shoot* with the slow-fire hold and *cock* with a full-hand hold. This latter prevents shifting of the gun during the cocking action and by simply easing the finger-tips off, I can fire with my accustomed and correct slow-fire hold.

But, let me assure you that the moment you start *tensing* up or *pulling* the trigger, your targets are not going to be worth looking at.

I find it advantageous to teach the pupil to load 5 cartridges in such order that the first cocking will place the empy chamber under the firing pin. Upon hearing the "ready" command the pupil starts aiming and two or three seconds *before* the whistle, he squeezes on the empty chamber and continues his rhythm with the loaded chambers.

In concluding this chapter I am afraid I have to make a concession to my stubborn disposition.

Suppose, we take the case of a *police officer* who

is engaged in a gun duel with a gangster. (Such a situation would surely be quoted in support of rapid-firing). According to present precepts, the officer is expected to start rapid-firing. It is logical to assume in this kind of fast firing that accuracy must suffer. The chances are that, coupled with the resultant excitement, the accuracy of the officer's shooting is further greatly reduced and that the officer misses his antagonist entirely. After the last shot has been fired, the officer's gun will be empty and he is robbed of his most potent weapon until he finds time to reload again.

The officer knows that it is necessary to hit his opponent only once in order to demoralize him. But he has to be *hit*. The value of noisy display is questionable, only a direct hit is a powerful persuader.

Is it not then logical to say that the problem seems to be really one of "getting the drop" and, if necessary, to "hit with the first shot" and then to be ready for further emergency?

If the officer's training were conducted along these latter lines, the lawless element would entertain the idea of a pistol duel with an officer with a much greater amount of trepidation.

Since, however, target-rapid-firing in its present form is an established institution, (and God knows, it is the pet subject of some apostles who never saw action, either in peace or wartime) we must submit in order to be able to enter target competition at all.

My suggestion for competition, if I were asked about it, would be to replace the present form of rapid fire with the following:

Gun in holster.

Upon command the gun should be drawn and

fired once. The shot to hit a rather small target. The gun should then be re-cocked quickly and held up again at "ready fire" position, *aimed* at the same target. The whole action should be timed and the results be judged by "time elapsed" and "value of hit," the weight of scoring to lie with "time elapsed."

ADJUSTED STANCE

It happens sometimes that the group of your shots appears elongated horizontally. (If this distortion is caused by body sway (see First Chapter under "Stance"), then we have an effective remedy.)

By advancing your rear foot slightly you change the sway of your body. Instead of swaying from left to right with your gun-arm, you will now sway more up and down, thus causing the group to constrict horizontally.

If the group should appear elongated vertically, follow the opposite precept.

Remember, if you present more of your shoulder to the target, your gun arm will sway from left to right. If you present more of your chest to the target, the arm will sway up and down.

COMPETITION

And in the end there were matches—

Up to now, we have devoted everything to lapping up what there was in the way of technique— We are fairly satisfied with ourselves—Our slow-fire scores seldom go below "80" or "85" and our time-and rapid-firing is coming along.

We emerge now from our den and stick our nose up to see what is going on in the good wide world—a sort of "Bring on your fancy shots!"

Sure, we know that there must be others who studied and practiced just like you—And all of them think that they are pretty good—Just like you.

Wouldn't it be interesting now to compare notes among you fellows?

All right! I'll be on your side—rooting for you. I know what a diligent pupil you have been and, if there are any little crinkles to be ironed out, just holler!

You deserve to win your first match. But, you are on your own—No fear, with your equipment you should do well.

A little nervous? O—O—We all were, you know. —You'll get over that. Look at your opponent. (He must have heard of your lone scores—Maybe, you told him—) He seems to be sort of nervous himself—

All right, you start even.

Fun?—

Yes, matches are our ultimate goal. While we exult at good individual home targets, only competition, and competition alone, furnishes the real spice to our sport—Good, clean competition. Being gentlemen, we lose and win in good grace. We don't show any condescending pity nor 'do we sulk in disappointment—Competition is the crucial fire of testing our painstaking course and proof of our character stability.

Of course, if we had been negligent—just stumbling along, shooting indifferent or inconsistent scores, then competition is a bad thing! And that's why I warn everybody: Avoid matches like the measles *unless* you are fairly prepared. Matches should *never* interrupt a predetermined course of learning. You see, after you have graduated and you have made up your mind to enter into competition, in short, after you are sure of yourself—honestly sure, then you should go into *training*. You have to prepare for the matches. Don't tumble into any old match! Make up your mind to participate in slow-fire matches first. Your training consists now of firing this kind as often as you can, in your Club or by yourself. Try to create the *conditions* that you are apt to find on the competition grounds, such as distance, light conditions, weapon, ammunition, number of shots, etc. For your first opponents don't pick on the giants in the game—Choose men of your own calibre—"Tyros," I think, they call them, people that haven't won a match themselves. It is of psychological value that you do not lose every match, in the beginning. You should win some of them so that you may throw out your chest, put some fire in your eyes and swagger home.

If at all possible, try to practice on the range on which the competition is going to be held. I mean, go there several times in the morning, if the shoot is to be held of a morning. Light conditions in the morning are different from those in the afternoon. The target to the left will offer a different problem than the target on the right. On some ranges, the targets are hung higher than on others. Old hands in the game take *everything* into consideration —They know! Try to make notes—adjust your sights—Don't leave things to chance! Think of how golfers try to get acquainted with the lay of the land—how they practice certain difficult shots—

If your competition is an outdoor affair, there will be old "Boreas" to be figured with—it matters whether the wind is blowing from the rear or from one side or whether it is shifting all the time.

If there should be a target that offers special difficulties—a so-called "hard luck target," get most of your practice in on that one. If the sun is out, it may be necessary to smoke up your sights—oh-there are lots of possibilities. The idea I am trying to get across is that you should not get on a new range, entirely at sea. Those things depend upon circumstances, of course, but, if you can at all do it, get *acquainted* with the range and its conditions *before* the match.

Some people shoot only at night—they have no time for practice during the day. When they have to compete in the morning, they are up against different moods and conditions. You want to think of all that!

Some revolvers "spit" perceptibly and the competitors to the left or to the right get considerably annoyed and flustered. When the hot sparks touch their faces or hands, they are apt to muff their targets. I believe that it is the sporty thing to see that *your* revolver does not "spit" too much. Being overly smart does not make friends.

You are, of course, familiar with the special conditions of the forthcoming match. I mean, as far as the number of shots, the calibre permitted etc., etc. are concerned. If the match should call for 20 shots, SLOW FIRE, at 75 feet, you don't of course, practice over 50 or 150 feet. You just imitate the exact conditions: You fire 20 shots at 75 feet, within ten minutes. And then you count up your score. Make your sight-corrections, amplify your notes as to position of sun, direction and velocity of wind etc., etc. and repeat the same course. After shooting the course three times, stop for the day. Sixty shots per day is ample for you. When scoring, be honest with yourself.

Don't pick out the two best targets of the day and add those up. You are fooling nobody but yourself. And then, when the day comes, your confidence will be supreme. In order to save you some confusion, I have concocted a little nursery rhyme. If you learn that by heart, it may help you—in a pinch. It's terrible, I know; but better than nothing:

> *If your shot-group is too high,*
> *Up with your front-sight just a fly.*
> *If too low the group should be*
> *Lower the darn sight just a wee.*

> *With an adjustable rear-sight job,*
> *Raise it if too low the shots;*
> *Do the reverse if you want to stop*
> *Shooting above the bullseye-spots.*

> *Adjust the notch to "port" a mite*
> *If your gun shoots to the right,*
> *But use the opposite direction*
> *If your group has "left" deflection.*

Don't start adjusting sights right away. Fire a few sighting shots first. Sometimes, one's hold on the bull changes after a few shots. The experienced shooter is the one that changes his sights only when *absolutely* necessary. You may get a little excited and tense when you start. Look at page 79 and read again what I said about "One-Two-Shooting" and relaxation before the shoot.

If you participate in an individual match, that is if you are shooting for yourself and not as a member of a team, see that you take some means along, to spot your shots—a pair of good binoculars or a telescope. There is nothing so distressing and disappointing as not being able to correctly see your bullet holes. You must know all the time what you are doing on the target. This holds particularly true for the 150 feet outdoors match, where even a pair of 7/50 Zeiss glasses would fail. A rather high-powered telescope would be the answer there. When you are on the firing line, throw a sort of "isolation aura" around yourself— Not that you should be sulky or impolite—Just retire into yourself and concentrate on your work. Don't pay *any* attention to what your neighbor does—and close your ears to any commotion or conversation around you. Don't be worrying about the other fellow's scores—your own need all your attention.

After the final shot is out, become sociable again. You have done consciencious, earnest work and you are entitled to a little "let-off." Be sure, not to disturb the firing line, however. Some of the others may still be in the throes—If I were you, I would also curb my curiosity as to your scores—Be nonchalant! If your scores are exceptional, somebody will tell you and, if "lousy," some kindly soul will impart that information too, no fear.

When a member of a team, do about the same. The scores of the other team-members do *not* interest you—on the firing line. All *you* do is: doing your best!

You know, if you start worrying about things, the match will be no fun! And you *did* go out to get something out of life, something worthwhile, even if it should turn out to be nothing but "experience." That will come in handy in your future matches. You have nothing to lose in your initial matches but the opportunity to enjoy yourself.

And, who would be so foolish and forego pleasure just for the sake of being able to do some fancy worrying?

All through this manual, you must have gotten the impression of cheerful enthusiasm—Even when we are hard at work, we never let down. Our sport should exercise an optimistic influence upon our character—If we do a little bragging at times over an exceptional score, that should constitute nothing but a little slip. All in all, our sport should be kept wholesome—a friendly feeling of "belonging" should prevail, a helpful spirit—In short: our sport should be worthwhile, not only in the way of achievement, but also in what it can give us in spiritual values—Friendship—Comradery—

REPUTATION

My friends (I hope that I have, by now, earned the right to call you that)—there is one thing in Revolver Shooting with which I have never become entirely reconciled. I should like to talk about that a little.

It is human for every one of us to desire to be a top-notcher, to be known as a marvelous shot—as a dangerous opponent—as a champion—in short to have a reputation.

If you should reach this stadium you have a perfect right to be proud of your achievement. Hearty congratulations are in order. You yourself know best what an amount of diligent work you had to go through to get this far.

You will come face to face with the realization by and by, that your work is not ended then—that you must go on and on. It is not possible for you to rest on your laurels. Remember, my friend,

there is reputation not to "have" but to "maintain"
—a very fickle thing indeed—and a danger.

Do not let this thing grow into a curse.

I shall illustrate: You have a reputation. You
are invited to a friendly shooting party—You go
there expecting to have a good time—but you have
to show your stuff first—and woe to you if you do
not show in top form. Nobody considers whether
or not you feel right or that conditions are different on every range.

Just because I was known to have done it, when
in form, I was asked time and again to hit a
cigarette at 60 feet with one shot with weapons I
had never even seen before. I was too good-natured
or too vain to refuse. I want you to believe me
when I say that, although I succeeded, many a fine
day was spoiled for me. Praise and admiration
are not sufficient recompense for the silence which
follows if you miss.

You are not permitted to experiment anymore.
Every shot is expected to be perfect. You are under constant pressure and, sometimes, you wish
that people would leave you alone.

The only way out seems to be to make light of
your reputation. You may state that any average
shooter could duplicate your shooting if he were
to try seriously (which, we know, is true. Say
anything—but don't let the thing get you.

YOU AND YOUR GUN

We have seen, after getting this far, that there
is a little more to revolver shooting than many perhaps anticipate.

You don't just resolve some fine day to take up
shooting, buy a gun, step up to the range and bang
away.

You have found out by now that you have to get a foundation and that you have to *work* to get it, that you have to discard and to rebuild, to bend and submit to other judgment—until you can stand on your own.

Although everything is fundamentally simple, you have to make yourself "absorb" these simple things—and you have to practice—practice and then practice some more.

We have filled many pages with fundamentals and what will be considered as aids and hints, but, although we have criticised its technical weaknesses, we have not spent much breath upon what I would like to call the soul of our gun.

Do not, even for a moment, get the idea that your revolver is just a tool of the trade.

Every revolver has its peculiarities, although it may have been made with fine factory tolerances along with thousands of others—peculiarities,—indeed. I am tempted to say that every revolver has its own character. Don't smile, just switch guns and your face will lose its sanguine expression.

Let's pick a simile. Once you have chosen a gun, consider it in the light of a sweatheart, court it, fondle it, treat it with care; but, beyond all, study it, try to find its characteristics, solve its soul.

The rewards will be ample.

Your gun is very jealous and will not permit a rival (that is, not within eye-scratching distance). So, do not switch sweethearts (even though you may think that you have solved them individually) during a shoot.

Just try to do that very thing and your sunny disposition will suffer.

Therefore, don't!

THE POSSIBLE

It is timely that I should say now that within the scope of a manual it is not possible to completely cover a subject in all its aspects. This would really require a volume. It is not even feasible. My aim was to show just the skeleton; to strip the difficult matter, as much as possible, of all finesse—unadorned with (for a beginner) unessential detail. I trust that this task has been covered in this handbook.

There may come a time when the advanced shooter, if he be ambitious, believes that he has reached his limitation. His hope is still that, one day, he will accomplish the "Possible"—but a sort of resignation seems to settle upon him. He may still take pleasure in knowing that he is considered a dangerous opponent, yet he recognizes that he is at a standstill.

However, a state of mind of that order is not at all in conformity with the hopeful enthusiasm which I have tried to instill into my reader—not at all.

Now, my friend, the battle has really only started.

If, so far, you have only followed suggestions, now is the time to start analyzing the cause of your apparent limitation.

Let us look the facts in the face. There is no reason in the world why you should not reach the "Possible" (10 shots in the ten-ring). I go even further and say that there is no real reason why you should not be able to shoot the "Possible" more than once.

But, if you are seriously and conscientiously after the "Possible," you will come to shoot in the "nineties" pretty consistently. And why should you not have a little luck once in a while?

However—and here is the really important part —even if luck should turn her shoulder, you are still shooting in the high "nineties." Get the drift? With high nineties, you are a *top-notcher*. That can be and should be your goal. To get there, the word "limitation" should disappear from your vocabulary.

Use your head.

The fathers of the Standard American Target were wily rascals, indeed. They settled upon the smallest possible ten-ring. Still "Possibles" have been shot. Luck does play a part in it, since even a machine-rest will not always shoot "Possibles"— with today's ammunition.

There must be some things which you are doing wrong. There must be! It is not the target, elusive as it may appear; it is not the gun. The ammunition, it is true, could be a whole lot more uniform.

But don't look outside of yourself.

You are the only one responsible.

It does not do for you simply to accept my statement. You should, inherently, discover it yourself.

What then is the purpose of this chapter? It is to make you realize that you are doing something which is wrong—What is it?

Find out! Study your problem. Experiment.

Why not re-read this Manual carefully? Some little thing may not have been absorbed. If, while experimenting, you were to discover for yourself an apparently more or less unimportant, yet very helpful expedient, and in glancing through this Manual you should find the subject already

treated, would you not think yourself rather foolish?

Maybe, it is your hold, or the non-discovery of
the infinitesimally short periods where coordination brings about the disappearance of all tremor,
just when six o'clock is easing on your front-
sight.

Maybe, it is a number of things, and possibly
only one single error.

Go ahead. You are on your own.

A complete coverage of all intricacies cannot
possibly belong in the realm of a Manual. Consideration for the many who have not reached
your status would forbid that. They must 'not be
confused by chapters which really should go into
a "Manual for Distinguished Experts"—maybe,
sometime—later on—

> Get your chin up—
> And study—
> And work—
> To success.

FUN GALORE

We revolver addicts are a cheerful bunch as a
whole, cheerful in the sense that we meet adverse
happenings before the target with all sorts of
alibis—alibis which sometimes are so extremely
funny as to provide hearty amusement,—first for
the other fellows and then (to a lesser degree)
for ourselves. We go down, but we always come
up again—for more. The bug has bitten us. We
are addicts—hopelessly so.

Although afraid that lour total sum of available
amusement may be severely curtailed, I rather like
the thought that your more or less sorrowful moments (which run concurrently with our bursts

of humorous appreciation) should be lightened some way or other.

Take an acute case, a case to be found at any gathering of shooters. We find our friend exultant at the first signs of improvement. His bearing is full of exuberant vitality. He pats everybody on the back. His eyes glow. He struts around, and he is generally very happy. Life surely looks sweet to him. During the intervening week till the next gathering, everybody is his friend, even his next-door neighbor. His relatives do not pain him half as much. He is an amiable creature. And he confidently attacks his new target. But, for some reason, things seem to have changed. A cloud has passed over the sunny sky; friendship somehow does not seem quite as sweet. What in the world—? A pungent string of expletives indicates a frigid score on the target.

Something he ate the night before—the ammunition was faulty—not to mention the gun. That's it—the gun—no good—he knew it all along. He remembers having seen this or that fellow shoot some other model—that was the gun par excellence. All right, he'll get that other gun! His alibi is complete. He'll try again with the other gun. He's up again, bouncingly confident. Wait till he gets his hand on the other model.

And the cycle all over again—ad infinitum.

Brother, I wouldn't want to miss you among our bunch for anything. Life would be too drab otherwise. However, next time remember that there are ladies around.

Now, I know, you yourself didn't enjoy the show nearly as much as we others. I have a faint suspicion that you didn't enjoy part of it at all. You wish to avoid that in the future? Then:

Don't make an ass out of yourself by fooling around with all kinds of guns, and fail every time. *Stick to one gun*—stay with it until you have it licked.

If you should get a stupid target:

—Don't alibi your way out

—Don't swear—and

—Don't blame your gun.

If you follow these "Don'ts" you will, probably, take half the fun out of our lives, but you'll enjoy yours just that much more.

If you are down, try—try again—with the same gun, and you will be up again—and improve again. Because you are one of us.

SOME KICKS

This manual is of the Revolver. The metacentric unbalance of the revolver and the ramifications caused thereby had already been treated in the first "Elusive Ten." My diatribe must have sounded quite startling. One friendly would-be reviewer sweat blood and finally refused to comment because, he said, that manual contained too much dynamite. And Boy, did I strut—I never knew I had it in me—Of course, in a manual of this kind, I can have no other interest at heart than that of the reader, the beginner, the pupil. If, while writing, I have to step on the toes of the mighty ones, here and there, it can't be helped. I am independent of them, thank God. Take the lamentable fact that some guns are too muzzle-light, unbalanced, thus accentuating tremors and vibrations. In exasperation, the shooter is forced to experiment, with insufficient knowledge and equipment, using steel rods or other means to overcome a deficiency which the manufacturers should have avoided in the first place. And that brings me to Gun-Grips—When looking over the crop of guns that has been put on the market, one is almost tempted to think that the manufacturers spent all their brains on barrel-and action-construction—After designing these, they seem to have run out of grey matter—Unfortunately, it was necessary to stick a handle on the darn thing so that the fool shooters wouldn't burn their fingers. So, the boys went ahead and put a handle on—any old handle, any old way. Durn it, even the people who make porcelain cups, try to use their heads by putting comfortable handles on them. It moves me to tears when I remember that these alert cup-makers were considerate enough to put a clever bridge across the abyss, just to keep the handle-bars of our forefathers out of the cup—Modern people, these cup-makers. But, of course, coffee cups are scientific instruments—Handguns are just—

Ah, Nuts! I believe, I shall have to take the boys to task! What the hell did you have in mind when you fastened those funny doodads on the frames? Or *did* you have anything in your mind? (Boy, I am enjoying this—See them squirm—) Eh? Come, come! Speak up, venerable ones!

Must we go on buying miscarriages? Must we? Ah, I know, you will say: "This bird tries to amuse his readers at our expense."

Righto, brothers. If we can't get the guns we want, we might as well have some fun! Don't tell me, you poor orphans had nobody with brains to advise you—What is that? You say that your "naked" stocks must meet the requirements of most shooters? Oh, there would be nothing wrong with that *if* your stocks "as are" really *did* fit *most* shooters, which they don't, of course! It isn't that the shooting world hadn't hammered away at you, begging you, imploring you—. Well, I am going to take matters in hand a little. Thousands will read this and will grin at your discomforture. I know this much: If an experienced shooter steps up and corrects me, I can take it in good grace. But just direct some well meant criticism at the manufacturers or their representatives and watch the stubborn glint in their eyes—Ah well, boys will be boys. They think that since they cannot or will not give us the sensible thing, all we shooters can do is to hand over our hard-earned cash and say "Thank you!" Who are we anyway? How nervy of us to want the guns that *we* want and not the ones that our betters *think* we should have—Isn't it so that we shooters have become so meek that, whenever the boys lay an egg (Be it ever so insignificant), *we* do the cackling for them? Why don't you big handsome things get among people and feel their pulses, instead of having some long-bearded "Know-it-all" harrumph you into your green table splurges?

Don't tell me, you ravishing brutes, that you never heard complaints about muzzle-lightness, about wrong angle of stock to frame, about unscientific grip-design, about silly trigger shapes and positions, about lousy sights—Am I the first one to kick? Or the only one? Why should European pistols be generally superior to ours? Oh, I know what your answer will be—But, let me implore you: *Wake up!* And respect the intelligence of the shooting world. To hell with the few who lick your hands! I am talking PROGRESS, such as we meet in every other line of endeavor: Heating-Radio-Motorcar-Industries, etc. If *they* had been content to sit back on their tails, we would still be chugging along on one cylinder!

The way things are now, we buy a gun from you for so and so many dollars and then, in order to have something serviceable, we have to go ahead and spend some more money on Grip-Adapters, new sights, muzzle-weighting devices, etc., etc. Just imagine buying a car and, in order to be able to drive it, having to go out and buy a steering wheel from another party—Your godsends may be alright for the average lousy shot, but we, with our ambitions, we demand more! Who is going to give it to us?

I am afraid that my good friend Colonel Whelen, a gentleman if there ever was one and our ranking expert on fire-arms, will read this phillippica with a slight shock. My dear Colonel, forgive my language—You know that I am really a nice chap, but my heart bleeds for my fellow-shooters and somebody, still recklessly aggressive, will *have* to speak up! I simply don't give a rap if the big Methusalems get heart-failure. We pay good money for our guns and we want them to get busy and give us our money's worth!

(I have told Tom Samworth, the publisher, that, either he lets me write what I *must* or he can't have the manuscript.)

What do we want? Well, boys read the manual and weep!

And don't skip what I say about "sights" and other things!

The shoe fits all of you!

Get modern, you producers! *Think* modern!

Have initiative! Don't let the sports-world go on squawking!

Experiment! Consult your serious critics! Don't ask for easy endorsements and sit back on your haunches and smirk! You are only fooling yourself! Quit laying tiny eggs! Follow the example of other successful American industries! Discard your outmoded junk! Sit down and give us *Modern Guns!* And, if your work shows merit, it will not be necessary for us to sing your praise, because the shooters themselves will do so.

Well, well, dear Reader, we have had our lil' fun! It's time to get back to work! When I laid into the manufacturers, it did not mean that their products cannot be used at all. Don't get *that* into your heads! Certainly, we can do fine work with them! All I set out to do was to point out a sort of "rut." There are endless possibilities and we want them explored! Not in ten or twenty years—but: Right now! Hell, with our American inventive brains—

SIGHTS AND SIGHS

Here we come to another sore spot—Sights are, probably, the most neglected part of the modern handgun. Just think of it: In order to do accurate shooting at all, one must line up the sights accurately or give up—That's the law!—and yet "Sights" have been the stepchild of the manufacturers ever since somebody invented the darn things.

Why the important item "Sights" should have been thus neglected, is one of the things that will, forever, stay a mystery with me. Hell and damnation!—Wait a minute! Cool down, old chap! Ladies will read this chapter and they might object to strong language.

Listen, my dear Lady, what would *you* do if, at

an important match, a match that you have set
your heart on, light-or target-conditions demanded
a sight-adjustment and you couldn't budge the
—sweet thing?

Alright, my dear, I understand; Don't mind me!
I am used to cussing.

Now, there are certain apostles (I like that word
—it suggests long beards and friendly, if slightly
vacuous eyes) who go in for "fixed" sights and
claim that changing sights is for the "imagina-
tive." Maybe, they are right! But their celestial
scores are too lousy to carry much conviction.
Stand aside, you bewhiskered ones. We'll see you
later, after the match. No time now!

My dear friend, will you accept a statement from
me? An unequivocal and modern statement? Here
it is: Don't buy a gun, *whatever* it is, *unless the
sights are adjustable!* Look for sights that are
easily and positively adjustable. Not sights, where
you have to fumble around, ruining small screw-
slots and guessing at what that and that adjusting
screw will do. We've done that too long! It's
time somebody outlawed the abominations that
are foisted on us. Stand pat! Insist! Keep on
insisting and, one day, maybe, somebody will wake
up, what? In the meantime, turn to people like
King's in San Francisco who have made a study
of this thing called "sights" and who are offering
sane and practical solutions. True, you won't get
their things for nothing. But, listen carefully, they
are worth *many times* more than you pay for them,
in the way of better scores, better health and
sweeter dispositions. Don't get the idea that I
owe these people money or something. I don't
know King's from Adam. But, damn it, I admire
their work.

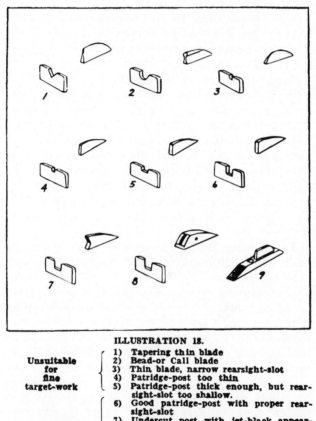

ILLUSTRATION 18.

Unsuitable for fine target-work

1) Tapering thin blade
2) Bead-or Call blade
3) Thin blade, narrow rearsight-slot
4) Patridge-post too thin
5) Patridge-post thick enough, but rearsight-slot too shallow.

Recommended Sights

6) Good patridge-post with proper rearsight-slot
7) Undercut post with jet-black appearance. Rearsight-slot tapered (Wider toward frontsight-post)
8) WHITEX-sight
9) King's red-post block with chromium mirror.

All sights must be adjustable for windage and elevation.

Being such a nut on scientific sights, I naturally spent some thought on them:

> *If the sights on your favorite gun*
> *Are fixed and not adjustable,*
> *Shooting won't be any fun and*
> *Tempers grow combustible—*

I thought that up, all by myself.

Well, of course, you and I agree to throw fixed sights in the ash-can. That's where they belong. And our attitude is firm whether we talk about target-or practical shooting. Show us any gun that is to be used for fast draw and we will show them that modern sights needn't interfere, what?

Everytime I hear that stuff about interfering with the draw, I am reminded of a "Belly Sigh in the desert"—offensively pungent, but, oh—so futile—.

The guiding idea in our modern sights should be their ample proportions, their contrast and their easy adjustibility.

Theoretically, a very fine blade, instead of the broad posts we use, should give the smallest errors. If you set a thin blade under the bull—Pardon me: If your front-sight were a thin blade and could be held at right at 6 o'clock, there should be no deviations and every shot should register in the exact center of the "Ten." That's what our bewhiskered big shots had in mind when they put these thin blades on the military guns. Practice shows, however, that these thin blades suffer from lack of contrast—they dissolve under our agonized iris. I bet that our forefathers, the troglodytes, recognized this and the front-sights on their clubs—Ahem! I believe, one must ridicule fool things, rather than argue about them.

No, we work best with a front post which is at

least 1/10th inch thick. That size will not shrink
so much, optically speaking, particularly if we have
a *wide enough* slot in the rear-sight. Many shooters put too much of a strain on their eyes by trying
to balance their front-post within too narrow a slot.
You want a distinct "light line" on both sides of
the front post, wide enough so that you can juggle
the post comfortably. The human eye has sufficient geometrical ability to juggle the post so that,
in a wide slot, it appears right in the middle. At
times, conditions prevent the "light lines" from
showing clearly. Hold your black sights against
the dark green of the woods and the whole sight
apparatus becomes useless. I've had an idea for
years that we should emancipate ourselves from
the bizarre and impractical color schemes of nature. What gives us the "light lines" on both sides
of the front post, is the background. Why not discard the natural background and substitute an artificial one? What ho—?

Suppose, we put a snow white piece of card board
in place of our front sight and *paint* a post on the
card board. What do we see when we line up?

Well, there will be the black rear-sight with its
slot. Within this slot there appears the painted
coal black post surrounded on both sides by two
snow-white lines, which are part of the artificial
background visible through the slot.

It is true that we cover up part of our target or
game, but we can well afford it. We see what we
want to hit, *over* the post.

Put into practice: We could fasten 1/8th inch thick snow-white ivory blocks on each side of the front post and undercut the latter in order to intensify its backness, and our artificial background is there. In Indoor-shooting, of course, this artificial background would be in the way and we would have to remove the ivory posts. I have cunningly inveigled you within the confines of "contrast." In Outdoor and practical shooting, contrasting sights are a conditio sine qua non.

Maybe, my idea was worthwhile playing around with—

Just think: You can hold right into the bull, instead of holding at 6 o'clock.

Through one of those queer quirks of chance it appears that, while I wrestled with the above problem theoretically and incorporated the result in my notes, another genius in a different part of the country did not stop at such a futile gesture. A chap by the name of R. J. Tappehorn in Louisville, Kentucky, after independently tackling the same problem, took out his tools and *made* the thing! And a good job too! Yes Sir, while my M/S was stewing with the Publisher, friend Tappehorn was putting the thing on the market. And, let me tell you, fellows, you want to get one of his sights! They are really great! Your uncle recovered from his amazement over the erratic whims of coincidence, put the new "Whitex" sight on his K .22 (Having received a sight model in the mail) and exulted over the clear definition. I say again: You will want that sight! Not because I was a sort of platonic father to this same brainstorm, but because you should not go without it! Come on, Tappi, ol' Boy, shake! You did a fine job! Just hold that sight right into the darkest green in the woods or into the bullseye where it is blackest and your bead will be as distinct as you could wish! I found that opening and deepening the rear-sight slot a little (So as to get more ample white lines on both sides of the black front-post), enhances the usefulness of this modern and immensely practical sight-innovation.

For Indoor-Shooting under artificial light conditions, just open one screw and remove the white side-pieces and you have an efficient, undercut patridge post equal to any on the market.

Yes, things are starting to move all right, all right!

Right now, I am wracking my brains to conceive a sight arrangement that can be used under *artificial* light conditions. Holding "dead center," instead of at 6 o'clock, has always been my contention. It is so much easier for the human eye to gravitate toward the center of a circle, than to balance a ball upon the top of the front sight. The bullet strikes where you hold the bead—How natural—Under artificial light conditions such as we find in most of our Indoor ranges, we are compelled to hold the bead under the bull so that we may see our black sights at all. Again we were looking for "contrast" and found it in the white paper of the target. Unfortunately, our unacknowledged craving for contrast sometimes leads us to overdo things. Mostly, our targets are vastly "overlit." The halation effect often found and which so exasperates the retina, is attributible to too much candle power. It is not the object here to go into range lighting problems. But, a good thing to remember is: to try and get along with as few lumen as possible, rather than the other way around.

Indoor Sights—yes, yes! What is to prevent us from reversing the two sights, that is: to put the present frontsight at the rear and the rearsight at the muzzle?

Oh no, I am not crazy! Not yet! Listen:

If the slot in our promoted frontsight were wide enough so as to embrace the bull—and if our new rearsight consisted of a "T"—

NEW FRONT SIGHT

NEW REAR SIGHT

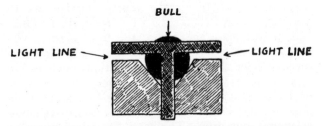

Both sights imposed. All shaded sections will appear black in artificial light. The horizontal light line halves the bull.

See, what happens? The fact that the slot is further away from our eyes (Being now located at the muzzle of the gun), would tend to keep the slot rather narrow. You know, the further a thing is away from the eye, the smaller it looks. Just look at a standard bull from 60 feet away and you will agree that we don't need much of a slot—say no more than 1/8th inch at the most. It has to be slightly wider than the apparent diameter of the bull—(It may be a "V" slot) so that we can snuggle the latter in the center of the slot.

Our "T" bar (or a thick wire—of triangular profile, fastened in a frame) cuts the bull horizontally, allowing for light-lines between the bar and the top of the new frontsight.

In my estimation, there is no need, when sighting, to pay much attention to anything but the light-line which separates the bar from the top of the frontsight. Although part of this light line, namely where it crosses the bull, will not be visible, our eyes will automatically make it look continuous. If the light-line is too wide, then the frontsight is held too low, etc.

The thing may look a little unusual, but so did our present day automobiles at first. I shall continue to fool around with this idea as soon as time permits. By golly, if we could solve the problem of holding dead center, in indoor ranges—

TRIMMING YOUR GUN

If we admit the necessity of "perfect balance" as a generality, we shall be in a much better position to "trim" our gun. (The term "to trim" meaning to shift the center of weight, the "hang" and also comprising intelligent work on the trigger and hammer, etc.) The gun must rest comfortably and naturally in your hand and the muzzle should steadily tickle the bull; the trigger should have no unnecessary travel and the hammer fall should be short and sweet. Sure, perfect balance would be desirable—but that definition cannot be dismissed by simply saying that the point of fulcrum should be in front of the trigger or at any other definite

point.   It is much more subtle than that!   You
see, each shooter is an individual with his very
own peculiarities, physically as well as mentally.
What may be perfect "hang" for one, may feel
quite the contrary to the other.   There are very
few instances where a gun model seems to have
a more universal appeal, such examples being the
"Lueger" in the Automatic field and the .38 Officer's Revolver, just to mention two.   A model becomes a favorite not because it is just better than
the others, but because it satifies more people with
the sort of "universal hang" it has.   There is little
reason why every good gun could not be adapted
so as to offer the individual hang a shooter might
desire.

The trouble in general is, however, that most
shooters don't know what they really want!

For general guidance, I would like to suggest
that they "trim" their gun so as to have more or
less (Rather *more*) muzzle weight.   The advantage of moderate overbalance near the muzzle will
be acknowledged particularly by nervous or high-

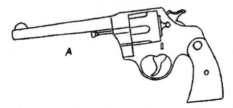

**This gun would dip because the angle of grip to barrel axis
is too near at right angles.**

strung persons.   If we admit that, under shooting
stress, most people are somewhat nervous and
highstrung, it would follow that muzzle over-
weight might benefit 90% of all handgun shooters,

Now, if a gun is overbalanced forward, then there will be a tendency of the muzzle to "dip." (I am nearly overcome with the importance of this deduction).

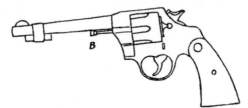

This gun with correct angle has been made to dip by adding weight near the muzzle.

Hah, Watson, the needle! Use your cerebral faculties—Your bean, in other words! Suppose, we look at the following sketches?

You can make the muzzles of both guns perk up (without changing your natural hold) by trimming the shape of the handle, thusly:

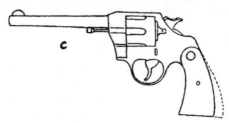

Add to the lower end of the backstrap and the ball of the thumb will "poosh" the muzzle up.

You may feel, on the other hand, that the muzzle of your particular gun "stargazes" like 'D' (Happens mostly with extreme angle between handle and barrel axis) If such a gun is muzzle-heavy, but "points up," because of extreme angle and, if further weighting down the muzzle would make the whole assembly too heavy for you, add something "low front" and, if possible, take something away from the lower backstrap and your handle will look like this:

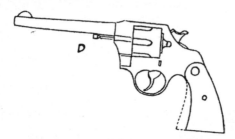

You see, it's amazingly simple, theoretically, to change the "hang" of your gun either by adding weight near the muzzle (Never lighten the muzzle) or by changing the shape of the grip, or both.

What we really do is to change the "angle" of grip to axis of barrel, as a study of the sketches will quickly show. What the correct angle (If there were such a thing as a universally correct angle) is, I don't know. I believe that this angle is more or less individual. Doubtlessly, certain guns show an angle which facilitates the endeavors of the shooter to "get used" to the particular hang. In the above I have shown, however, how anybody can ascertain his own angle, possibly suited only to himself. With the media of Plastic Wood, Dental Wax, etc., everyone can gradually and studiously develop his own "hang" and, after the final shape has been arrived at, it is a simple matter of having it carved into permanent form. Of course, any schoolboy could have told us that but, it seems, none were around.

Whatever correction is attempted, special attention should be paid to providing a comfortable resting place for the little finger. There is a wider space between the bend of the little finger to the ball of the thumb, than with ring-or middlefingers. Logically, one needs more wood behind it. There must be no feeling of skimpiness under the little finger, a sort of "nothing there." You will find that all my sketches, whether stock is added front or rear, show a widening of the stock under the little finger. With the regulation stock, the little finger angles for support and, not finding it in a natural spot, it tenses more and more in its search for wood. And, if you tense your little finger, just try to keep the others loose—the tension transmits itself through the whole hand, the wrist and the arm.

The lower end of the stock, (Shall we say: its "foot"?) must always be considerably wider in proportion to the other sections of the grip. If a grip is evenly wide throughout its length, even if there were enough support for the little finger, it always feels uncomfortable and awkward—Take, for instance, the old .45 Automatic.

Having achieved the right "hang," the next important matter to be attended to should be the "trigger travel." With the exception of the automatic pull (where the trigger travel partly covers the "take-up"), the trigger in every part of its short travel (Seldom more than 1/16th of an inch) should do actual work, namely that of overcoming the hammer-spring tension until the hammer slips the sear-notch. There should be no loose motion *after* that! It is often possible to terminate the trigger travel by a small stop-screw in the trigger-guard, behind the trigger.

Another good "trimming" point is to lighten the hammer by reducing its mass (To "skeletonize" it, as it is called by confirmed bugs) and to shorten the hammer fall, eliminating all jars. These mechanical manipulations with trigger and hammer had better be left to a good gun-smith. It is too darn easy to lick off just a mite too much here or there, with stone or file. But, if you are one of the "Guild of Guileless Ginks," then—

For the Tinker-Nut there is no hope!
Seeing a gun, he is interested
And grabs the thing, applying the dope
Which his brain has scarce digested.

His eyes aflash, his hands atremble,
He loosens screws and smirks insanely,
And as the gun starts to dissemble,
Parts fly around and clutter inanely

The landscape. Our friend not heeds!
That gun had, by gar, too many parts.
Tch! Tch! But what it really needs
Is tinkering. Wait till the "filing" starts—

And being put together again,
It may look like a gun, fit as a bell,
But its shooting days are gone, my fren',
Another "pet" has went to hell!

When the nut gets through with the bally thing,
Put in his nose an iron ring
And yank with might and curb his fun
And don't let him touch your own pet gun!

Personally, I never touch my guns with tools. I *know* that I am too dumb! And I am given to cussing.

GRIPS

I was of the impression that the matter of scientific GRIP—design had never received the close attention due it.   Of course, any fool if he be stubborn enough, might get used to almost anything. But, why trudge in the mud of mediocrity always?

Whenever guns are discussed, the topic revolves earnestly around the accuracy of barrel, calibre, number and depth of grooves, pitch and direction of twist, length of barrel etc. etc., ad absurdum. Lesser attention is paid to the action of the gun, even less to weight distribution, balance, hang, etc. But, when it comes to "Grips," the buzzards are mute.

True, we see, here and there, an attempt by an amateur to acknowledge the importance of "Ideal Grip," but there is nothing concerted or conclusive in these sporadic endeavors.

When Roper introduced the H. & R. Grips, the shooting world perked up, but the very variety of these handles made a decision very hard for the average amateur.   You see, nobody really knew what he wanted.   When later, Roper, departing from his former variety, sort of consolidated his ideas and brought out the now quite well-known new Roper-Grips, the advent was hailed as an important revelation.   The enthusiastic response from the shooting world vindicated him.   Still, nobody seemed to be able to accurately name the factors that contributed or were responsible for the good performance of these grips.   The most sensible, if slightly vague reaction was that the "belled" shape gave a feeling of comfort, of being able to "bed" the hand.

On a single plane, it is difficult to depict intricate functions of the shooting hand.   Still, I be-

lieve that a careful study of the following sketches
will convey the drift.

Some time ago, the author developed a grip of
his own in which he tried to incorporate all his
theoretical ideas about what he thought con-
stituted the "ideal" grip. This grip of mine, because it is highly individualized, may be somewhat
awkward for the production line. However, closer
analysis of the behavior of the shooting hand in
shooting position made me realize that the "foot"

ILLUSTRATION 19.

Arm in pronation. Weight of arm is held up by the shoulder.
In semi-prone position, that is when hand is turned so that
the thumb is up, you will notice that when the turning is done
slowly, the fingers tend to close. The palm in that relaxed
position suggests a definite flare for the lower end of the ideal
revolver grip. See Illustration 20 (Shaded area).

of the grip, where the little finger seeks its support, should be considerably wider than at the
"neck" of the grip. The ratio of "width of neck"
to "width of foot" is, of course, dependent upon the
individual size of the hand.

My first consideration was to determine the
curve of the backstrap. In the instance under discussion I found that the "hang" of my Officer's
.38 model permitted the use of the original back-
strap curve as outlined by the factory frame.

My second thought was to flatten the curve behind the trigger guard so as to bring the middlefinger about half an inch lower, thus permitting a
more natural position for the trigger-finger.

I then chose the width at the "neck" to suit my
personal preference. In my case, the neck is rather

wide as I had intended to keep the whole grip rather "flat."

I had now three boundaries or measurements, namely 1) the curve of the backstrap, 2) the curve behind the trigger-guard and 3) the width at the "neck."

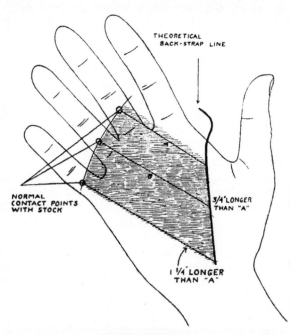

THEORETICAL BACK-STRAP LINE

NORMAL CONTACT POINTS WITH STOCK

3/4" LONGER THAN "A"

1 1/4" LONGER THAN "A"

ILLUSTRATION 20.
When hand is in semi-prone, relaxed position, the proportion of the length of lines a-b-c should stay about the same as in the open and stretched hand.

Now came the most important speculation, namely, the placement of the other fingers, especially of the little finger.

With my hand stretched, I found that the distance from the middle of the first joint of each finger to a "theoretical" backstrap-line (Which extended from the middle of the "web" to the middle of the wrist), varied for each finger. In my case, the little finger showed a line which was 1¼" longer than that of the middlefinger-line. Although in the relaxed hand these distances shorten, I assumed that the ratio would not change materially. Thus, I secured a fourth point of measurement at the "foot" of the grip.

I had to "curve in"!

I then had a Walnut Grip carved, using the data which I had so assiduously and empirically obtained and—my grip was a success! Don't write or order grips from me! I am not selling them.

In studying Roper's grips which came out a few months ago, I found that Roper has, inadvertently, complied with the anatomical requirements through "belling inwards." What we picked up laboriously through the above learned discourse teaches us that Roper was right in the first place—only he didn't know it! His grips deserve fullest support. They are positively swell. He makes them, as I understand, in various sizes to suit different hands. Thus, Roper went a lot further than your uncle in his lone studies, in that he created grips which are more "universal" and will fit more shooters than my abortive product.

I am positively happy over the thought that friend Walter knows now *why* he made his grips the way he did. You are perfectly welcome, Walter, ol' sock. Nothing more consoling than to be sure about a thing, what?

And the world goes on serenely—and guns continue to come from the factories, showing the same old handles rejected by Methusalem, with a persistance that is almost touching.

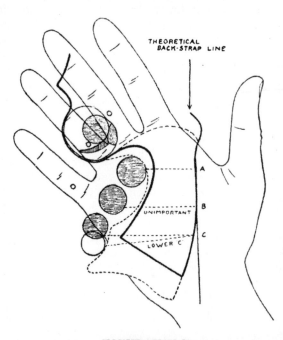

THEORETICAL
BACK-STRAP LINE

A

B

UNIMPORTANT

C

LOWER C

ILLUSTRATION 21.

At point A the author has given the handle a width comfortable for the average hand.

At points B and C, the differences ascertained in sketch 20 for ring and little fingers were added, a little modified.

The dotted outline gives the contour of handle developed by author. For the sake of pleasing appearance, the author has tried to avoid too wide a flare at C, by placing the little finger lower than normal, away from the ringfinger.

The shaded circles represent the cross-sections of fingers. The thick line is the contour of the frame as delivered by factory.

It will be noticed that the curve behind the trigger-guard has been flattened by the author's grip, thus bringing the trigger finger into a more normal relation to the rest of the hand.

The small circles on the fingers represent the contact-points of fingers with frame, when they are bent. When shaping the stock, no importance need be given to the placement of ringfinger. Middlefinger and little finger however, must have definite contact which latter effect is achieved through "flaring" the stock at the bottom.

I seriously think about forming a "Society for the prevention of lousy grips"—Contributions are in order. I think, as its President, I could get along with $10,000 a year salary—It will be a lifetime job!

As for the scientific critics that may read my exposition and who would doubt my qualifications: You, who know all about "interior" and "exterior" ballistics, hark ye: I have studied "anterior" and "posterior" ballistics at the University of Timbuktoo. While you fellows keep quiet on subjects that are painful, I go right ahead and soliloquize to my heart's content—After all, the reader can't talk back. Come to think of it, I have reason to be quite satisfied with myself—Just a young scientist trying to get along—and, all of a sudden, he develops an astounding theory—But, modesty is his middle-name—Let's compromise! Let's call it the "Reichenbach-theory"—Einstein? Bah!

AMMUNITION WRINKLES

Oh no, I am not going to talk about hand-loading!

Our publisher, doubtlessly, has a whole book for you, devoted to that nutty pastime.

In this chapter we shall not look inside the shell.

The cartridges (Which provide those sumptuous mansions for the kindly lords who make the cartridges for us), look pretty in their boxes, what? Lined up like soldiers—One looks exactly like the other. And, to tell the truth, they should *be* alike —but they "ain't." Their "innards" differ sometimes—You know: varying powder loads.

Now, one would think that with the way in which our technical era progresses so amazingly, a little thing such as a machine to measure powder accurately, could have been invented. Well, brothers, there's no doubt in my mind that the mansions of which I spoke, have all the latest improvements available, but dammit, you can't get a batch of shells in which there are not some "Aviators"— Primadonnas of the air—irresponsible—erratic— baffling—exasperating—Aviators, what? They cavort whether the shooter is an expert or a dub. Of course, the very fact of the possibility of shells running "amok," provides us with most excellent alibis. Personally, I prefer alibis which I can make up *myself*, not those that I have to pay for. I want to own a mansion myself, some day. I shall, therefore, not give thanks to our cartridge manufacturers!

If we eliminate the human element in testing cartridges, by using a machine rest, we find that nine bullets will punch paper, with holes touching. The tenth shot whizzes an inch away, sometimes more! Reason? Sure! Different powder loads. By the beard of Mahomet, don't they inspect these damn shells at the factory? Sure, they do! Then, what the hell?

Well, my friends, we shooters have had this grievance in our craw these many years!

You know, I don't profess to understand the first thing about cartridge manufacture, but I know enough to snarl: "What the h—?"

This isn't Denmark, you know. These are the United States, where we boast of gauges that distinguish tolerances of 1/1000000 of an inch. But we are too dumb to measure—and repeat in production—a predetermined amount of say three grains of powder. That is: one hundred times the measure will be right and then an over-or under-

load sneaks in. These occasional aviators are the
ones that may spoil our scores in an important
match! We sort of sit on a keg of powder, with a
live cigar in our mouth. We never know when
it is going to happen, what?

Not satisfied with baffling the patient shooters
by sneaking in erratic powder loads, the manufacturers get a more artistic delight out of varying
the bullet weights—Not in a coarse way, you understand, just subtly so—

Maybe, we shooters are too stingy and squawk
too much about the cost of our cartridges—It's all
so confusing—

Well, Rome wasn't built in one day—But, somebody has to tell the Moguls that Rome has to be
built sometime, what? And I am telling them!

What can we do, in the meantime?

In the .22 ammunition field we shooters are sort
of helpless. As for the larger calibres, we have the
expedient of "weighing" the shells — (A thing
which could easily be done at the factory, of
course.) Those shells that deviate in weight from
their brothers should not be used for serious practice. Although the weighing method is not infallible, it will at least *assist* in weeding out the
most glaring discrepancies in either powder-or bullet weights.

Since normalization in cartridge manufacture
has not been achieved as yet, we will find that different brands perform differently. The thing to
do is to test the various brands in the machine rest,
using your *own* gun for which you wish to ascertain the most suitable ammunition. After you
have found the closest groups with a certain make,
stick to it! It is true that the batches as they come
from the hatcheries, are not uniform but, generally,

they will perform better than if you were to change to some other brand.

Now, I have repeatedly said that the field of "ballistics" is a "quantité inconnue" to me. But it appears to this ignorant observer as if the science of ballistics were, somehow, musclebound.

Listening to the big Wags—selfstyled or acknowledged—who oracle about ballistics in their superior way, one cannot help thinking that they, too, must be musclebound! To them, the whole thing is pure mathematics and the fellow who can rattle off the most formulae from the books, is "cock of the walk." If the thing were really reducible to pure mathematics, then the ballistic science has not been explored enough! And that is what is probably the whole trouble! Half-cocked, I calls it! Should it not, academically at least, be possible to design a gun and a cartridge on paper and "predict" their exact performance? Ere the thing is shot?

No! Most things are still done empirically— And I shall go on getting innocent fun out of reading or listening to the vitriolic pratings of the "Know-it-alls."

> *There is a pest, called KNOWITALL*
> *Who sneers at those who trustful grope—*
> *With lifted eyebrow he will call*
> *His fellowman a silly dope*
>
> *For knowing less of things ballistic—*
> *Stealing, himself, from better men,*
> *He struts and shows sadistic*
> *Pleasure, by wagging his almighty pen.*
>
> *Conceited fool in overalls,*
> *You callous ass with caustic mind!*
> *These damn olympic KNOWITALLS*
> *Give me a pain in my———err neck!*

In order to be consistent, I cannot very well recommend certain brands of ammunition, as the best or the most accurate. It would be easy if one had a sort of standard barrel in the machine rest and knew, or could ascertain, the deviations from standard, in any given gun barrel. I say again: Have your *own* barrel tested in the machine rest and find your own ammunition—and then don't change around!

I am still insistent in my demand that energetic steps be taken to *normalize* barrels and chamber dimensions, angle and direction of twist, etc., and, no doubt, the ammunition manufacturers will follow suit, with the result of generally better performances all around.

GUN LEGISLATION

Let's take a little walk—to the dump-heap over yonder—We do not expect to find pretty things there, but I must show you something. See, I take a stick and poke it into the nearest heap— Ugh! Phooy! See that? Cockroaches—a whole nest of them—Here, take my magnifying glass! Look closer—What? You see the lettering on their backs? Sure—it says "Criminals" — But, look again—There's an especially fat one—Ah—What does it say?—"Shyster Lawyer"—? Pick out the fat ones and they will all bear the latter stamp. You see, they are fat because they live off the other ones—No, you can't destroy them all—Too much of a job—But, you can step on some of the fat ones, those that don't hide—If it weren't for them, the others, the "Criminals" wouldn't thrive so well—

Oh no my friend, there is no moral to this excursion—I just wanted to kill some printing space.

What was it that I wanted to write about?

Oh yes! Legislation—I mean, legislation that concerns itself with the crime situation. Let's you and me, look at it intelligently—Not many do it, you know. We'll confine our thoughts to crimes that are committed with the help of fire-arms, handguns. Who commits these crimes? The criminal element, you say—Right! Where do they get their handguns? They buy them, they rent them and they steal them—Right again! Who sells or rents them? Ah, shucks, we'll never get any further that way—

In order to make it hard or impossible for these criminals to lay their paws on handguns, some bright lads invented laws—Sullivan-laws and similar laws—but violent crime goes on! The laws were strengthened—and crime goes blithely on, unabated—The laws were again strengthened— Oh, doesn't it make one sick? As if laws were obeyed by those they were meant for—That's the criminal's *business*: to *dis*obey the law—That is what *makes* him a criminal! If he obeyed the law like we do, he wouldn't be what he is. That's logical, what? So, what good are these laws? They aren't worth a damn! But, they do a lot of harm to us sportsmen—*We*, who do *not* wish to commit violent crimes such as hold-ups, murder, etc., we are the only ones who suffer under these gun-laws.

Our peaceful hobby is to follow a fascinating sport—a sport worthy of gentlemen—But, these damn fat cockroaches—Oh, pardon me—There I go again!

What can be done about it?

Gun-laws don't do any good—Even the best ones—The fat cockroaches know all the loopholes.

"Regulation" of some kind? Well, let's see—We have certain regulations over automobile drivers— In order to get a license they must submit to a driving test—They must show that they know how to handle the thing—But look at the yearly casualties—It's quite confusing—But say, here is an idea—It may not be very effective in curbing the criminal element directly—You really *can't make* them obey society's restrictions—But, the idea might help—It might!

Suppose *everybody* were permitted to buy as many handguns as he wants (See, how the gun-manufacturers prick their ears?), but he must hand over to the seller a certificate from the Police, with fingerprints and photo, saying that he is competent to handle a gun safely, that he is not a fugitive and, is, on the whole, sound of mind, stable of character and not objectionable. The buyer takes his purchases back to the Police Department where the gun-characteristics are recorded. The applicant is given a booklet telling him all about hand-guns, how to use them under certain conditions.

It would encourage him to seek practice and perfection and counsel him to join a shooting club in his neighborhood. It also warns him of the legal consequences of any misuse of his arms, and the necessity of renewing his license every year. If he should decide to discontinue having a gun around, he could dispose of it to anybody who presents the aforementioned registered police certificate or to an accredited dealer. Or he could turn it in to the Police Department which should hold auctions from time to time, auctions where the distribution is again subject to restrictions drawn up to meticulously follow the whereabouts of *every gun in the country*, from the time it leaves the factory up to the moment when it is destroyed.

All such records to be centralized in the Department of Justice in Washington. And, above all, such pistol permits should be recognized and honored throughout the entire country, the way our various States recognize automobile registrations and operator's (driver's) licenses, issued by other states.

The cost of the additional organization necessary for the administration of such supervision could easily be covered by the licensing fees. The actual testing of the applicant could take place at the nearest police station which should have a pistol range anyway, for its officers. Anyone, who does *not* pass a certain sensible test, does not get a license—Such a man should not be trusted with a gun!

Anybody who is caught with a gun and *no* permit, goes into the jug for ten or twenty years. See the fat cockroaches shiver—

Sure, we may have a few more shooting crimes of passion. I mean, instead of using a knife, or an axe or poison, the perpetrator might want to use a handy gun—Why not? It's much cleaner! But Hell! These "crimes passionelles" are only a drop in the bucket.

The prospect of ten or twenty years in stir— That might make any criminal think twice—We must, somehow, force the criminal to enter into this scheme—He should *wish* to try to own a gun *legally* and take a chance on his bullets being traced—The ten or twenty years he would get for not having a license, are *inescapable*—(The fat cockroaches are useless)—But actually hooking the criminal up with a certain crime of violence

through evidence alone, lies in the lap of the Gods
—The percentage is with the criminal.

Just think, what would happen to all these nice
hold-ups etc.? The little cockroaches like to
threaten or kill, but they don't care for the medicine for themselves—Hell, it would be a dangerous
thing to hold up somebody—The other fellow
might shoot first—

"Regimentation?" Of course!

(Wait a minute! Somebody up near the rafters
is hollering—A little louder, please!) What's that?
—Liberty — 100% Americanism—? Listen, you
Sap! Isn't our automobile-control also "regimentation?" Do you squawk about that? You do not!

Aren't the fool gun-laws that we have now, the
worst kind of "regimentation?" If a decent citizen
can't be trusted with guns, the way we have it
now in the State of New York, for instance, what
do you call that? A state of affairs which robs the
law abiding man of means of defense against the
criminal who *flaunts* those very laws? Shut up
with your meaningless stock-ejaculations! "Regimentation"—I realize that bureaucracy might stultify even the most intelligent rules but, all in all,
what could really be more stupid and degrading
than our present American Gun-Laws? *Only* cockroaches, fat and small, shyster-lawyers and criminals, thrive under the present laws and God knows!
they do thrive—

One thing is painfully obvious: It couldn't possibly be any worse than it is now. Many an eager
sportsman cannot get a license. Our silly gun-
laws, thickheadedly interpreted and enforced by
zealous (Let's call it that—) Police higher-ups balk
most of the decent citizens—It's one hell of a mess!

Now, your vote is as valuable as the next one,

theoretically. Any Assemblyman or State Senator from your district who introduces silly bills or votes for them, does *not* get your vote again! Tell him so—or write the bastid! Kick up a row! Squawk as loudly as you can! Step on the fat ones! And, maybe, we sportsmen will have a chance, after all—The National Rifle Association is doing valuable work in this field by consolidating all sporadic efforts—Their legislative experience and legal training have helped to kill or soften many a bill that was proposed by the Abramowsky-and-Stinkovitch-tribe. Join the NRA! And, Boy, after we have become sensible again and free again, just think what fine guns we will have—How the manufacturers will vie with each other—And, when the supreme necessity arises again, we will have competent material and not a mass of young boys led to the slaughter, untrained and inexperienced—doomed because in peace-times their government did not provide—

One may think about the necessity or futility of "WAR" what one pleases—That point is not up for discussion—But: Let me say this: *As long as humanity has not become entirely and intensely cultured,* there will be disputes fought *with violence* —Not by loudmouthed politicians or doddering statesmen who fail to avert disasters or even *arrange* them—*Their* job is finished when they have agreed to have a little war—No! The *youth* of the nation is sent to the front—to finish what they themselves hadn't begun—They *must* go! They *must*! What a thoughtless and futile crime to send them out—the farmer, the laborer, the white-collar-man—all of them absolutely unprepared, unfamiliar with guns, the tools of war—How silly the oriental propaganda, to agitate against preparedness—Let our diplomats stick their heads in the sand and somebody will kick them in the pants, as long as there are other diplomats around that cannot resist when they see an invitation. And, brother, if a diplomat gets his pants kicked, that's sacrilege and the youth of the nation must avenge him—Ah—Hell!

FINIS

Well, all things must end sometime, whether they be good or bad.

I expect that now, after having gotten this far with your reading, you feel like leaning back in your arm-chair—with a hopeful sigh. Of course, we know that there must be much more that should have been said—But, this was to be a MANUAL and not a book.

Some of the things I did say may have sounded a little blunt, or, at times, sarcastic. But, how in heck, can one expect progress unless someone speaks up?

Our sport is so close to my heart that I cannot help but love everything and everybody connected with it. However, as long as there is room for improvement, I suppose, I shall go on "prodding" —and I must make a prodder out of you!

The whole-hearted reception of the first crude "ELUSIVE TEN" forced my publisher to get out this second edition, enlarged and refined.

Conceiving this "Sixguns and Bullseyes" was a pleasure; writing it was hard labor, but the thought that so much more was left unsaid, was agony. My publisher took pity on me and, hoping that I may really have something more on the ball, told me to go ahead and, for Pete's sake, write what I must. I grabbed the chance and broke out with another blurb.

In it, I dabble in Automatics and "practical" shooting. The Woodsman, .45 Auto, Lueger, Walther, etc.

If you liked the Manual you have just finished, you will want to gobble up the wisdom I dispense in my Automatic book. I promise you a whole lot more fun!

But, dash it, the "well" will not dry out.

That is the way that I shall feel about handgun-shooting until I go West—As long as there is life—

Won't you tell me what you think of my stuff?
                    Good luck, my friend!

AUTOMATIC PISTOL

MARKSMANSHIP

With towering strength, foreboding, yet beautiful, it looms
sky-high...........

AUTOMATIC PISTOL MARKSMANSHIP

By

WILLIAM REICHENBACH

ILLUSTRATIONS
by
RICHARD KROTH
AND
EDWIN BENDER

Skyhorse Publishing

CONTENTS

INTRODUCTION

There is, my dear Reader, a quandary in this Manual—If I could assume that you had read *Sixguns and Bullseyes,* my book on the target revolver, I could safely overcome most of my scruples. In that case I would have nothing to fear from you—since we grew acquainted through that medium. Therein we wandered together, hand in hand; we looked at problems together and put some light into them—in short, we became friends.

However, there is a bare chance that you may not have read *Sixguns and Bullseyes* and, in order to put myself over, I should have to start all over again. Ah yes: A quandary indeed!

Continuing where I left off with my old friends and striving hard to please you, the new adjunct.

Oh, Ye Gods, who guide my inspirational splurges, give Ye me the power to entertain both.

The trouble is that I face limitations, of which not the least are those of space.

In vain did I remonstrate with my Publisher to let me put my pets, the Automatics, right into the first volume. "Nothing doing," was the peremptory answer, "we don't want a book that would have to sell for $4.00. This here is a series that shall reach everybody—If you have anything to say on Automatics, you better reserve that for another occasion."

Of course, one cannot argue with one's Publisher, what? And, by Gar, the jasper is right too! Allthemore, since he continued: "You go right ahead! We have been waiting for just such a book on Automatics from you. Go on and tell the world what you must!" You can imagine how eagerly I grabbed the chance.

So, here we have a Manual on Automatics only. I do not know yet what all I shall have to say, but you may be sure that I shall get a great kick out of saying it. Talking about "kicks," some of them will be directed at august persons and organizations and that should give you a kick too. Service to everybody: That's me!

This here is a sequence to *Sixguns and Bullseyes*, but while the latter dealt with the Revolver and its use as a target weapon, this Manual is devoted to the Automatic and it treats "practical" shooting. Of course, one can do practical shooting with a Revolver and do fine target work with an Automatic. This writer believes that success in practical shooting is based on prior good performance in target work. We might as well get that off our chests.

If you want to be a good practical shot, it is essential that you be a good target shot first. Oh yes: a practical shot can develop by himself, but he must be wondrously gifted with patience and lousy with money. On the other hand, all a target shooter has to do, is to sort of "speed up" his methodical target work and he can be both: a good target shot *and* a good practical shot. It's more sensible to start right. It's like horse-back riding. You can pick it up, somehow, and be fairly good. But the portals to higher equitation are closed to you. You would have to forget the many painful falls, you would have to unlearn too darn many faults which were picked up since you didn't know any better. I have met some self-made practical shooters who, with astounding infallibility, will hit that ol' barn-door with every shot, even at 45 feet. But, when you ask them to step back to 60 feet and hit the keyhole, they laid down. Yet, a target shooter will do the latter, although he may be a bit slow about it. But, give him a little practice and he will get that keyhole as fast as the other hits the big door. The difference is that the target shooter can be taught to do difficult things fast, but the self-made practical shot will never hit anything small. Who wants to wreck "barndoors" anyway? Let's get down to business.

The advantage in any controversy lies with the Author. All he has to do is to make a statement and then say "Enough of it. Let's get down to business." The Reader can't talk back, you see?

So, I shall settle this thing again by saying: One *must* be a target shooter first and then advance to practical shooting later.

But, I must not teach you target shooting in this Manual, because I would curry the danger of repetition. In covering my allotted space, the best I can do is to give you a quick outline and dwell more extensively on the points wherein the Automatic technique differs from that of the Revolver. The rest you will have to glean from *Sixguns and Bullseyes*. (How is this for a "plug," dear Publisher?) Having agreed on this, if somewhat assiduously, we can proceed.

It seems there were seven little devils and these seven little devils formed a union and proclaimed themselves: "The solution to the mastery of the handgun." First: Hold, then Stance, Relaxation, Bringing the Gun Forward, Sighting, Squeeze and Breathing. Seven of them. Count them! With the exception of numbers one and six, the principles hold good for Revolvers as well as Automatics and since, in this Manual, we are concerned with the Automatic only, we shall delve more fully into the discrepancies.

Of course, you will have guessed by now that I have an affinity for the Automatic Handgun. Its relative modernity (Technically as well as artistically) in contrast to the ancient stolidity of the Revolver, always exuded powerful fascination for me. Not only in friendly match-competition, but more convincingly during the dark days of the 1914-1918 debacle, it seldom failed to substantiate my faith in it. Is it any wonder then that I felt very much disappointed when the limitation of space forbade the inclusion of my thoughts in *The Elusive Ten* and later in *Sixguns and Bullseyes?*

However, since Tom Samworth the Publisher, himself an enthusiast in everything that has a tube and a trigger, foresaw the existence of a livid interest in Automatics among the American shooting fraternity, his commission to incorporate in this booklet what I know and think about the topic, seems timely.

Talk about my pets? Why, I'll go without food if I have to. Just mention Automatics to me and watch my eyes.

From what I have observed, there are only a few Automatic models in marked favour at the present time, pistols such as the "Woodsman" and the "Ace" in the .22 class; the "Lueger" both in the .30 and the .38 calibres and last but by no means least, the .45 Automatic and the .38 Super Auto. Occasionally, one finds some other guns such as the "Mauser," also the "Bergman," the "Ortgies" and others, designed more or less after the "Browning" patents. Responding to the popular tendency, I shall make an attempt in this Manual to confine myself to a few guns and to add only a few personal pets and not waste time and space on the lesser fry.

The guiding idea is to concentrate on models which are suitable and safe for either competition or practical shooting. I cannot, for the life of me, find a warm spot in my heart for the socalled Pocket-Guns or Vestpocket-Guns. They look cute, doubtlessly, but they belong in a Lady's handbag, particularly if they have mother-of-pearl-handles or if they are goldplated and—yes—even alluringly perfumed.

We mean business here!

Now, it seems that we must establish some sort of personal contact between us, in order to clear the table for action. Those of you who are acquainted with my Revolver Books, will already know of my little peculiarities and will be accustomed to my style.

However, there are the others. So, let me tear down the barriers of conventionality and call you all: My friends!

Suppose, you pull yourself a comfortable arm-chair and relax. We'll get on much better. There! That's fine!

Before we plunge into a description of the various models that I intend to parade before you, there are a few thoughts—

I don't know whether you ever handled an Automatic or not. If you haven't there are things which you must know before you touch them. (Those of you who know all, may sit over in the other corner and skip my pratings.)

Know then that you can't just go out one fine day and buy yourself an Automatic, go out to some range, fill up your magazine and pop away. Heavens no! It isn't done! It's impolite! It's dangerous! Besides, the law may have something to say about that.

First, I should make sure just what Gun Legislation exists in your State. Maybe, you need a permit—

Then, you must familiarize yourself with the Automatic. We are not puzzled over crude things such as: Where the hole is that's where the smoke comes out, and similar stuff. We also have to agree that only a pedantic person with a flair for inquisitiveness will want to look into the muzzle and pull the trigger just to watch the ol' bullet rotate around the grooves in the barrel.—That's scientific stuff. What it teaches won't have time to percolate—

Suppose, we make up our minds to stay away from dry science altogether? Let's be practical!

Alright then: We shall have to acquire the *safety* habit first and we set up two initial rules. The first one: An Automatic is always loaded! Secondly: Never point the damn thing at anything you don't want to hit!

On this I need your faithful promise!

Will you keep these two rules in mind?

Then we won't have any trouble!

I shall endeavor not to bore you with a lot of dry statistics or "holier than thou"-preachings. There are parts in this book where I do have to speak about the "technique of shooting" the Automatic. But you will not find the topic overly dry, I hope.

Then, interspersed with the text, I have put down some turbulent thoughts which, if they do not please some of the "High and Mighty," may draw an affirmative nod from you or, possibly, an occasional mischievous grin.

What we have had offered to us in the way of books, was mostly too ponderous, too lectural. Why not have a little fun at the same time? I have always found that one picks up things much faster that way.

Generally speaking, there are some points in which the Automatic Pistol differs vitally from the Revolver. The latter, as its name implies has something that revolves, turns. Its the Cylinder which holds the Cartridges. As the Revolver hammer is cocked, the Cylinder turns until a Cartridge lies directly behind the barrel. When the trigger is pulled, the hammer falls, hits the Primer of the Cartridge and the resulting ignition tears the Bullet loose and forces it through the barrel. After the Cartridges have all been fired, you push a doodad and the empty shells fall out. Now, in the Automatic we have a Magazine into which the Cartridges are stacked. We insert this Magazine in the grip, pull the Slide back with our hand, thus cocking the mechanism, and let the Slide snap shut again. In its forward travel, the Slide peels off a Cartridge from the Magazine and shoves it right into the barrel. Upon squeezing the trigger, the firing pin ignites the Primer and the Bullet is expelled through the barrel. The recoil of the explosion throws the Slide open, extracting the empty shell and cocking the hammer. The

Slide shuts again by spring action, loading another Cartridge and so on until the Magazine is empty. There is no hammer to be cocked by hand after every shot. All one has to do is to squeeze the trigger. These are the principal differences in the actions between the Revolver and the Automatic.

But, the Automatic also has a different trigger travel and it has to be held differently. More about that later.

The advantages of the Automatic principle are so manifold as to outweigh by far its few shortcomings.

Despite the inescapable logic of this comparison, the controversy on the part of the Sixshooter Fans is as hot as ever, and that includes some Revolver manufacturers, what?

Well, as you go along, you will form your own opinion and I trust that I may have been instrumental in making an Automatic fiend out of you.

AUTO *versus* REVOLVERS

From what you will read below, you might get the impression as if I seemed somewhat prejudiced against the Revolver. Damn right! Let's get down to brass-tacks! What changes have happened to the Revolver, say within the last thirty years: I mean, has the Revolver kept up with modern times and developments? All sentiment aside: Unless the Revolver in its inherent form was the "ideal" instrument right from its inception, did its development point to an ideal solution to the handgun problem? Of course not! Let me ask brutally: Isn't the Revolver like a dead-end street? Sure, you can polish it up here and there, put on better sights, do this or that, but you *can't* change the inate nature of the Revolver materially. The Revolver cannot possibly develop beyond itself. It will always be a Revolver!

I know that many of my good old friends will shake their heads in regretful disapproval. Yet, deep down in their hearts, they know it's true. Cherished memories form the barrier to a brave admission. I don't blame them! It is hard. The early history of modern America is closely wound around the Revolver. It's a specifically American institution. It still holds its proud position in the target field, a position which the Auto has not been able to upset. But, that is threatening—

When the first .22 "Woodsman" Automatic (A wholly

1

American conception, by the way) was introduced, I surmise that the makers did so very reluctantly. I mean, they
may have acceded to some demand from the outside, urgent
enough not to be disregarded, and not because they themselves felt that the Automatic was the coming thing. Well,
I don't really know— So, let's give them the benefit of
the doubt. The "Woodsman" was a darn good job too,
for an initial introduction. I am not being paid to say
this. In fact, I have a sort of general aversion against the
—let's call it bluntly—thickheadedness of our manufacturers. Wouldn't you think that they would snap up
valuable suggestions from the shooting world, as quickly
as they could? You know, ideas that really mean
"progress"? But, all they can think of, the playful lil'
things, is the cost of retooling and, from a business point
of view, that may be considered sensible. But we poor
shooters— Where was I? Oh yes! The Automatic.
The ballistics of the Automatic are generally considered
somewhat inferior to those of the Revolver. But, even if
that were true, the Automatic is a comparatively young
gun and there are *endless* possibilities. Principally, as I
said before, a comparison would reveal that in the Revolver
the shell rests in the cylinder. When the pin strikes the
primer, the explosion takes place in the cylinder where
the bullet is wrenched loose from the shell and tumbles
toward the barrel. The bullet jumps a gap, skids about a
bit and then staggers into the bore to be straightened out
for its travel through the barrel grooves which impinge a
rotary motion upon it. If there is the slightest misalign-
ment between cylinder and barrel, the bullet, upon hitting
the chamber, has to pay a tribute first in the way of violent
lead shaving. The gun "spits."

In the Automatic, on the other hand, the shell with the
bullet is seated right in the barrel itself, in but one chamber
which is shaped to exactly conform with the profile of shell
and bullet. When the primer is hit, the bullet does no

tumbling around, looking for a barrel. Instead, it is pressed forward into the grooves immediately in front of it and starts its rotary movement, the same way as in a rifle.

Which of the two methods described above is the better, the more modern?

It is said that the Revolver permits of more tolerances in shape, etc., of the ammunition. That, of course, might be considered advantageous under adverse conditions. On the other hand, such interchangeability of ammunition has its definite dangers. Nobody considers such interchangeability in the rifle. You just use the ammunition made for a certain rifle—and that's that! Well, this principle applies equally to the Automatic.

Further experimentation, doubtlessly, will develop ammunition that will assist in the faultless functioning of the Auto. That's up to the ballistical sharps! One thing is certain: If the Auto-cartridge had received as much attention from the munitions-makers, the Auto ballistics would be far superior to those of the Revolver. I believe, a stricter normalization of bore diameter and chamber measurements would encourage the scientific development of the Auto-cartridges.

So much for the ammunition part.

Now, let's view one of the stereotypical objections against the Automatic itself. There is the subject of "unreliability," the pet-idiosyncrasy of the mossbacks. I have seen actual warfare during the last crash. Not once has my Lueger refused to function. True, I did not neglect it or permitted it to get filled with dirt and loam. Given reasonable care, a good Automatic of approved design is just as reliable as the Revolver. I am being reminded of the public attitude toward the motorcar. The cars turned out today are all good, engineerically speaking. Treat them right by changing oil regularly, attend to greasing etc., etc., and they all will give more service than you pay for. But, there is a great number of car-users who judge the merits of the car by the amount of "ABUSE" it will stand and, naturally, some cars are more rugged than the others. Our automatic handguns are, to some people, not rugged enough to absorb the abuse that the Revolver may stand. Hell, my attitude is very definite. One shouldn't abuse *anything!* Not even the good nature of the reader. Maybe, I better get along—

The Automatic itself, as I said, instead of being blocked technically like the revolver, offers unlimited possibilities for further mechanical development. Who can say what our present-day Automatic is going to look like in ten years? I have no intention of speculating scientifically. I'd never get through. And, besides, I mightn't know enough! But the necessity of thinking modern, of abolishing things which are stagnated, impresses itself upon one's mind every day. Although the public may have recovered quickly enough from its surprises at the initial success of the Wright Brothers in the aerodynamic field, (Comparable to the advent, in a smaller measure of the first crude Automatic) the constant changes and rapid improvements which have taken place over a relatively short period, fill us with wonderment and greater and still greater expectations. Just compare the present day Airliners with the first Wright models—The change is amazing. Instead of being satisfied with these achievements, our minds refuse to accept these Airliners as conclusive. No, we are actually disappointed if, throughout a given year, a new and major improvement fails to materialize. We have become impatient—New ideas are accepted with casualness and promptly deposited in the archives of permanent and self-understood evolution.

Yes, in the Aero-Industry everybody is wide awake, impatiently straining forward and things crowd each other.

We are filled with regret and pitiful disappointment, however, when we look at what has taken place in the

Automatic Handgun province. The inception of the Automatic principle, in itself of course, wonderful and inspiring, has not been followed by development. We are today still fooling around with what transpired 30-40 years ago. Naturally, there wasn't as much financial interest, or even public interest, in the Automatic handgun and one might not expect as fast an evolution there as in things of wider public value.

At times, like for instance during war-times, an artificial respiration takes place. In these times, immense quantities are produced because they are sorely needed. That stretches over into the neighboring field of Machine-guns and Automatic Rifles. Despite this influx of need, of capital, during the last war, the poor goddess "EVOLUTION" was shunted and instead of eager experimentation and impatient betterment, we saw mass-production of standardized fossils. Scientific probing displaced by haste, by greed. The thought was that the need won't last long and let's take what we can get.

The significance of encounters lost through inefficient equipment, of human lives thrown to the reaper needlessly is of no importance in times like that. Greed!

And, when the disturbance is over, orders stop and so does whatever interest there might have been.

In peace-times, the very times when there *is* leisure, the thing is forgotten. Aside from a few individuals, everybody has lost interest. And what will be there if another supreme upheaval takes place? The same old junk will be put in mass production—ad nauseam! In this year of 1937, that is almost 20 years after the great war and, possibly, 30-40 years after the inception of the Automatic idea, we are about where we started from—

People are not breaking their necks anymore with crude flying crates—

No, they ride in comfort and on schedule.

But the Automatic—

And it *is* an important necessity!   Not a luxury!

Not only in war times, but also in quiet years—There is Police-work going on all the time and the training of the Military, so vital for efficiency in the emergency—And there is the Sport-field which surrenders excellent human material when the draft-bills are passed by old men on Capitol Hill.

What right have we thinking Citizens to permit our brood to be sent to the front, wholly unprepared?

Of course, we are not militant, chauvinistic—No, we don't want war!   We want to stay away from war!   But, what happened the last time?   We didn't want it!   Others did though!   And they started "drafting" and then— what?

We carry fire-insurance, although our house may never burn down, but we are careless and hate to think of the possibility of major disasters like the last one.

One single human life lost is too much to pay for in-efficiency!

Our Military are issued the .45 Auto as their official side-arm, to protect them and help them do what they must.   What kind of a side-arm is this .45 Auto?   Is it modern?   Does it do what it should?   We'll see about that, further on in the book—

This Manual sponsors the Automatic handgun as an in-herently sound principle.   The Revolver, for major pur-poses, is obsolete and, the sooner we make up our minds to that, the better off we will be.   Let's concentrate all our efforts on the evolution of the Automatic handgun! Don't let's fool around anymore!

We have learned things, plenty of them, but we have not applied in practice what we know.   We haven't even exchanged our ideas on the subject.

Once put into practice, new experiences will turn up, evoking new thought trains, new suggestions to be worked out—

At the present, the thing is confined to a few experimental stations where work is carried on faithfully, but uninspired. I say this with conviction, because nothing "new" ever shows up. And, by Gar, we need new things and need them badly!

There must be, among you shooting fans, clever mechanics with probing minds, same as there were and are in the Radio field. Get interested! Get busy!

That's one of the ideas behind this book!

As we near the next chapters in which I put the various Auto models through the mill, I would like to register a definite reservation. I can deal only with guns which are offered in the market, that is as we can actually obtain them. Wherever I make certain recommendations they can, naturally, only apply to the guns as are and not as we Moderns should "wish" them to be. When I say, for instance, that this or that gun constitutes the ideal thing, never forget that indicated reservation.

You see, my plea for general modernization extends not only to shapes, weights, etc., but especially to changes in ballistics, whether internal or external.

In this book we deal with guns that have been put in production within the narrow confines of our present ballistic knowledge. Now, we may find occasion to recommend changes and improvements, all based on actual experience, experience gathered by practical shooters who are neither scientists nor even mechanics.

If one of you alert Readers should conceive an idea here or there, an improvement for instance, something which escaped me, he will be on the right track. Let's think and study ways. Let's *do* something!

◆   ◆   ◆

MATERIAL

THE "WOODSMAN"

We'll start off with our best American Small Calibre Automatic. It's the "Woodsman"-Pistol with a 6″ barrel, made by Colt. It is an excellent instrument to learn Auto-shooting with. I am not conversant with the antecedents of this gun, but I declare it a surprisingly original idea. It must have slipped through the watchful brigade whose duty it is to preserve moth-eaten traditions and to prevent the cropping-up of revolutionary young ideas. Well, fate was kind and we shooters received the makings of a very fine weapon. I wish the perpetrators had gone "whole hog"—but, nevermind: The world wasn't made in one day. For instance, I believe it would have been a good safety idea to have the slide stay open after the last shot.

The "Woodsman" is at present confined to the .22 rimfire calibre only, but I see no reason why the idea should not be adaptable to larger calibres, after necessary constructional changes, of course. I should say that, if fitted with a proper grip and a shift of weight more toward the muzzle, this inherently fine gun should be superior to all the costly Free Pistols in Slow Fire. Illustration 1 shows this pistol equipped with a "Roper"-Grip. A hundred per cent improvement. Not only does this grip bring out and enhance the innate beauty of this little handgun, but it improves the holding qualities to an amazing extent.

The remedy for the most glaring fault in the Woodsman, namely that of extreme muzzle-lightness, suggests

itself. Our own experiments in that direction were somewhat variegated. One can, of course, weigh down the
barrel by taping bars to it or cast huge lead-chunks, to be
clamped there. Such measures are, while probably achiev-
ing their object, at best only temporary ones and, mostly,
they look it too. I had in mind to have a wooden fore-
stock made of pleasing design, hollow inside, so that one
could pour lead-shot in, to suit one's needs and plug the

Illustration No. 1

WOODSMAN .22 cal. (Colt) with King-Red post and chromium
mirror frontsight. King adjustable rearsight. Roper handle.

Insert shows Roper walnut-forestock (hollow) filled with lead
to suit the shooter. King, San Francisco, are getting out a
ventilated rib sight for the Woodsman, similar to the one shown
on page 1C of "Sixguns and Bullseyes"; the rib in two parts so
as not to interfere with the movement of the slide.

thing up. Of course, being so set on doing it right, we
demanded of our design that it carry all the lead near
the muzzle and none further back of the barrel. Because,
doing the latter would only make the assembly heavier,
without steadying the muzzle as effectively. It developed
that the wooden forestock idea is practically out of the
experimental stage. Walter Roper made me a beautiful
forestock as you can see from illustration. It is held to the
barrel by the pressure of two screws. The fact that the
barrel tapers toward the muzzle would, theoretically, cause
the forestock to shift forward. However, there being so

much carefully measured contact surface "pinching" against the taper, no actual shifting takes place. Just to make sure, I put a strip of friction tape under the barrel. Before this book is out, our Springfield friend will have effected a slightly different distribution of weight in that the lead-weight (which is placed inside the hollow forestock) will have been shifted a little closer to the muzzle. That fore-stock is not only artistically pleasing but also very effective in shooting. Those of my friends that have seen and tried my beautiful gun are simply crazy over it. The muzzle just refuses to jiggle. You will want to have that fore-stock, so you had better get in touch with Walter. Further-more, we got ahold of an engineering friend of ours and by putting our heads together we figured out that a thin steel-shell, properly shaped, blued, and weighted, might do the trick. I append herewith a few drawings which convey a third idea. As can be seen, one may choose the number of lead-plugs oneself. However many one puts in, they will all be nearer the muzzle and thus conform with our credo that a proper "shift" of weight along the barrel, rather than a thoughtless increase of barrel weight, will steady that shivering muzzle. Please don't write to me on that score. By that I mean: Don't write me! I shall know no more than you. You know, I pleaded some-where in *Sixguns and Bullseyes*, not to write to me in con-nection with that nutty handle that I designed and illus-trated, because I don't sell them. I am not in that kind of business. But, will you believe me when I tell you that, at this early stage, a number of friends wrote in, asking for blueprints, etc.? Of course, I appreciate, nay: I welcome, the intense interest that shooters take today in current problems, but how in heck can I be expected to write numerous letters? When I write a book, that should be the end of it. So, don't write me! Unless, of course, you want to—

In this matter of the Woodsman assembly, I am only

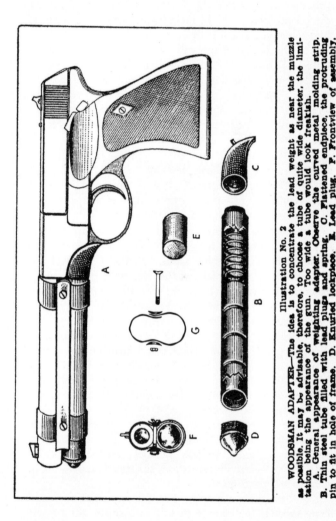

Illustration No. 2

WOODSMAN ADAPTER.—The idea is to concentrate the lead weight as near the muzzle as possible. It may be advisable, therefore, to choose a tube of quite wide diameter, the limitation being the appearance of the gun. Too wide a tube would look freakish.

A. General appearance of weighting adapter. Observe the curved metal molding strip. B. Thin steel tube filled with lead plugs and spring. C. Flattened endpiece, the protruding pin to fit in hole of frame. D. Knurled lockpiece. E. Lead plug. F. Frontview of assembly, showing clamp, metal moulding and bolt. (Two of each needed.) G. Clamp, cross section of moulding, also bolt.

interested in the conception, not in the making and distribution of "thingamajigs." For that matter, if you had
the proper dies or could make them, you could manufacture something much better, for all I know. A steel-cast-
ing of the proper shape will not work well, even if you
were to lighten the steel toward the trigger-guard-end by
drilling, etc. You need "Lead" and you need it near the
muzzle. But, whatever correct assembly you employ, you
will find that the Woodsman performance will improve
considerably, particularly if the new King-rib-sights are
fitted, which have a click-adjustment.

The "Woodsman" has comparatively fast lock time
without jarring and shoots anything in the .22 Long Rifle
class of cartridge. I myself use Kleanbore and get excellent results. This pistol comes also equipped with a
4½"-barrel, but I don't particularly care for it.

I advise any beginner or expert who contemplates buying a fine Automatic, to get a "Woodsman" (6" barrel).
I know what I am talking about. You will find sufficient
evidence in this Manual for the fact that my regard for
manufacturers is sort of "tinged with ironic mistrust." My
recommendation therefore should have double weight. The
"Woodsman" is a fine instrument. I understand that
the Colt boys intend to bring out a heavier barrel of
elliptical profile. I am afraid that I shall not be able to
give any data, as they are still fussing around with it. I
do hope that they don't just make the pistol heavier but
use their noodle by putting the weight in the proper place,
that is: near the muzzle.

But, new model or not, you cannot go wrong on the
"Woodsman" as now obtainable and, if you should be
ambitious (As you eventually will be), get the "Roper"—
and "King"—improvements as suggested above. You
won't need much more.

The mechanism is simple. But this very situation tempts
many shooters to tinker with this mechanism, the trigger-

pull for instance. Not being a good mechanic myself, I carefully refrain from doctoring guns. It so happened that my gunsmith (Accidently?) stumbled on just the right adjustment for the Woodsman, namely, a smooth take-up and the shortest pull imaginable. I leave that gun strictly alone.

A friend came to me the other day and showed me his Woodsman, asking my opinion of the trigger action. I told him what I thought, naturally. But I warned him at the same time, *not* to monkey with it himself, Nonetheless, our enthusiast went ahead and unwittingly converted his Automatic into a single shot pistol. He was quite impressed with his deed, but hasn't made up his mind as yet whether to feel pleased or not.

Many a fine Woodsman have I seen that shot "fully" automatic in places, after they got through with them, or the trigger action was too sloppy, so that I have become quite a confirmed "Non-Tinker." At best, gun-smithing is not an easy art.

THE "WALTHER P. P."

The following is the outcome of an accident, or rather: I came across the thing by accident. Ladies and Gentlemen, let me present the "Walther P. P." Automatic. Take a look at Illustration 3 on page 15 and if slick, convincing lines impress you at all, this little model has everything. You see, I happened to be on the look-out for a small .22 caliber holster-automatic, not too heavy, yet accurate and efficient enough to be of value. I fell in love with the looks of the Auto. I then went out and shot it and, believe it or not, this little thing actually *outshot* special target-models, not once but many times. It became a menace. One night, I must have felt particularly good, but I shot a "292" over the Standard American 20 yard course, in club competition. That means, out of a possible

"300" I was only eight points down. I had other people shoot the gun and *all* of them made higher scores with the first try. What do you deduct, dear Watson? Ideal balance? Right! Good pull? Right again! And, although not built for target purposes, I believe, it would be a crime to leave this sweet little thing out of our collection. I consider it my little "pet" and anybody that shoots it, will grow to like it. It is a pity that it has to be imported. It is worth being an American gun. It is a greater pity that the people who import it, instead of being satisfied with a reasonable profit, put the thumb-screws on the buyer. Well, we shooting nuts take it and take it—

It is said, that if one were serious and conscientious enough, one could master any pistol, even the abominations. But, with this Walther, things are made easy. The angle of stock to frame has been scientifically ascertained and the magazine with an extension piece gives you a full grip. It has a clever action and, despite its short barrel and correspondingly short sighting radius, the ballistics are so favourable as to put the gun alongside of special target models, within reasonable distances. Your club-friends will have to look to their laurels, if you introduce a Walther. For general purposes, it has several safety features and, most unusual, it is a "double-action" Auto. That means, you don't have to pull the slide back with your other hand, for the first shot. All you do is to pull the trigger and that action will cock the hammer and fire the shell. From then on, it functions the same as other Automatics, that is by recoil. The initial trigger pull of the Walther as delivered, is too heavy. If adjusted, however, to a four pound pull or less and, if fitted with proper sights, you will have a pistol that *is* a pistol. Stack it up against any target gun! The fly in the ointment is that the sights are not adjustable and, of course, the outrageous price. Maybe, the importers if they should condescend to read this, will beat their breast in remorse and sharpen the pencil. I am afraid they are of the same breed as some domestic dispensers of nut-material.

Another product by the same factory, is its longer brother, a target-model with a 7½″ barrel. Remarkably accurate. It appears that, in an unguarded moment, the

Illustration No. 3

WALTHER .22 cal., P. P. model, with long ramp and special frontsight. Rearsight adjustable for windage.

Insert shows gun in "double-action" position, that is: pressing the trigger will cock the hammer and fire the cartridge; successive action is automatic. This model is also made in .32 and .380 calibres, with less favorable ballistics.

makers bethought themselves of the fact that this model might have the same disadvantages of most of the other Automatics, namely, that it might be too muzzle-light, which, of course, it was. They therefore invented a short hollow tube attached in front, which can be filled with lead—a sort of make-shift and not a very bright one at that. This tube resembles the bow-end of a Zeppelin and, God knows, it looks terrible. But, if you can forget looks, the intended weight-shift is a good step toward the ideal.

THE "LUEGER"

I suppose it seems natural to favour things that have a sort of sentimental past. I must confess that my next selection, the "Lueger," is kind of tinged that way. I carried it during the last lamentable debacle and had a chance to get well acquainted with it. Its powerful slenderness appealed to the artist in me while its deadly accuracy overshadowed any of its possible shortcomings. I played around with it after the war and my attachment grew deeper, if that had been possible.

In the minds of the public (Myself included), the Lueger is classified as a German Automatic. Imagine my surprise when I read in Hatcher's latest book that the Lueger idea was conceived right here in America, by a fellow named Borchardt. It seems that the Germans knew a good thing when they saw one, faster than the American Official circles. Anyway, the Lueger has been manufactured in Germany these many years and any improvement over the first crude model, was, probably, made in that country. The reason why I touch the history of this Automatic casually, is to sort of underline a certain irony in the affair. The Parabellum (significant name, by the way) is an American invention, but, despite its superiority over other models, it is American no longer—What a pity! And what a joke! When American Officials *did* need an Automatic for military and other purposes, they had to shop around and fool around with European models and finally adopted and bought the rights of one, which cannot even hold a candle to the Lueger. And here is the joke: The model which they adopted and bought from Europe, was invented right in our own back-yard—Ho—ho—ho—. Now, we heard about all the intensive tests that were made with all kinds of different guns at the time—Again, the most modern, the most progressive, the most promising among the models tested, was not recognized. For the

second time, America did not grab the chance to manufacture the excellent Lueger gun right here.

I am not a historian, certainly not on astral affairs, but
there is no doubt in my mind that the fellows who were
responsible for rejecting the Lueger are not playing the

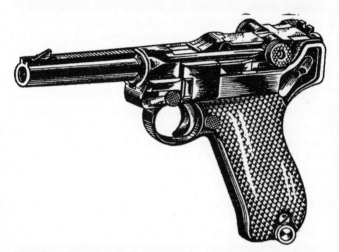

LUEGER 7.65 mm. with factory handle. Disappearing frontsight
when gun is used with conversion assembly.

harp among Elysian clouds. I only hope that it is warm
enough for them down in Mephisto's inferno.

Now, in discussing the Lueger, I don't want you to
rely on my testimony. I am too prejudiced. Ask anyone
who has ever handled a Lueger—(Of course, I am talking
of the "genuine" Lueger and not the oriental fakes that
the gullible American public was fooled with, shortly after
the war—I am being shown some of these relics at times
and they impress me like a demimonde imitation of an
aristocratic lady.)

Well, let's get on! Take some of the mossbacky objections against the Lueger. It was claimed that the gun jams.

The story goes that the various models under test were put in muddy water for a day, fully loaded, and then hung up to dry. Without cleaning they were then put to shooting tests and the model that still functioned, was selected for its ruggedness and abusibility. Of course, a soldier is trained, before an attack on the enemy, to put his .45 in muddy water, let it dry and then try his luck. As far as I am concerned it would not matter much. He can't shoot the damn thing anyway. Would a commission bent upon finding the best wristwatch, throw the various models from the top of the Empire State Building and condemn any make that couldn't stand the shock? Why should a gun be watertight? I thought it was built to be shot? Maybe, I am all wet myself, but if I were on a commission I would test those features that are vital and important for the thing under scrutiny. Most assuredly. What good are sound-proof tobacco pipes? Heck, if a gun jams because it was thrown around in the dirt, it is the shooter and not the gun that should be condemned. From what little I know of war-conditions, I remember that any sonofagun who didn't treat his tools with kidgloves, was in for merry hell. And, do you think for one moment that a man, when he knows damn well that his life may depend on the proper condition of his tools, will neglect to keep them in condition?

Let the scientists get busy and invent primers and powders that won't corrode the barrel.

How about the metalurgists finding an alloy that won't corrode or erode nevermind *what* you put in the cartridge?

Where the hell is the man in the trenches to get hot water from to clean the barrel of his gun with, so that it won't rust, etc.? With our Luegers and ammunition we used an oil-rag and were safe. My Lueger never jammed, but then I had no ulterior motive to find the gun faulty and—I treated it right.

Then they said: "It has an awkward trigger pull!" My

Lueger and many, many thousand others, has the finest and smoothest squeeze that you will ever find in *any* gun.

As for the ballistics, they were so far superior to anything in existence then, that all they could dig up was the lame pretext of insufficient calibre. These Santa Clauses had their minds already made up—Obviously. Just because a few Moros had been tickled with some .38 Revolver shells and had the audacity to survive, the ".45 calibre craze" became the credo. "Knock the bastid down so that he stays knocked down." And "Shocking-Power" assumed such importance that it makes one sick. As ballistic science grows up, more and more actual data are made available and many a mossy concept will be thrown in the ashcan. Among them the famous "Shocking Power-Idiosyncraziness."

Well, the damage is done—I was, in contrast to a number of the "Wags" who waggle earnestly about ballistics, compelled to work the trigger in combat, that is with the targets spitting back at one. And, being done under duress, the memory is unpleasant in the extreme, but in retrospect I can assert that less extremely large calibres do more effective work than the .45 calibre. It all boils down to the question of how good the shooter behind the gun is and I claim that a calibre unnecessarily large, is not conducive to good handling.

I am quite serious when I say that the Lueger is the most accurate handgun ever built. It was modern and far ahead of its time when it was invented. It still looms sky-high over other large calibre Automatics.

With adjustable sights and trigger-pull adjusted to a nicety, its accuracy is uncanny. It has a scientifically designed grip, good lock-time and is an easy shooting gun. By that I mean: You don't have to buckle down and *lick* the thing. You just get acquainted and it will almost shoot itself.

The only outstanding technical objection I have to the

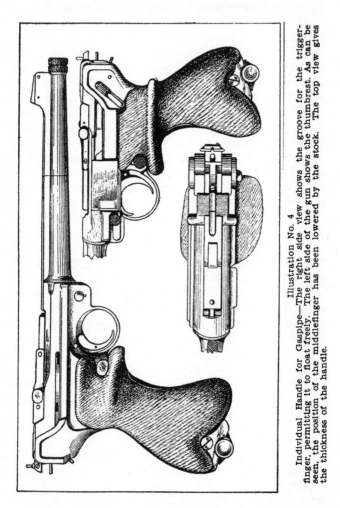

Illustration No. 4

Individual Handle for Gaspipe.—The right side view shows the groove for the trigger-finger, permitting it to float freely. The left side of the gun shows the thumbrest. As can be seen, the position of the middlefinger has been lowered by the stock. The top view gives the thickness of the handle.

Lueger, is a certain muzzle-lightness. A heavier barrel could take care of that.

Another objection (that of a civilian) is the cost of the shells.

And the price of the gun asked by the Importers is, probably, too high also. These foreigners are not used to American methods of quantity turnover and resultant drop in cost. They want to retire into fortune in their own thickheaded way. Speaking for myself: I would pay *any* price for a good Lueger and so will all the other dumb gun-nuts.

One of the crowd of infernal pluggers, tinkerers or what have you, a fellow who seems to like me, offered to make a handle for my Lueger that would, as he expressed it: Knock my eye out. I viewed the offer with misgivings—After all, I like to keep my organs in good shape. I gave him a few pointers, still sceptical. But, when I saw the handle and tried it—Have you ever heard a gentleman audibly "smack" his lips over a plate of some exotic, exquisite soup or other dish? Well, I "smacked"— Look at Illustration 4 yourself and judge—Can you blame me? Boy, am I exclusive. That handle has everything— everything but an automatic bulletholepunch. I told that philanthropist that he should manufacture the thing—He said, he would.

THE "GAS-PIPE"

Here in Illustration No. 5 we have our "Mystery Gun." I've put it in, not because I wanted to show something sensational or exciting, but because this combination is proof of a really serious attempt at modernization. It has always puzzled me why we should not have a powerful Center-Fire-Gun and a *conversion* that is easy and economical to shoot for the .22 Long Rifle Rim-Fire shell.

Practicing with a large calibre gun costs so darn much

in the way of support. If you have to pay around a nickel for every squeeze, your pocketbook will feel it, particularly in Time-and Rapid firing. The consequence is that most shooters lay off and stay very much "average" in these calibres. I suppose these larger calibre shells do *have* to be expensive—Well, since they are, matters are not helped along. Now, if we had an attachment suitable for the cheap .22 shell—You fertile minds of America, you inventors, you clever gun-tinkers: Here is a field for the better mousetrap.

The attempts made so far have been sort of feeble and unsuccessful. Somebody thunk and thunk and finally came down with a .22 attachment for the .45 Automatic. He blew his horn lustily and the dumb shooting world pricked its ears. But it turned out to be a "fizz," just a poor and unintelligent brainstorm. Hell, that thing isn't worth a nickel, since it works only "Single-Shot," when it works at all. Still, one should praise even that attempt, dumb as it was. Somebody, somehow, realized a crying need—That's something! Now, I know that there must be hundreds of intelligent gun-nuts with mechanical ability in this country of ours. Fellows, let me tell you: Get out a mousetrap that works and your fortune is made!

Over in Germany, somebody approached the situation with a bit more initiative. It concerns a conversion for the Lueger-Automatic. When introduced in this country, it was received with lukewarm mistrust. I became interested—and I am still cursing the day when I laid eyes on the damn thing. Mind you, a clever approach, but as painfully a termination as a caesarian miscarriage. I don't know how annoying a miscarriage can be, but let it pass.

Like other nuts, I was stubborn though. I fooled around with it. Spare me the recount of what the darn thing has cost me so far—But, here is the point: I have up to a short time ago, not been able to contact a clever gun mechanic who was willing and able to cooperate.

If, among you readers, there should be one ambitious soul, let him get in touch with me. He can have all the credit and financial rewards—as long as he succeeds in perfecting an ideal conversion. Look at the picture: You see the original 7.65 Lueger. The centre-fire breechblock

Illustration No. 5

LUEGER 7.65—Conversion into .22 cal. Factory handle. Note special breech-block and junction of centrefire with rimfire barrel. Frontsight of centrefire-gun is now out of the way. The sights for the conversion are adjustable for both windage and elevation. Insert shows gun with Whitex-frontsight.

has been replaced by a rim-fire-block. A .22 rifled tube was stuck through the 7.65 barrel. Theoretically, it should be possible to fire either rimfire .22s or centrefire 7.65s by exchanging breechblocks, with or without the .22 tube.

The conversion I have *does* work, but it does not work ideally. (I wish I were a mechanic. I would show you fellows something!) The firing pin travel is too long, the blow too weak and the trigger too sloppy and indistinct. But each shot that *does* go out shows remarkable accuracy. I don't dare enter the conversion in Time and Rapid fire competition because I never know beforehand whether it will shoot "fully automatic" or just "jam."

A simple mechanical problem—Here I wrestle with my thoughts and ideas and hundreds of clever technical guys are worrying about where their next Rolls Royce is going to come from.

I *want* that ideal conversion, damn you! And all the other Lueger nuts want it too. How about it?

I want to be able to participate in serious competition with my 7.65 Lueger, but I don't want to spend a fortune supporting the ammunition hounds. I want to practice every day with my conversion on cheap .22 shells and when the match approaches, I will be ready to blow a box of the gold plated 7.65s.

Isn't my "Mystery Gun" a beauty though? It is true that people who profess to be friends of mine, call it the "Gas-Pipe" or the "Buck Rogers" or even the "Mouse Trap." When they see the high "nineties" on the target, they just shrug their shoulders, but, as soon as the thing jams or acts up, the comments become sarcastic. Is it "I" against the whole world? Well then: So be it! I'll get that damn thing to work yet and all the sneerers can go to hades!

I know that I am, basically, right in my demand for a conversion and I know that, after this book gets around a bit, things will start to move.

Let me dwell a little on the performance of the insert-tube, in slow fire. The long sighting radius is an advantage. The converted gun holds rather well, although it shares the common fault of most Automatics in that it is somewhat muzzle light. That is mostly caused by an unnecessarily heavy magazine. (Another cause to shake one's head at the thoughtlessness of the designing engineers. I am sure that if the designing were supervised by "shooters," our present day guns would be much more satisfactory. And that makes me ask a pertinent—or impertinent if you will—question: How many experienced shooters are there to be found among the designing engineers, in any one gun factory? Aaaah—no answer, what? Am I getting old, crabbing all the time? Oh no, fellows! Others before me, better men, have pleaded and cajoled—It's ever the old, old story——)

With the trigger function so adjusted that there is a smooth "Take-Up," a distinct point of resistance and a rather light final squeeze, the Gas Pipe is a peach. It is easy to master—and just think what could be done with the 7.65 gun if the .22 cartridge conversion permits of fine results—You could practice to your heart's content, grow onto the gun, its grip, its squeeze. Now, I am not just talking for myself: I shoot the large Lueger well— always have—It is such a remarkable gun that I like to see all my good friends get similar results with it. The answer is the successful solution to the conversion problem —And so to bed.

Ere I close this chapter, I must tell you of an experience. I *did* meet a gunsmith who can think and plan and whose meat is "Automatics"; a chap by the name of Hyde, a German expert over in Brooklyn. Friend George, after being told of my ideas, looked at the thing —a few handshakes and the Lueger fell apart in the manner so puzzling to the uninitiated. At first, George seemed stumped—I tell you, he actually sweat blood—However, his thickheadedness would not admit defeat, especially after I told him that nobody else could do a thing with my idea. I left him alone for a few days. He had a tough job on his hands—and we knew it. First off, we had agreed that the action should, necessarily, be confined to one type of ammunition. In view of the fact that as much recoil as possible was needed, I settled on a certain High Speed L. R. cartridge. I also had in mind to use "Trombone Oil" for the slide so as to diminish any trouble on that score. When George rang up after a few days, he informed me simply that the thing works. I inquired breathlessly what ammunition he had been using for testing and he came back with "*Any* ammunition, ordinary or high speed, mixed or alone" and that the slide was riding dry, without any oil. You can imagine how quickly I hied me there. It was as he said. No ticklish picking of special ammunition or of a special lubricant. My troubles were over! I found, however, that the trigger squeeze was not as desired by me. A few more licks and I had what I wanted. We removed the insert barrel and exchanged breechblocks. The gun, practically, worked faultlessly on both blocks. All that was necessary was to raise the firing pin shoulder on the 7.65 block.

The way it is now, the conversion has weak points, naturally. There are things still to be ironed out.

So, you Lueger fanciers, you see, . . . ?

I am vindicated!

The centrefire-to rimfire-conversion.

MAUSER

Somehow, I never cottoned on to the Mauser pistols. Their workmanship is superb, but workmanship alone isn't what makes a pistol. The big 7.63 m/m model is an abomination and can be used effectively only in combination with the holster stock. With the latter arrangement, the accuracy is unexcelled—and I mean it. The cartridge is very powerful and shows, I believe, ballistics not approached by other shells of like calibre. However, in conjunction with the holster stock, the gun is practically a carbine and we shall therefore not waste many more words on this monster.

Used without holster stock, the gun punishes the hand fiercely and one needs iron nerves for continuous shooting —positively not the gun for sewing circles. The grip looks ridiculously like a blackjack and is out of all proportion with the heavy machinery. In short, the big Mauser is an unlovely, ungainly piece of apparatus and I hold no brief for it.

The .32 Mauser (7.65 m/m) Pocket model is, to my way of thinking, inferior to the .32 Colt Pocket. If you should happen to own one of these small Mausers, I recommend that the same changes be made as with the .32 Colt, although adding to the backstrap will not improve the already impaired appearance of the gun. When modernized, the .32 Mauser pocket will be much more valuable as a defense gun and, after being licked, it should show good results at Melee distances.

◈　　◈　　◈

WALHAL

(A tale of stone and heads and anger and more stone)

I now take you, my Reader, into strange happenings—Up yonder steps—They are wide, round steps such as one finds on war-memorials—They lead up and up—to the pinnacle where stands the Grecian temple—We are out of breath as we reach the landing and stand under the imposing portal—The white marble edifice awes us—We blink into its cold shadowy depths—Austere—Prim—Sterile pillars. Invitingly forbidding—Nothing but impressive, oppressive silence. We whisper in undertones. This, my friends, is "WALHAL" wherein puny man preserves that which is magnificent.

Will you follow me? No? All right then, wait here. I must go in! I clamp my lips and resolutely take the first step—Row upon row of alabaster pilasters—Cold and smooth to the touch. The sound of my heels clatters blasphemously through the aristocratic stillness and I put foot before foot, carefully, filled with uneasiness, as if stalking. Through the overhead dome shafts of sombre light fall on the rotunda—The floor a geometrical pattern of greyish, polished stone.

Beyond, in the forest of pilasters, lie deep, motionless shadows—Irresolutely, I pause under a ray and peer nervously around me—The all-overawing stolidity of masses, of costly stone, transfixes me. I feel as if I must leave this minute—the way I came. I must get away from under this imperious silence! Hesitatingly, I put a foot back—when a sound arrests it in mid air. A deep, resonant sound like the murmur of water flowing swiftly over and around rocks. The sound swells in volume and recedes—There is a disturbing note in it—Am I intruding in this hallowed hall and do the Gods resent my presence? My eyes grow accustomed to the twilight under the pillars—I see the circular wall in the background, dimly but recognizable, broken by deep "niches"— at regular intervals—jet black niches—The shrines of the Gods. The murmur comes from my right—I strain my eyes—and I see figures moving restlessly before a niche. I must get to this group, must satisfy my earthly curiosity! With the first rude impact of my sole, the sound rises—But I labour forward—forward—and I see whiterobed old men with long flowing beards—Somes faces are turned toward me—They do not move their lips, yet the compelling waves of sound rise and echo from the ceiling. Every step, careful as I am, magnifies in my ears—and now I see the first face clearly—A martial face, as if carved of stone, reigned over by harsh eyes, burning with fanaticism—The face turns away from me—slowly—as if in contempt.

I have gone this far and I shall go on! All have their backs turned now, their faces uplifted to the niche before them. I waver a little and then I touch the man in front of me, shyly—He shakes his shoulder impatiently. I walk carefully around the half-circle of forbidding backs. The murmur, I flatter myself, cannot be for me—It sounds like the deep, low sing-song of Tibetan priests—not unmelodious, but monotone. I stretch on my toes, but I cannot see what they revere—these old men. I shoulder

one of them and he steps aside unwillingly. I shoulder
another—and another—and as I get deeper into the
ranks, I see rapt old faces—fanatically inflamed old eyes—
And ever the murmur, rising in cadence and subsiding—
I notice that as the men step aside, they seem to click
their sandals. Incredulously, I watch again—Yes! The
man before me whom I touch, stiffens his spine and, with
a measured half-step opens the passage—Like a man with
martial training. How absurd! These cannot be soldiers—These are priests! Priests, immersed in their cult.
I stand now before the niche. From its black recess a
white cararian pedestal shines immaculately—and there
is a marble tablet—and I read the inscription "The Sacred
Cow." What? Here in Walhal? My eyes stare out
of their sockets. But I see no Moloch—no Idol—But,
there must be something—and I look again and on the
circular stone disk on the pedestal—No, it's impossible!
But, there it is—Am I crazy? Can all these men be sane?
I turn around and see their faces. Despite their long
beards I somehow know that these men are military officers—high ranking officers—But, they don't seem ludi-
crous in their robes—Everything seems to fit the situation.
Cold brained military officers, yet fanatically intent upon
this ritual of offering homage to the monstrous God—I
open my mouth and instantly the murmur recedes and
dies down—Stillness—Awful stillness—and this stillness
is pregnant with antipathy, vibrant, resentful antipathy
against me—I must say something now— to break this
awful suspense—this imperative something—Suddenly,
there rises a raucous voice from the stillness: "Intruder!
Mocking Defiler! You have sneered at tradition—Have
insulted our Apostles!—"

I am stunned—and again the voice vibrates, harsher
now and menacing: "You dared despoil our temple. But
you shall not hurt us again as you did with your last
book! Avast!"—And there is a sea of angry imprecations

—maledictions and raised fists—The ranks surge toward me—My knees tremble—Before I flee in terror, I must again see the "Sacred Cow"—I must—My head turns—and I again see the thing in gleaming, polished steel on the pedestal—My senses whirl and—then everything breaks loose within me—A maniacal shriek wrenches from my throat—and I shout: "You—you—" And I rush head-long into the wall and break my skull.—

The idol on the pedestal was a ".45 Government Automatic"—

❖   ❖   ❖

THE COLT AUTOMATICS

This is going to be a long, long chapter, I am afraid. You better lean back some more in your arm-chair and prepare yourself.

AND IT CAME TO PASS that the clouds gathered overhead—and they covered the sun—until the light faded altogether—and it was dark on this earth—and—the .45 Automatic was adopted as the official side-arm for the Military.

That's the way things began. This .45 Automatic has wide distribution—I don't know how many, many thou-sand are in the hands of sportsmen alone, but it must be an imposing number. This number is enhanced by the many owners of the brothers to the .45, namely, the .38 Super and .22 Ace. These three models look alike, outwardly, but thank God, they are as different as brothers usually are.

Well: Let's not put off things—Let's get at the .45 calibre. I shall, in the space allotted, not dwell on the inception and the practicability of this large calibre gun. My choler, you know—Principally, the ballistics are rather poor, but, brother, do the bullets make "holes." And we

Americans, peaceful as we may generally be, when we shoot at a man, we want to knock the bastid down and put him " hors de combat" once and for all. The bigger and uglier the exit hole, the more bloody and hopelessly crippled our victim, the better do we like it. Oh—Oh—I wanted to constrain myself and here I go—

COLT .38 Super. This gun has the same appearance, generally, as the .45 Automatic.

Anyway, some fine day, the need for better ballistics was felt, even by the perpetrators and kindred, and the .38 Super was called into being. Although of smaller calibre, the .38 Super Auto. shell showed vastly increased velocities and greater penetration. Obviously, somebody had made a mistake in the beginning when the .45 calibre was adopted—No, I take that back! Although at that time better performances were known to exist, it took some time to percolate and, I believe, we better call the final acknowledgment of the superiority of the .38 Super, an "Evolution."

Still, the .45 Automatic is the official side arm yet—
Over shorter distances, say up to 50 yards, its accuracy
is undeniable but not remarkable—and that distance is
about the extreme limit within which such a hand-gun,
in a serious melee, would still prove useful.   When I
spoke about "accuracy" I had the commercial model in
mind, a gun with better fitting of the parts, with honed
action, a total trigger squeeze of about four pounds and
equipped with sensible and adjustable sights.   It seems
that in the "Issue" guns everything goes.   Anything that
might tend to reduce accuracy was incorporated.   I spoke
somewhere else about the uselessness of the thin military
sights.   Let me tell you: I can shoot almost anything that
has a tube and a handle, but trying to line up these military sights is agony.   In endeavouring to untangle the
divine purpose behind the adoption of these silly sights,
one assumes that other sights might interfere with the
quick drawing of the gun.   Have you ever seen the
official holsters that the .45s are toted around in?   Are
they "Quick Draw" holsters?   No, *that* couldn't have been
the reason!   What else?   Oh brother, don't be so infernally inquisitive.   "There are the sights as issued!
Take them or leave them!"   I could say that it isn't my
funeral—But, I feel so generous that I don't mind opening the eyes of some of the big wigwags.   After all: If
you can't line up a gun properly, what the hell good is it
anyway?   But, of course, you can never tell—Dumber
things than that have happened.

Take, for instance, the "Grip"—Unless you are over
six feet tall with fists like North Carolina Hams, that
grip feels mighty uncomfortable.   It's a handful, brother—

Now, we don't want any toy things in the Military, but
heck, we are not Vikings!

While we are at it, let's take some more of our objections: The .45 Automatic is, what I call a "Flutter" Gun.
"What the h—— ?" will you exclaim.   (I sometimes say it

myself) "Flutter-Gun" is not a scientific term and I will
have trouble in making myself understood. "Flutter-
Gun" means a gun that—errr "flutters," what? Observe
the behaviour of the upper part of the gun when somebody else shoots it—Stand to his right!—You will soon
see what I mean by "flutter"—It is a sort of crazy twitching along the slide, particularly after a few of those
healthy recoil kicks—It does not seem to affect the performance (Maybe, only the shooters). Or, maybe, it
does. I haven't found out. It's one of the antics of
the .45 and, possibly, wholly unnecessary, useless, but
certainly annoying.

One thing more, have you ever tried to hold the gun
steadily in any kind of wind? Breasting the wind with
its ponderous sides? Ouch! Has it ever occurred to you
how few outstanding experts there are with the .45 Automatic? Everyone is willing to make allowances, somehow. If a fellow shoots a .45 Automatic and shows fair
scores, everybody will praise him. He has done a thing
that he could have done much easier with some other
gun. But he choose to make things harder for himself
and, ergo, he deserves credit. (Like the fellow who
unscrews the hinges of a gate, then walks thru' the hole
in the fence, with the gate under his arm, and puts the
thing back again.)

Well—Well—

But, of course, the fact that ammunition costs so much,
makes extended practice very costly and that may be one
of the reasons for the generally poorer showings of the
.45 Automatic. Because, I *will* repeat here: The .45
Automatic is not an altogether badly shooting gun. It
is accurate within reason. And it *can* be licked—No question about that! But, brother, you have to lick it with a
capital "L."

Now, I am not the wise uncle who discovered all this.
Oh no! Others were there first. One knew all about

the handicaps. So, they put their heads together and concocted the .22 Ace Automatic. These benefactors figured
that the main trouble with the .45 Automatic was lack of
practice. That a gun which could shoot the cheaper .22
ammunition, might provide this practice. Inherently
sound! But, what resulted was a bastard gun. A .22
Pop Gun with the large frame of the .45 bellybuster.
The shooter was supposedly enabled now to practice with
the same weight, trigger squeeze and general handling,
whether he shot the .45 or its .22 brother. Of course,
the recoils were different, considerably different! The
functions of the two guns were as unlike as black and
white. But, the Colt boys are busy on something to overcome part of that difference; something along the lines
of the machine-gun sub-calibre attachment. Maybe, I
shall be able to whisper some more about that. Anyway,
something is brewing, some initiative is in the offing and
I solemnly propose that we stand up and bow our heads
in admiring acknowledgment. Let's hope, it's not one
of those eggs—I wish that it could have been a .22 attachment to be used on the original .45 Automatic Frame.

The .22 Colt Ace, as now delivered, is quite formidable
as a target gun. I really mean it! I shoot about as good
with it as with the "Woodsman."

Then, why all the "ribbing?"—Well, it means two guns
to buy, two guns so different in characteristics, behaviour
—Just my playful impatience—Things move too slow for
me, I suppose.

Resumé: The .45 is moderately accurate and the .22
Ace is most certainly, a very accurate gun.

How about the .38 Super? Ah—There is a gun for
you— I wish I could say that, unequivocally. There is
practically no recoil felt, despite its powerful shell. But
don't shoot that thing indoors. Its vicious flash and blast
are kind of hard on the system. I believe I should call
the .38 a strictly "Outdoor" gun. Put a pair of decent

sights on the thing and a not too heavy pull with proper "Take-Up" and you have a powerful and very accurate Automatic. Main objection: The cost of the shells and resultant curtailment of practice. And "practice," we agree, is necessary for *any* gun if we want to lick it.

Already as a wee lil' baby, one outstanding trait of mine was a constant source of annoyance to our factotum Elsie.

COLT—ACE, .22 cal. with adjustable rearsight. (For windage).

She had a word for it. Translated into polite English, I believe, it would have meant something like "Head-strong." Of course, in the vernacular, it sounded much stronger, very much stronger. Well, friend, I am still that: "Headstrong," what I mean "One-track-minded" —plain "thickheaded." So, don't be surprised if I take up that "Convertible" again, at this point. Since the .45 Automatic *is* the official side-arm (A thing for which *I* was not responsible), we must make the best of matters, I suppose. As said before, this gun can, with certain changes, be shot with accuracy.

Disregarding for the moment the possible improvements in the gun proper, we still face the high cost of the ammunition. (I don't mean the Government ammunition which is being doled out to our Reserve Officers, but the commercial ammunition.) It is unreasonable to expect a .45 enthusiast to dig into his pockets and spend a fortune on practice shells. Most of us are not related to Rockefeller and rather than going bankrupt, we prefer to put the .45s away and play around with something that we can afford.

Of course, that's all wrong! A sane solution lies in the direction of a conversion. What is to prevent us from conceiving a conversion that would, after the change-over, permit the use of the economical L.R. cartridge? Have we no brains in this country of ours to solve so simple a mechanical problem? I don't say that I can do it. I am not an inventor nor a mechanic. I am just a shooter. But, how about the bozos that have the ability? Yes, how about them? You complain about "Hard Times?" Your own damn fault. Sit down and design a .22 conversion for the .45 Automatic!

You know: An insert-barrel bored to fit the .22 ammunition so popular at present, a change-over breech block or a separate slide built for the reduced recoil of the smaller cartridge; a provision for adjusting the recoil-spring or a separate provision. There is a theoretical possibility of "boosting" the recoil-effect (As it affects the backward motion of the slide—An interesting idea as it would simulate, to a certain extent, the dissipation of forces within the frame and the shooting hand.) Last, but not least, would attention have to be paid to the similarity of trigger-travel in both calibres. By that I mean: Everything should engage and disengage under exactly the same angles and spring pressures. So that we would truly and honestly have an identical action (Including recoil-force-dissipation) in both the .45 gun and the .22 conversion. Something that would permit us to practice with cheap ammunition and, without change in hold, squeeze, weight, action, to go into the larger calibre—

There we have something to think and work over, you gifted Enthusiasts—something entirely possible and feasible, yet never seriously and intelligently attempted. (One lame—very lame— attempt was made in the .22 tip-up-barrel affair which was peddled around some time back, and which worked "singleshot" only—Tch! Tch!)   No, I am talking here of something on an intelligent plane, otherwise, I would not plead so earnestly.   And, after you have solved it, some alert manufacturer will buy you a home, free and clear, and will give you enough pocket money to last for the rest of your life.   You don't even have to "sell" the idea.   All you have to do is to shout: "I have a conversion for the .45 Automatic that works!" It's as simple as all that!   Because there is a crying need for it!

Here we have had the .45 Automatic for years.   For an equal length of time it was felt that a conversion was needed.   These many years have gone over the land and our austere gun manufacturers have not met the demand. They have all the machinery and, supposedly, all the brains necessary, but they keep on twiddling their thumbs.

Ah—Why not forget them?   This is an appeal to the real patriots.   Give us that conversion, you Nuts, you Cranks, you Wizards!   You will be hailed as the saviours and you will get a pot of gold besides.   Don't let some foreigner solve the thing for you!

After the advent of the successful conversion, watch the national Matches and count the .45 Automatics that will be shot and will take honors.   And how many potentially good soldiers would that mean?—American soldiers would be known and feared as dangerous Automatic fiends.   I only hope that these clever foreigners don't read this and thus get a bee in their bonnet.   By Golly—

maybe, somebody there might invent something adaptable to their large calibre handguns and then: Where would we be?

No! Don't we lead them in things technical—all the way? And shall we let a little thing such as a conversion stump us? Hell No!

Now, boys, you heard what I said! You sit right down and invent and don't let me hear any excuses! And don't come down with any more "Aces."

What fits the .45 Automatic will also fit the .38 Super. Two flies with one swat.

> Those of you who love the fun
> of shooting the .45 Automatic gun,
> if your brains are nimble enough
> and you have sufficient ambition,
> Go ahead and do your stuff
> and break the deadlock of drowsy tradition.
> Invent a conversion for Twenty-twos
> And chase away our forty-five Blues.

I know, it rhymes terribly, but so does the fact that our .45s lie idle.

I can see the face of my publisher. He expects me to part my hair in the middle and talk sedately about the ballistics of the .45s, etc. Hell, I don't know the first thing about that and, besides, there must be heaps of literature on that score. Every lousy catalogue tells you all you want to know. (Say, if this stuff ever sees print, then my publisher must be a good egg, what?)

Oh—Oh—I am forgetting time—and everything, I can get so wrapped up in a thing—that I could go on rambling, without ever wanting to stop. This .45 Automatic topic is what the red blanket is to the bull. Just wave the damn thing and I charge, horns down. Is there a remote possibility that I am just a poor fanatic? But then, did I not give you an array of splendid arguments? Is there really anything in favour of the damn gun? Oh—there must be some things—But, if there are, I am not going to lose sleep over them.

However, I like to close my diatribe with a consoling word. I don't want you to throw your gun away in disgust—No, no: Like other Automatics, so has the .45 Automatic possibilities. Only: they have to be brought out, developed. Even though I may think that the inherent principle is wrong, it is only one man's opinion and who can tell what the future holds, in the way of experiments etc.? If only we had that pesky ol' conversion, suitable and workable, our intensified practice with the cheap rimfire ammunition might adapt us to handle the poor jalopi with much greater confidence and enthusiasm.

Our last gun, the COLT .32 Pocket Automatic, is a pleasant looking piece of defense apparatus and it shoots! The cartridge is viciously dangerous for the short distances in which it is used. The accuracy, I should say: the practical accuracy, is very fair.

For greater convenience it is recommended to add to the backstrap so as to keep the thumb-tip apart from the finger on the depressed trigger. The sights should be modernized by substituting the 1/10″ Whitex frontsight and a rear-sight, of sufficient height, with a wide, deep slot.

The quick-draw holster, if it is a cross-draw belt holster, should leave the rearsight uncovered and the leather should be cut away so as to leave the trigger section exposed.

More on that topic under the "Holster" chapter.

FACIT

There are, as we know, a great many more Automatic babies and miscarriages in the market than I have described. Unless you already own a pistol not mentioned here, I would advise saving your money. Generally speaking, there are very few intelligently and independently designed Automatics in the market—Most of them are copies or adaptations of some leading principle.

It is rather significant that in this fast moving era, with inventions and discoveries crowding each other, the Automatic field should show no new and distinct departures from the inherited pre-war humdrum. I believe that we are about due for a decidedly modern novelty!

Jules Verne didn't know what he was talking about when he penned his fantastic stories, but most of his ideas have become facts now! Even if I dare not put myself in a class with this departed brilliant dreamer, I have the audacity to speculate.

Let's dream of vastly greater velocities, not because we want a longer flight of the bullets, but because we want to flatten the trajectory and because we want to shorten the functional time of the recoil materially.

Let's think of the possibility of slow dissipation of recoil, maybe using the hydraulic principles, so that the "mass" of a gun doesn't have to increase as the chamber pressures rise.

Let's study the human anatomical conditions as they affect or are affected by the function of a hand-fire arm—and design shape, weight of gun, angle of grip etc. etc. in accordance.

If, in order to create the modern superior gun, we need chemicals other than our present powders, let's develop them!

If the 1937 means of ignition, namely the primers, are insufficient or too slow, use something else, maybe an electric spark from a tiny battery with booster—But, here we drift into caricaturing the thing—and yet—quien sabe?

Going back to our present day Automatics, I would think that actions in which the barrels are tightly screwed to the receivers, should give greater accuracy than actions with "floating" barrels. The easy exchangeability of the latter is often quoted as a sales feature. I beg to discount that. We treat our barrels sensibly and we don't care to compromise on this floating barrel stuff.

Although it would be, academically at least, desirable to have the sights on a fixed base (Like in the revolver), the deficiency of the moving sight base is negligible. The action takes place so fast that the inertia of the average human retina cannot detect anything but a continuous sight picture.

Somewhere else I ruminate about the "Ideal Automatic."

But, as long as we are still hoping, we must try and get along with what we have. Each gun paraded before you has something or other the matter with it. In some cases, we can do something ourselves: Add to muzzle-weight, adjust triggers correctly, change the handle around, improve the sights.

We should make an earnest attempt to overcome the deficiencies of the object, if necessary with the help of clever gunsmiths. But even if there were an "ideal" Automatic in existence, it would not shoot itself. We would have to get thoroughly acquainted with it and we would have to practice—practice—

However, trying to do something with one of the abominations which I have carefully refrained from describing in this Manual, is wasted labour.

I like to say that it is my honest opinion that the models shown you, are the best of the present day crop. They are fully capable of contesting the revolver results in the competition field and even surpassing them. Naturally, we are not satisfied with that. We must have automatic weapons which are so much better (Ballistically), so much more practical and reliable and cheaper to shoot than the revolver that the latter should become definitely obsolete. We must hope—and experiment—and prod—and, some-day, maybe, we will get there!

A word here about mal-and misfunctions, a thing that the opponents to the Automatic like to gloat over. If a cartridge does not go off (A dud, in other words), there will be no recoil. (Say Watson, my dear fellow, wasn't there something—err—profound in my last remark?) Now: No recoil, no exit of bullet, no—no nothing. Reason: A faulty cartridge—Not so elementary—It may have been a weak Firing-pin blow. Don't, I beg you, leave that ol' spring under tension for months on end. No spring will stand that.

If the slide, after recoil, jumps back, and forward again and omits to pick up a new cartridge, it may be that there was not a cartridge in place because the magazine spring, tired out after many months of tension, refused to stretch sufficiently.

In the popular .22 L.R. cartridge, the lubricating grease (A benediction in other ways), will prove a hindrance to the smooth disposition of the cartridge from magazine to chamber. The cartridge, caught lying in an almost level position (In the lip-section of the magazine), has to raise its nose, climb an incline leading to the chamber, where it has its tail raised, by forcefully holding its nose down, until it again lies horizontally in the chamber proper. Quite a brutal procedure and as brainless as—as—Never-mind. In all this, the sticky grease will prove a handicap, as will also the softness of the lead bullet.

If you carry your pistol around with you all the time, certain body emanations (That's delicately enough ex-pressed, what?) influence the chemicals in the cartridge—Also the oil with which you lubricate or protect the metal of your gun, has mysterious and detrimental neutralizing effects upon powder and primer. Don't soak your gun in oil, therefore, but dry it from time to time and oil it afresh. And then use fresh cartridges too. When you clean your gun, watch out that you don't damage your barrel muzzle with your brushes or patches—Try to do it from the breech-end rather.

And above all and everything: Don't throw that valuable gun of yours around in the dirt. (That's strictly a matter for test commissions.) Dirt in the gun means trouble—But so does dirt in your eye—

With reasonable care, there should be no mis-or malfunctions in your Automatic. And I don't care what anybody says to the contrary!

TECHNIQUE

The title may sound just a trifle forbidding. However, the necessity of possessing a technique in handling the Automatic need not be emphasized.

And, although I may wish to say that I shall be short about it, I cannot, in fairness to you, skimp in this chapter. I shall, however, try to avoid all dryness to make this as pleasant reading as is within my power. Everything in this Manual is meant for the good of the Reader and I hope that I shall acquit my task with grace.

Are you on?

Somewhere else I harped on seven little devils—seven points in our little system, which I feel must be mastered by you. This is as good a time as any to enumerate them:

1. HOLD
2. STANCE
3. RELAXATION
4. MOVING THE GUN INTO POSITION
5. SIGHTING
6. SQUEEZE
7. BREATHING

If we except the 1st and 6th points, all the others apply practically unchanged whether we handle a Revolver or an Automatic. Reference will have to be made where necessary to my Revolver Manual *Sixguns and Bullseyes*. The two exceptions mentioned we shall go into at greater lengths as we come to them.

Well brother, these little devils will turn out to be your best friends. Therefore, get set and follow me.

HOLD

When we favoured a tenseless hold in *Sixguns and Bullseyes*, we knew that we had in the Revolver a gun whose metacentre was unfavorable. The peculiar shape, weight distribution and action of the Revolver demanded a cunning understanding of the particular problems it offered.

We were satisfied to admit that a tenseless hold, confined mostly to the front- and the back-lines of the handle, would interfere least with the effects of the trigger, hammer and recoil-actions. We, therefore, decided to hold the Revolver handle in the following way:

We placed our middlefinger between trigger-guard and handle so as to enable us to support the weight of the gun. The position of the middlefinger thus forms a fulcrum for the dipping and tipping of the gun. We arrested these movements by placing the ball of our thumb against the back-strap (the rear of the grip) and resting our thumb on the latch. We then proceeded to curl our other fingers, the ring- and little fingers, around the front line of the grip, right under the middlefinger. We then took care *not* to touch the stock of the gun with our fingertips. We agreed that using our fingertips might, and would, divert the recoil-motivated muzzle to the left. Well and good. We knew that the forces which we unloosened in squeezing, those of the mechanical action inside the gun as also the recoil, would work along a sort of diagonal line, from the muzzle down to the point where thumb and wrist join.

Now, all this we shall have to amend with the Automatic. You see, in contrast to the Revolver, all action in the Automatic takes place *over* our hand on a horizontal plane, not diagonally *through* our hand. The delicate balance of mild pressures in the Revolver need not be maintained to the same degree in the Automatic. I mean: If we curl our fingers around the stock and let the fingertips casually touch it, no harm is done. There will be little, if any, side deflection of muzzle by the recoil, since the latter is not dissipated diagonally through our hand.

All we have to do is to hold the grip and let the slide shoot back and forth over our hand, horizontally.

Now, this hand- and finger-contact must not be of the hickory-club-order, but more on the order of holding a banana. This is not a joke. I mean: No one would think of gripping a banana with a vise-like pressure. He would squash the poor thing and it would do nobody any good.

Now suppose, just suppose, we treat our Automatic handle like a banana—careful not to press hard. After all, even if we were fanatic and surmised some kind of juice in our Automatic handle, what could we possibly do with that? No earthly use, I tell you.

Alright, my boy, just think of a banana when you grasp that Automatic handle, what?

I could lean back now and, with a smug smirk on my facade, lecture about the theory of the thing. But it would be dry stuff, me lad, dry stuff indeed. Let's skip it, therefore. Just you take my advice. Uncle knows best.

What's that? You insist?

No—No!

I can't possibly repeat a lot of stuff that has already been dispensed in *Sixguns and Bullseyes*. Well, just this then:

The Automatic has more "kick" (not more recoil, mind you) than the Revolver—Let's not go into ballistics and all that. Suffice it to say that part of the recoil-gas-pressure is employed to throw the slide back. (The slide extracts the empty shell, as you know, a new shell jumps into position as the slide closes again by force of the recoil-spring.) The force required to throw the slide open has to compress this rather heavy recoil spring— In the Revolver some of the gases fizz out harmlessly at the cylinder-gap, right into the air, while in the Automatic they have to wrestle first with that pesky ol' spring, ere they can go prancing. Hence, the greater kick in the Automatic. Now, all these functions take place over your hand on a horizontal plane as repeatedly pointed out and, naturally, you may use a grip slightly firmer than for the Revolver. Your fingers, therefore, encircle the stock with that banana-touch. We don't use any violence or strength. We try to get along with as gentle a hold as possible. We don't want any tremors, caused by tense gripping, to disturb our work.

To resume: We have placed our middle-ring-and little fingers.

We find now that the thumb sticks up in the air like— err—a sore thumb, what? Simple that. Just lay the poor thing over your middlefinger and—presto—there's your thumb rest.

Some people, when they handle an Automatic, hold their thumb up near the slide—like a hitch-hiker. Down with it on your middlefinger! It should lie on the middlefinger and lock itself there. (Unless your handle has been provided with a special thumb rest).

Your thumb—You know, one of the reasons why we hold the thumb down, is to keep it out of mischief—The same bright lad who sticks it up in the air, aside of the slide, may one day look for his thumb and not find it. The scientific reason—There I go again. I have a hard time to prevent the scientist in me from spilling over all the time. Suppose, you simply accept my statement that the thumb should be locked over the middlefinger— what's wrong with that?—Well, being so stubbornly methodical, I must say that holding the thumb up can only be considered as an affectation, because it serves no practical purpose there, even if there were no danger of injury. Contrarily, by keeping the whole hand *below* the slide, a sensible principle is followed. As said before, there is no cause when shooting an Automatic, for counterbalancing forces such as one meets in the Revolver. And, I repeat again that all actions, recoil as well as mechanical, take place in a straight line back, *over* your hand. There is no tendency on the part of the Automatic to deflect the recoil—I have gone into this question quite fully in *Sixguns and Bullseyes* and I must refer the curious Reader to that blurb.

Now, in certain Automatics, the construction of the stock is such that the end of the trigger-finger when crooked will touch the tip of the thumb. A situation like that is very annoying. The trigger-finger, instead of "floating," leans against the thumb and is actually stopped from functioning freely. Some genius thought of using this defect to advantage—He claimed that, as soon as his forefinger touched the thumb, it knew where it was and would start to push the thumb—Peace in the family, my children! After all, the thumb was there first. In a case of that kind, the remedy is to build up the backstrap until the thumb won't be in the way of the trigger-finger anymore. The general tendency to rest the trigger-finger against something, instead of having it "float" and thus preserve its sensitivity, is a fundamental error. (It's one of the reasons why the European "set-trigger" in the Free-Pistol causes us Americans so much trouble.)

Ah—me—It seems we have covered the old grip question—

Oh no, not quite! When we hold the Automatic up in shooting position, we must try to remember that not only the hand should be kept without appreciable tension, but more so the wrist, the arm, etc.

All that should happen from the shoulder onward is that our gun arm is held out laxly. Let the shoulder joint support just the weight of the lax arm. Don't employ any other muscles. If you feel your biceps, your triceps and the lower arm and wrist sections, they should appear flaccid. I know this demand may appear unorthodox to the Reader who is unacquainted with my system. This Manual, I wish to emphasize, is not of wrestling or of weight-lifting but of pistol shooting, the art of pistol shooting.

Again reverting to the grip proper: After you have found your very own method of holding your gun, in a manner that feels comfortable, it's essential that you memorize this individual grip of yours. That is to say: You must endeavor to assume this particular grip every time you lift the pistol for action. To use an example from *Sixguns and Bullseyes*, imagine your gun stock covered with a thin film, which upon correctly placing your hand, records every little skin wrinkle and skin fold. Every time you place your hand around the stock, all your skin folds should match the first imprint. It sounds harder to do than it really is. Whenever your hold on the gun is changed, you also change the point of impact of the bullet. And, since we will have trouble enough with aiming and squeezing correctly, we should not make things harder for ourselves by changing our hand-and finger positions.

STANCE

Generally speaking, there's little difference in the position of our feet whether we shoot Revolvers or Automatics. Where one could introduce any doubt is in comparing target—with practical shooting, but I assure you that there need be no difference.

We can, therefore, assert that we place our feet so that our toes do not point directly at the target. That would make our chest also face the target. Neither do we turn a quarter to the left. (For right handers) No, we arrange our feet so that our chest faces between the two points just described. The reason (Of course you will want a valiant reason, durn your hide) is that the human body "sways"—It sways in the direction in which our chest faces. If your chest were facing the target, you would sway back and away from it. Stretch your arm, pointing it at the target, and you will observe that the hand will move up and down as it is being influenced by your sway. Likewise, if you were to turn your body a quarter to the left, with your gun hand still pointing at your target, the body sway would cause your hand to travel from left to right and back, horizontally, across the target.

Both positions and their resultant sway are detrimental to good shooting. We can't afford them.

Now, we cannot entirely eliminate body swaying, not as long as we have to get along with two feet only, but we surely can minimize the effect of body swaying by taking the mid-way position described before, somewhere between the two bad ones.

I have no time here to argue the point further, you just believe me.

Alright: Our chest faces one-eighth of a turn to the left, our gun arm points at the target, our feet are something like fourteen inches apart. (You have to find out for yourself how many inches). Withal, you will stand naturally, without the slightest tension. There's just a slight half twist in your shoulder.

When we shoot at targets, we put our left hand in a convenient pocket, as we want to forget having to worry about it.

With a fast draw from the holster, or any other practical or fast shooting, we may want to use the left arm as a balance somehow, and we, therefore, do not imprison that member.

This much about "Stance." Short and sweet, eh?

Now we come to

RELAXATION

Very important, although easy to explain. Whenever you observe some dub shooting a handgun, you will find that he is all tied up in knots. I disremember how many thousands of muscles there are in the human body, but somehow or other, the poor gink manages to tighten and tense everyone of them. I can understand how a saber fencer is all springs and vibrant energy, but pistol shooting is something entirely different. I say that of the whole bunch of muscles, there are only two single muscles that are required to do work in this art of shooting the pistol and they are the contractor-muscle of the trigger-finger, and, possibly, that ol' shoulder-muscle which holds up the weight of the gun arm.

The expert knows that and he stands "relaxed."

Suppose you make up your mind that you will not do a lot of fumbling and experimenting, but resolve right here to practise "relaxation" while shooting. You certainly will save a lot of time.

But not only our body should be relaxed, our mind should equally be at ease. None of the tenseness of the mind, none of that zealous eager desire—Be nonchalant, devil-may-care.

Heck, you may learn all there is to know about pistol shooting: But just tense up—just don't relax and everything goes for naught. That has been the trouble with all the thousands of bum handgun-shooters in this country: Too damn tensed up in muscle and mind. Forget it!

Just try it my way.

MOVING GUN INTO POSITION

Whatever we do around Automatics, remember they are always loaded, even if they are not. We must acquire the habit of handling the thing in a safe manner. As soon as we take an Automatic in hand, the muzzle points, right away, *forward* and *upward*, at an angle of about 45 degrees. If the damn thing goes off, no harm will be done.

Never, not even after having made sure that it *is* unloaded, point it at anything or anybody you don't want to hit!

Bring your gun hand up to your shoulder, direct the muzzle up and forward and control all movements of your gun hand toward and away from the target so that the muzzle points forward, in the direction of the line of fire.

One shot gone wrong and nothing can undo it.

As you handle the Automatic for any length of time, your familiarity with it grows, but remember all the time: The thing is loaded!

In order to do any accurate shooting, we have to know something about

SIGHTING

There are two sights on your gun, the rear—and the front-sight. These pesky things were invented by some evil spirit to make life harder for us shooters. However, there they are and we better get acquainted with them.

Suppose we observe a shooter on the firing line. He stands in correct position and looks serenely at his target. We can draw an imaginary line from his (right) eye to the aiming spot on the target. That imaginary line we will call the "sighting line." Alright, he now brings his gun arm up slowly and aligns the top of his Automatic with this sighting line. Looking over his shoulder, if we could do that, we would find that the sighting line, starting from his eye, travels over the exact center of the rear-sight-slot to the exact center of the front-sight-top, to the aiming spot on the target. He has taken a "bead," as we high-priests of the art call it. The whole thing is simple. The expert holds the front sight post right in the middle of the

rear-sight-slot, thus that the tops of both sights are even
and level. I said level! Because if the gun were not held
level, then he would have "canted" (Another expert
idiomism) it and canting will influence our point of
impact.

What ho —? The expert keeps both eyes open? Ah—
That's what makes him an expert! He uses both eyes. He
figures that God has given him two eyes—Might as well
use the two of them. He doesn't screw his face up to keep
one eye closed, because he knows: No muscles are supposed to work when shooting a handgun. He also knows
that he wants a binocular, a stereoscopic view of his target.
Sometimes, particularly in the beginning and if the shooter
persists in looking *through* the sights instead of *at the
target* only (He could not *help* noticing the sights the
moment they appear within his vision anyway), there will
be two images. Each image is the stereoptic part of a
plastic composite view furnished by *both* eyes. In stereo-
photography there must be two pictures and each picture
is slightly different from the other. One, the left, gives
the picture angle as perceived by the left eye and vice versa.
These two separate (And slightly different) pictures are
brought together by viewing them through the "Stereop-
ticon" which has *two* lenses (or eyes). If we look *through*
our sights, we will see these two pictures, the left and the
right one, of the entire "bead," but they cannot merge into
one composite. If, however, we look *at* the target with
both eyes, the "master-eye-image" (In my case the right-
eye-angle picture) is predominant and the "left-eye" version just merges. I, therefore, register only *one* (The
composite) picture. My left eye, being kept open, assists
me therefore in encompassing the two views over a wide
field on the target end and that is very important in practical shooting.

How did the expert determine his "Master Eye"?
He held a pencil at arm-length and lined it up with a

vertical member of a window frame. He then closed his right eye and saw the pencil jump aside. He opened his right eye and closed his left and—the pencil didn't move. Whatever eye is open when the pencil doesn't move (In this case the right eye) is the master eye. It's the one that does the actual sighting, the other one supplements the task, rounds it off, so to speak.

The bead goes from the master-eye-pupil over both sights to the point of aim on the target.

Clear?

We make up our minds now to sight correctly with every shot we let go. It doesn't matter whether we shoot at targets or are engaged in practical shooting. None of that "from the hip"-shooting stuff! It's the bunk. Not that I say you can't shoot from the hip. Of course you can, but I am interested in making you "hit" things and this hip stuff is out! At least in this Manual.

One of our most famous exponents of practical shooting, my old friend McGivern, out in Montana, aligns the old sights with every shot, even when he bangs five shots out under two seconds and he hits small things, don't fool yourself.

One hears, once in a while, people argue heatedly about the best way to connect the bead with the target. One side claims that it is best to *go up* with the muzzle to the target, while the other party wonders whether it wouldn't be much more logical to take aim upon *coming down*. If we keep in mind that the recoil throws the muzzle *up* and that it would be simpler to just bring it *down,* back to the target, the controversy should loose much of its steam. It would be too impractical to force the muzzle down, after the shot, and then to bring it up again, back to the target. Altogether too much work!

❖   ❖   ❖

And now we come to

SQUEEZING

In this chapter here we touch "terra nova," new ground. While the peddling of the intricacy (if you will) of the manipulation of the Revolver-trigger caused me quite a few headaches in *Sixguns and Bullseyes,* my task right now is much simpler. I have devoted a special chapter to the technicalities as they bear on the "mechanical" functions of the Automatic-trigger, but here we are only concerned with our trigger-finger. In contrast to the Revolver, where we squeeze right from the start against a trigger-resistance of, say three pounds, and continue the squeeze until the hammer falls, in our Automatic we have (Or should have) a light "take-up"; that means: The trigger travels backwards a way and nothing happens. This "take-up" is the approach to the "resistance point." This latter serves as a sort of signal. The moment we feel this "resistance point," we know that we face the trigger-pressure itself. The total pressure, including the "take-up-pressure," is best fixed at, say four pounds. Our task is to overcome the *last little hill* by judicious "squeezing." With a properly adjusted trigger-action (About which more in a separate chapter), this squeezing is made so simple that we don't have to waste many words on it.

Suppose you run over the thing?

Alright then: Take your Automatic. See that it is empty! Magazine *and* barrel! Sure about it? Pull the slide back to cock the hammer! Take your proper hold, stand correctly and relaxed. Bring your gun forward and sight it, properly aligned, at a small black paster on the wall.

Now: Depress your trigger-finger slowly until all the "take-up" (Appropriate word, that) is taken up. Feel the "resistance point"? Go easy! It isn't much of a resistance —We have to feel for it carefully. From now on your finger will have to work a short way against a few pounds pressure. The real squeezing starts now. And now is the time to correct your bead—carefully and slowly now—a little more—give a tiny bit of pressure—go on—slowly—without interruptions—another minute particle of pressure—Bing!—the hammer fell—but keep on squeezing—squeezing until the trigger will not go any further—There! Fine!

The whole thing was done slowly and carefully—If you had thoughtlessly and vigorously pulled, you would have disturbed your delicate grip on the gun and you would have missed your target altogether. The more careful and deliberate you are in the beginning, the better you will be able to keep the sights aligned and to overcome any tendencies on the part of the mechanics inside your gun to disturb your acquired hold.

Now later, very much later, when we get to the phases of faster shooting, the whole procedure will be speeded up; that doesn't concern us here.

My predicament as mentor is very obvious at this stage. I am firmly convinced that you have to become a deliberate target shot before you can go in for practical shooting. Limit of space and the nuisance of repetition forbid me to be as painstaking in this chapter on "Technique" as I was in *Sixguns and Bullseyes*. In all sincerity I shall have to ask you to buy, borrow or steal that book and soak up the wisdom dispensed there. The treatment of technique in this Manual doesn't claim to be anything but very much condensed.

And now we can present our seventh fundamental, that of

BREATHING

In deliberate firing, you have to hold your breath with every shot. Fill your lungs and expel a portion of the inhaled air, lock your throat and hold your breath for the short time you need for your shot.

In competitive rapid firing, you take a deeper breath and let that last you for your entire string.

In practical shooting, conditions as they vary, demand individual treatment.

COMMENTS ON SUSTAINED AND RAPID FIRE

We may not be very much wrong in assuming that the inventors of the automatic principle were inspired by the possibility of eliminating certain manual maneuvers such as ejecting the empty shells and cocking the hammer. I mean, they may not have been intrigued so much with the notion that, in the Revolver, a lot of gas-pressure was going to waste and that such vagrant pressure should be utilized. Yet, both ideas merged and the thermal efficiency (Don't kill me, please!) of the mechanical functions was raised considerably. The whole problem was highly scientific but also eminently practical.

This, I fear, was as far as the progenitors cared to go. It was for the shooters themselves to discover that the durn things offered also the opportunity to be shot very rapidly and the old syrup of emptying a gun as fast as possible was revived rather than discouraged. And that is the one phase that I distinctly disapprove of.

Our present day Motorcars are capable of going 80 miles an hour (All right, fellow, your's goes 87 miles) but, where in blazes can one utilize this feature? Speeds like that are considered dangerous and numerous punitive restrictions make one wonder why the carburetors are not sealed up for the permissible maximum speed-limits. The Automatic Handgun should have a speed-adjustment too, in my opinion, so as to curb this old fast-shooting-craze. In the Motorcar, the excessive motive power can at least be made use of by accelerating the get-away and thus its existence is justified.

I do not like to repeat myself too often, but let me say once more: The Automatic principle facilitates the manipulation of the gun, but the possibility of it being able to be fired fast, is detrimental. There will never be an opportunity for fast firing in *any* situation, unless it be for the sake of noise or deception. I remember that in certain tactical maneuvers, it was tried to confuse the enemy with so-called "pseudo attacks." Certain detachments were given orders to fire as rapidly as possible so as to simulate an attack, causing the trusting opponent to concentrate his forces at that point, thus weakening his position in places where the real attack was to take place. I believe that the experienced strata in the shooting world will bear me out. As long as the efficiency of the hand-gun depends upon the support of one hand and upon accurate alignment of sights and on judicious trigger manipulation, so long will Rapidfire be useless.

We have admitted in *Sixguns and Bullseyes* that our present competitive Rapid-fire-course, namely that of firing five shots within ten seconds, has a certain paedagogical value in that it aids us to moderate the pedantism of the Slowfire-school. And from that angle alone do we advocate practicing a faster firing schedule. Doubtlessly, the easier and simpler manipulation of the Automatic mentioned above, gives it a decided theoretical advantage over the Revolver. If we are able to fire five shots within ten seconds, in an evenly spaced rhythm and make *good scores,* we shall be that much ahead of the Slow-Fire pedant, *provided* every shot is gotten out under perfect control. Sometimes, a perfect Rapidfire score is not a proper criterion. It will be such only if it is perfect *most of the time* and if the shooter knows what he is doing *all the time.* Championships in Rapidfire have been won by people who grabbed their guns, closed their eyes and trusted to God. Consistent scores over the NRA Standard American course, namely 10 shots Slow, 10 shots Time and 10 shots Rapid-fire, are of much greater value than specialized scores in either branch alone. In this course of shooting we have the careful work of the Slowfire-artist, the transition to the easy Timefire target and the definite, rhythmic Rapidfire, done with consciously organized body fibres, under full control. The first offers the ground work for mechanically correct and accurate shooting at a difficult object, the latter breaks down the growth of "over-fussiness", of pedantism. I have seen Slowfire primadonnas who couldn't fire a damn shot if somebody dared to breathe on the range, but I have also seen Rapidfire nuts who didn't know and couldn't explain why the hell they had a perfect score one day and fell down miserably the next. Specialization!

The automatic principle gives these latter nuts a little more rope than is good for them and, I am afraid, will assert an even stronger fascination over the less experienced shooters who still have trouble with "cocking" the Revolver.

With the above warning still ringing in our ears, we will at once admit the superiority of the automatic principle. The gun, after discharge, stays bedded in the hand. There need be no dislocation of hold, no fumbling with the hammer. The contact of hand with grip stays undisturbed and that alone should constitute full justification of the automatic principle. We start off with a great mechanical advantage over the Revolver competitor. All we have to do is to bring the muzzle straight down on the object again and squeeze once more. The dissipation of the recoil forces straight over our hand, horizontally, will make the subsequent re-alignment of the sights very much easier than in the Revolver.

There is one feature of the Automatic though which needs closer attention. I might attribute this feature to the rather general unfamiliarity with the larger calibres. Through lack of sufficient practice in the larger calibres, caused by prohibitive cost of cartridges, the lack of proper instruction or other reasons, the behaviour of the gun irritates the shooter. Ordinarily, after the shooter has fired a .45 Automatic say ten times, he is all rattled, shaken up. Co-ordination is destroyed and he goes to pieces. To fire fifty shots with the .45 Auto, under target conditions, is an ordeal. The explanation lies in the greater muzzle-blast and flash and also in the fact that the Automatic has more "kick," not more recoil mind you. (At least not theoretically.)

A great deal of the gaspressure in the Revolver goes to waste between the cylinder head and the barrel cone. In the tightly sealed Automatic, the rear-gasses have to throw the slide against a heavy recoil-spring-pressure before they are released. We hold the pressure under leash a little longer and we will feel that in our hand. There is a vicious finality in this release, a kick that seems to say that if we had held the pressure just a bit more, it would have been just too bad.

Then, of course, the slide, being violently pushed back against the recoil-spring and the subsequent equally violent reaction of the recoil-spring and, finally, the clash of metal against metal upon closing, introduce other new influences in the behaviour of the Automatic in the gun-hand. These are things with which the shooter will have to become acquainted. The larger the calibre, the stronger this influence, of course. They are practically nil in the .22 cal. Automatics and that is why these latter enjoy their well-deserved popularity.

The Lueger, although larger than .22 calibre, has, instead of a solid slide, a sort of jack-knife breechblock which, when folded, cushions the rear-motion considerably and that is why it is an easier shooting large calibre gun.

Familiarity with the action of the solid slide can, of course, be attained by practice.

The main trouble, aside from the cost of ammunition, is of course, the unfamiliarity with the general shape, hang, balance etc. and that can be acquired by the use of a .22 calibre conversion. I claim that, if one had an ideal .22

cal. conversion for the .38 Super for instance, (Which would, of course, also fit the .45 Calibre Automatic) one could easily get acquainted with the details as enumerated above, including an identical trigger action. Upon going to the larger calibre, the necessarily greater gas-pressure and resultant slide movement would impose an additional feature which, I assert, is also easily conquered through a little practice. We sort of sneak up on the large calibre. We first lick balance, weight, trigger action etc. through the conversion and then tackle the stronger action, unencumbered by attention to other details.

All the above applies to Automatics as available now. (The conversion, alas, is still evading us) If one were to take into consideration any ballistical and mechanical improvements that are possible, this business of muzzle-blast and muzzle-flash and recoil-action could be greatly modified, of course.

We trust that we already are at the threshold of conversions and ballistical and mechanical improvements. I have great hopes!

The advantage of the automatic principle in target work has been acknowledged, as witness the hot controversies in competitive work. Many competitions do not allow the .22 Automatic against the Revolver. Our major shooting organizations, the National Rifle Association and the U. S. Revolver Assn., should probe this phase carefully and lay down guiding principles which should not only be confined to the small calibres but also include the larger ones.

My personal position is that the .22 cal. Automatics have it all over the .22 Revolvers. In the larger calibres, the Automatic, having been the stepchild so long, should receive greater encouragement. I claim that it is so very much harder to equal high Revolver scores with our present day large calibre Automatics, and that it will be necessary to rate the latter a few points higher, say 5%. This would, undoubtedly, encourage the Automatic shooters.

It is decidely unfair to rate a score made with a .45 cal. Automatic for instance, along the same lines as that made with a .38 cal. Target Revolver. Why not create special Automatic targets with slightly larger rings? Not because the Automatic *needs* larger rings, but because it needs more enthusiasts, people willing to experiment and to shoot the thing more often. It isn't the Revolver that needs a break, but the Automatic. The Revolver has reached its zenith of evolution. The Automatic is at the bottom of the ladder, the orphan of everybody, from the Manufacturer down to the Shooter. And why this should be, in view of the unquestionable, inate superiority of the automatic principle, is beyond me.

If the .22 Automatic already is the bug-a-boo of the .22 Revolver, its nemesis in the true sense, then there is no reason in this world, why it should not be so in the larger calibres too.

If the adjustment cannot or will not be done from the top down (By experimentation on the part of the manufacturers and ballistical experts for the production of better guns and ammunition), then we must work from the bottom up. (By encouraging the reluctant shooters through larger rings in the targets).

At present, we have only a few, very few, Experts in this large calibre Automatic game, although we do have many, many actual owners. If one were to judge by the Movie films, it would seem that the strange colony of Gangsterdom owns nothing but. If that were really the truth, it would look logical, because the very lack of bulkiness in the Automatic would make it an ideal weapon for inconspicuous concealment. And, when one considers further that Hoodlums seldom shoot at anything beyond the five- or ten foot limit, an Automatic may otherwise be as inaccurate as possible.

And that gives me a chance to open up on this self-defense-business. My advice, in general cases, has been to run—to run like hell. Get distance between you and the punk. At fifty feet turn around and let him have one from you. That's all he should need. At that distance he will be wild and you won't. The greater the distance the better for you.

Of course, this sounds a bit academical. If somebody sticks a gun in your back and you are proficient and fast in close defense work (Read up on that in Colonel Hatcher's excellent book), then take a chance—by all means. If your opponent is a few feet away from you, it might be better to *run*, zig-zagging away, ducking, as fast as your legs permit you. Every yard you gain will be in your favour— Have your Automatic ready when you plump down, behind some cover if there is any—And then, so help you Hannah, bring into play everything you have learned and absorbed. And remember, your bullet goes faster than your opponent will be able to run—and run he will if he sees any kind of defense at greater distances than ten feet.

We forgot to say that, alas, his bullet will also travel quite fast while you run from him. But, as a rule, he won't shoot if he hasn't lost his head altogether. He doesn't want any more commotion than absolutely necessary. He may give the thing up in disgust at your timidity. You, on the other hand, have realized his status as society's enemy and, from your long distance, you have the definite incentive of laying him low.

In order not to be accused of empty talk, I should like you to draw some kind of moral from the above, even if you don't follow my advice. It is really hard to say what anybody will do under given circumstances, but, if the Police and the Military were to make it their business to always try to utilize their greatest asset in a gun battle, namely that of *distance,* there would be fewer casualties on the side of society or what have you. This aimless and often insanely heroic rushing at resistance destroys this initial advantage. Distance, naturally, demands good marksmanship and it is to be assumed that this has been acquired.

Once in a while I meet up with one of the strange fast-draw-and-fire-like-hell brotherhood. He will tell you to imagine certain conditions. You imagine. Then, if he has his act down pat, he will make your eyes blink. You stand there—speechlessly—and wonder when the hell this man sleeps—or reads—or eats—Dammit, he's got to be on springs every damn moment of his life—For his act to have any sense at all he has to be able, from one second to the other, to pass from a harmless appearing Citizen to an "adder poised to squirt." If he isn't anticipating every second, if he permits himself to eat a Hamburger, why, that might be the very moment when he is called upon to deliver. And, durn it, you can't flash a fast gun draw with a Hamburger in your hand. If a fellow like that wants to impress other people, it's all right with me. We all have different tastes. I suppose it does no harm to be fast. In the contrary, our Police should train to be fast! But they should not sacrifice accuracy. I should really say that our Police should learn to be accurate and, after that has been achieved, they should train for this "fast-draw-and-one-hit"—business, hinted at several times.

And the value of distance, mentioned before, may be a tactical rather than an individual point. Or, if that should sound too muddled, let me say that while the individual member of the Police or the Military should be a first-class marksman, first and last, the disposition of forces in a raid or so, is more of a tactical or strategical consideration, subject to the administration by the commanding officers. They shouldn't permit any heroism on the part of their men, but only cold and efficient accuracy.

People sometimes ask me why I habitually carry an Automatic. The answer is very simple. I have developed, after much thinking, an affair which suits me perfectly. By affair, I mean an arrangement of gun and holster, of course. As I walk about my business of being a peaceful

Citizen, I feel that I won't be entirely at the mercy of any ol' bully of a stick-up-artist. I may fail dismally when called upon, but, at least, I have that proverbial ghost of a chance. Again, there might be occasions, where one might be able to help the law, or a damsel in distress, or some other situation. Just think what a humiliation it must be to read in the papers that so-and-so, the well-known pistol crackshot, was stuck up and submitted meekly because he had no hardware with him. I admit that it might sound worse, if the papers tell how, although heeled, the Expert was relieved of his gun by the hoodlum and robbed to boot. However, if circumstances permit, I shall always make an effort to run and lay the fellow by the heels from a great distance, if he should still be around.

All in all, the Automatic does something to me——. My chest is thrown bravely forward. My eyes are serene and my mind is at ease. I know that I have a little steel-thing with me that carries death if need be, death to the enemy, be he ever so big and strong and smells of garlic. I feel the instrument of utter security along my waistband and—alack, sometimes also a wee bit of weariness. The damn thing doesn't weight much, but it keeps it up—all day long. My tailor also objects to it because, he claims, he can't get the perfect fit which he so desires.

How goes that story again about having a cake and not being able to eat it, at the same time? Well, at times I feel like eating the damn thing and never mind whether I still have it or not.

You see, I am not entirely and insanely fanatical about this "constant-on-the-alert-self-defense"-wishy-wag. No, if I should meet up with an opponent, I should like to be able to arrange things in an orderly manner; say, for instance, to tell him to stay away for 300 feet and watch me pop him off. Or, if he should be extremely critical and should want to see a certain waist-button fly, he should give me, say 60 feet. Alas, he probably will lack the finer sensibilities for finesse. He may even be sneaky enough to step up from behind and tell me to elevate. And elevate I shall. Even if the Hamburger in my hand should lose temperature fast and the mustard should roll down my neck, while the mercenary knave takes my precious gun away and whatever sheckels I carry. I'll be hanged if I am going to be on the "qui vive" all the time, every damn minute of my life. I am certainly not going to wrestle with this bird either. He may be so nervous and coked up that his gun goes off on the slightest provocation—and nevermind the ol' newspaper stories about the Expert being shamelessly—unless—unless—Say, maybe I *can* be faster than he——

You must admit that I am quite magnanimous about the thing. If I should appear just the slightest bit ironic, don't forget that I have beheld, with my own eyes, the superclown, funny lil' "fast-as-lightning-Mr. Belly-Bluster". Except to himself, he is more or less a mild pain to everybody else.

Well, my friend, do you think that this chapter on technique was too dry or tedious? It's the best I can do in view of the fact that condensation must necessarily be a handicap.

TRIGGER PAINS

This chapter is going to drive the scientists and engineers frantic. Well, it's really their own hair they are pulling. You and I will just ignore them, what? (We know darn well that we mustn't be too technical in a Manual that will be read and, I hope, be understood by all sorts of people, nice people; What I mean: Good friends. But why the heck they should have a college education to grasp my stuff is beyond me.)

Here is the introduction into the maze: We want to describe trigger-pulls and functions by way of sketches, without formulae and other frowsy stuff. Now: A Revolver-Pull, for instance, is fixed say at 3 lbs. We have to squeeze against 3 lbs resistance. The moment, we reach 3 lbs, the hammer notch slips from the sear (Or vice versa) and the hammer falls. The work of the trigger is over. Expressed in functional lines, this revolver pull would look something like this:

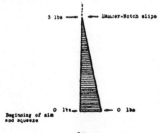

Well, I claim that sketch looks rather skinny and uninspiring. I like to compare the work of pulling with "climbing a hill." If I did that (And I am sure that everybody would enjoy my ravings much more), the picture would be more comprehendible. All right then: Let's try:

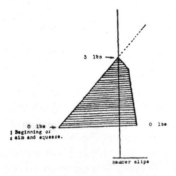

You see, the moment we sight the revolver we have to start climbing and, somewhere on the hillside (At a point which measures 3lbs), we suddenly and unexpectedly fall down the other side. We cannot, of course, exactly estimate 3 lbs with our trigger finger; we just climb and climb until, suddenly, we slip. We never know when. That's the revolver squeeze we inherited from the Eozene Period and it is still with us.

Now, a much more modern but not so new idea should be employed in the Automatic. There, we should have a "Take up," that is: the trigger travels a piece and nothing of importance happens within the gun. At the end of this Take-up we reach a distinct resistance. This resistance leads up to the trigger pull proper. We receive a sort of signal that, from now on, we have a short, smooth climb before us until the firing pin is released. When we lift our pistol, we start "taking-up" right away and the moment we feel the resistance point, we adjust and correct our aim comfortably and then get to work. The thing looks like this:

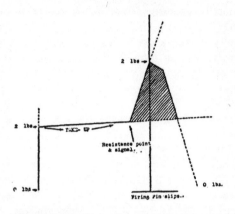

You see the difference?

This picture, of course, shows the "ideal" squeeze.

There are actually all sorts of squeezes to be found though, such as:

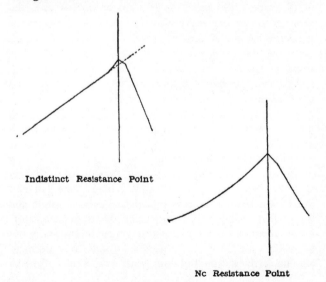

Indistinct Resistance Point

No Resistance Point

It must be understood that we are concerned only with the profile (I mean: the "outlines" of the hills we have to climb) of the above series of trigger-travel sketches. How we arrived at those profiles is, as you have seen, a matter of profound guess work.   To preserve our aura of semi-scientists we should claim that there is really no such a thing as the rear-line of the hills going all the way back to zero-pressure.   You see, the very moment that the hammer falls, in other words: when we fall down on the other side of the hill, the trigger ceases to function and we would have to terminate our line somewhere near the top of the hill.   But, we continued the line to the bitter end. Theoretically, this continuation registers nothing but a function of our brain.   We trust nevertheless, that our sketches are understandable for the intelligent layman.   We really are showing nothing but certain hills which our trigger-*finger* and not the trigger has to climb.

Furthermore (And this again only for the consumption of the super-critics who might want to trip us up), the lines of ascent are really sloping since the flesh of our trigger-finger has a certain "give", the slope, of course, depending on the hardness or softness of the flesh.   The shape of the hills is to represent the sum of everything, and for our purposes it matters little whether a degree too much or too little may have been employed.

So, you see, on the whole we need not be so very far off with our sketches. We simply want to enable the Reader, when testing trigger travels, to determine for himself whether certain travels conform to his ideas.   It is easy to measure the resistance of the Take-up and the resistance offered in the trigger-pull proper.   One can also "feel" whether the travel is smooth and even or rough and wavy. It is really not necessary to be able to make scientifically correct diagrams. The average gunsmith works not so much with theory, but he will be able to understand you perfectly if you tell him what you want.   And to make you know what you want, our sketches are supposed to help you.

The main thing is: to have a resistance point which you can distinctly feel. This should be about, say halfway between the top-and-zero-pressures. If you have a measured 4 lb. pull, you may do well to let the resistance point come at $1\frac{1}{2}$ lbs. The take-up starts from zero-pressure and should immediately rise to about $1\frac{1}{2}$ lbs. and offer the same or nearly the same pressure up to the resistance point. (Actually, of course, the line of Take-Up will always rise, but this rise should be held as low as possible above the initial pressure of each $1\frac{1}{2}$ lbs.) From the resistance point on, we only face a little hill of a mere $2\frac{1}{2}$ lbs. more and that should be "duck soup". In fact, it is so little that it won't disturb your hold much, even if you should squeeze a little less slowly than you have to do in the Revolver.

But the Take-Up must be smooth, as must be the hill. There must be no ridges or up-and-down waves in their path. Now, in instructing your gunsmith, you can say (He will, probably, only have an endulgent smile for you) that the seat for adjustment of the Take-Up is, in most cases, in the little spring that is actuated by the trigger lever directly.

The "hill" adjustment is sometimes done by working on the sear-or hammer notch-angles or by regulating various springs, or both.

In the Woodsman, for instance, in order to reduce the factory pull, the gunsmith will want to work carefully on the inner leg of the sear-hook friction angle and will avoid changing the hammer-notch.

The sear notch alone would not hold the hammer and it is supported by the sear-spring which latter also serves to return the sear body to its prefire-position.

We have, in the contemplation of the Woodsman-action no less than three spring influences, namely those of the trigger-spring, the sear-spring and the hammer-spring. I am afraid that, in order to show the functional lines of these three springs, coupled with notch-frictions, my hill-climbing sketch would not only be decidedly crowded but, more probably, rather confusing.

I cannot quite bring myself to admit gracefully that I couldn't draw the damn thing anyway. May I, therefore, submit that, in effect, the naked diagram should look similar to the one offered for the .45 Automatic? With the poundage changed to 2½ lbs. total, of course. (2 lbs. for the pull and ½ lb. for the take-up.)

Generally speaking, if too fine a pull is attempted, the hammer will not stay cocked and one shouldn't wonder if the gun should shoot "single shot" or, in extreme cases, "fully automatic." Quite a dangerous situation. Also the fact that the safety-fulcrum serves as pivot for the hammer, should warn of too low a pull since working the safety-lever might (And would) pull the hammer over, through friction at their mutual pin-axis.

The diagram for the .45 Government Automatic might roughly resemble this:

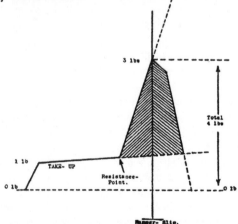

The functional line of the hammer-spring was omitted. It is possible to reduce the height of the hill (The pull proper) by weakening the hammer-spring. (The latter, as it comes from the factory, measures about 25 lbs., approximately 1 lb. to the coil. Given a five-pound-trigger pull with full spring, clipping off 2½ coils should reduce the pull by 10%, down to 4½ lbs.) In order not to weaken the speed of the hammer-travel, the spring should not be tampered with too much. Instead, a change in the sear- and hammernotch-angles would have to take place.

Total squeeze necessary is 4 lbs., of which 1 or 1½ pounds may be in the Take-Up and the rest applies to the hill. To demonstrate or prove a certain trigger-function, one should make use of a scale such as the gunsmiths use, preferably a scale that works with iron weights. Hooked over the trigger, the "Take-up" (in the case of the .45 Automatic) might measure 1½ lbs. By adding 2½ lbs. more of iron weights, the hammer should slip.

If you have set your mind on 1½ lbs. Take-up and a final Pull of 2½ lbs., see to it that the Take-up works when 1½ lbs. are on the scale. The take-up-travel of the trigger is stopped at a little over 1½ lbs. That stop is your "resistance point". When the gunsmith adds 2½ lbs. more of weights, the hammer clicks. That's your Automatic squeeze!

You will, by now, have guessed at the crux of the matter, namely that we actually "reduce" the total pull of, say 4 lbs. down to 2½ lbs., if we do put 1½ lbs. of it into the Take-up. The pull necessary to work the sear-notch is then 2½ lbs. net. No getting away from that.

Transposing the purely technical aspect of trigger-travel into the physical function of the trigger-finger, we find that we do not actually climb a four pound-hill by starting from the foot of the hill, but we "hit" it higher up, from a plateau of 1½ lbs. It stands to reason that the heavier the Take-up, the higher up we get at the slope of the hill. If we take, for instance, the considerable difference in pressure which exists between a Take-up of a mere half pound and a total pull of four pounds, such difference would noticeably decrease if the proportion were altered to, say 3 lbs. and 6½ lbs. respectively. In the latter example the proportion is approximately 1 : 2, while in the former it is 1 : 8.

Upon completion of the heavier Take-up-pressure, the finger already strains with an effort of 3 lbs. and will tackle the remaining 3½ lbs. with less additional effort than in the first example. In other words, the finger just needs to "double" the effort.

Although, in the case of the light Take-up, the same additional work, namely 3½ lbs., faces the finger, the preliminary Take-up-effort of half a pound is comparatively insignificant and the finger starts with too small a load ratio. It has to intensify it's work "eight-times" as compared with only "two times" in the first example.

Theoretically, therefore, it would be advantageous to have a high Take-up-pressure and a comparatively low final pull. However, we must be guided by the fact that all around safety and the reliability of function will set definite limits.

In the Woodsman, the lowest permissible "total-poundage" should be about 2½ lbs. We may put a certain portion of that (Say ½ lb.) in the Take-up and the rest would form the minimum-safety limit for the action proper. (A ratio of ½ : 2½, or 1 : 5.)

In the .45 Governmnt Auto with a total pull of 4 lbs., we may be able to lower the ratio to 1 : 4. (1 lb. against 4 lbs.)

All this depends upon the individual gun. None of them are alike!

And right here: I want to warn my Readers earnestly, not to fool around with this stuff themselves, without the help of an experienced gun-smith.

This exposition of mine is merely an attempt to draw my Reader's attention to the neglected and misunderstood "Take-up".

This Take-up has often and thoughtlessly been called "Slack" and was, in the Military Rifle, put in as a safety measure. If the man were to touch the trigger accidentally, the rifle should not go off.

But we make a virtue out of this feature here! We organize it along sensible lines and make it help us to manipulate the trigger with scientific control.

The crisp pull of the Revolver is a handicap, because the work of sighting and squeezing starts right away and the effect, namely the fall of the hammer, is fairly unpredictable. The gun goes off without the shooter knowing exactly when it will.

The true "Take-Up" puts a preliminary load on the finger; it enables the shooter to take his aim *later* (Upon having reached the resistance point) and the final squeeze will have less tendency to disturb the "hold", being that the hold is actually confirmed and fortified by the prior "Take-up"-action. The mechanism is already in motion before the shooting-action itself starts to function.

When testing the gun, close attention should be paid to the way in which the trigger is "guided" in it's path. In the .45 Government Auto, e.g., it is permitted to wobble up and down and also sideways. These wobbles must be taken out first, ere we can talk about intelligent handling of the trigger.

My friends, we can have our fun with the learned gentry, but we must not drive them totally insane with indignation. Poor fellows! I shall, therefore, apply the brakes now and say: I cannot, possibly, put my foot into all the technical possibilities of trigger-adjustment. (Maybe, I have done too much of that already?) To tell the truth: (Keep it to yourself) I am too innocent for that. All, I set out was to get all the other innocents to receive a general understanding, a very general understanding. You leave the actual adjustments to your gunsmith anyway. But you can impress that worthy one with the above quite handsomely, the more so if he doesn't get your drift. But insist with a firm voice (And stay thickheaded about that) upon a smooth Take-Up (No matter how long a one) of even pressure, a definite Resistance Point and a final even, smooth Pull. Total pressure not to exceed 4 lbs. More than that would be bad and less than 2½ lbs. may be dangerous. If he cannot do the job, don't do it yourself. Go to another Gunsmith. (I said "Gunsmith," not Blacksmith). When you get your gun back, see that it is empty, barrel and magazine, close your eyes, screw up your face, bend your ears—and squeeze the trigger. The travel of the trigger should resemble that of the first sketch on page 69, if it doesn't don't go into tantrums.   All right: One cuss word only!—Eh, feller, go easy—If there had been ladies around—Are you all right again?—Then don't buy yourself a bottle—Rather look through the ads in the *American Rifleman* and hunt for another exponent of the mysterious art of trigger adjustment.

Whew——

FLUTTERING

The fact that guns which are held and shot with one hand are very much subservient to the anatomical set-up of the shooting fore-arm, wrist and hand, is not generally recognized. The rifle e. g. is supported by the shooter at no less than four places and calls for the employment of the shoulder, cheek and both arms and hands and it is therefore less subject to anatomical influences.

The Automatic rests and is controlled by one hand only. One would assume that the designers would take pains to correlate the weight and balance of the handguns they develop, with the anatomy of the shooting member. However, so many products do not show such desired relation.

Let's look at our shooting arm. Assuming that no fractures have occurred, we may say that the bones, tissues, tendons and muscles look alike and function and react alike in all adult human beings. Our fore-arm has two long bones hinged at either the elbow or the wrist, namely the "radius" which is hinged at the thumbside of the wrist, and the "ulna" which contacts the little finger-side of the wrist and is hinged at the elbow. Both these bones are connected with each other by a tissue called the "interosseous membrane". This membrane prevents the two bones from separating and also offers surface for the tendons and muscles to grow on.

In a position of supination, that is when the hand is turned so that the palm is upward, the two bones are apart and the membrane is stretched. In pronation or when the palm points downward, the two bones cross and touch each other, with the interosseous membrane slack. Neither of these positions are used in pistol shooting. We assume a position between these two extremes, namely a semiprone position, that is: with the palm held vertically, thumb up. Not only does this latter position favour muscle relaxation, but it is also the only position in which a pistol can be shot, for accurate results. But it is also the position in which neither the tension of the interosseous membrane nor the actual touching of radius and ulna would help to steady or arrest "axial" movements of the wrist. The semiprone position allows of easy "axial" movement and becomes a handicap not only in that it facilitates "canting" of the gun, but it also encourages "flutter", if weight and balance of the pistol do not carefully counter-act this latter tendency.

I must ask your pardon for talking sort of semi-scientific, but then I did not invent these fifty-cent words. If this theme does not interest you overly much, you are free to skip it. You won't miss much. It is really addressed to our gun-makers, gun-designers and gun-nuts in general.

Proceed, dear Elmer!

It seems that when we hold a pistol which is predom-inently "butt-heavy" and "butt-bulky," we aggravate the flutter or twitching tendency. Empirical experiments have proved that a gun which is muzzle-heavy lessens this fault which is mostly found in Automatics. In the Automatic the recoil works on a horizontal above the hand, while in the Revolver the forces are dissipated into the hand, sort of diagonally. More so than in a Revolver, heavy-muzzle and reduced butt-weight and bulk are of paramount im-portance in an Automatic. It is not for me to say just how much the "flutter" influences the behaviour of the gun and its ballistics, but do we not all know about superfluous motion or, if you will, about the viscissitude of vibration?

A slow motion film of a faulty Automatic under fire would show a blurred slide—But, of course, I may be wrong.

Points at hand are, for instance, the .45 Automatic, the Lueger and the 7.63 mm. Mauser. The first named gun offers a heavy and bulky butt with lack of sufficient weight near the muzzle. The other extreme namely a little bit of a handle and an enormous piece of machinery above the hand is shown in the 7.63 mm. Mauser. Against these two, the Lueger seems to present the most satisfactory solution. It shows a comfortable grip and fair weight above the hand, although it would prove advantageous if the barrel were a little heavier.

This chapter was primarily meant to point at what I call the "flutter"-tendency of a gun and, possibly, to encourage research work on the question of whether "flutter" is undesirable. If so, then our amateurish anatomical exposition might point the way. The questions to which answers would have to be found would be:

    (1)   What is "Flutter"?

    (2)   What causes "Flutter"?

    (3)   How does "Flutter" influence the ballistics of a given gun?

    (4)   How can "Flutter" be minimized or eliminated through proper gun construction?

I have tried, in my crude way to form an opinion. If this opinion of mine should lead to concrete results, that is: better guns, I shall pat myself on the back.

If, however, the whole thing is only a crazy bee, than I should do penance by keeping quiet on the subject—until the next time. Talk about thickheadedness.

LICKING THE .45

It seems to be the experience of most people that just one reading of a treatise or a technical manual will cause many salient points to miss their due emphasis. It is like seeing a boxing-film. The events roll by in smooth sequence. Our mind registers the general flow and the outcome. One would be at a loss to describe certain effective blows or to analyze accurately the tactics of either opponent. Only a second or third review of the film, if possible in slow motion, will bring important details into focus.

You did read about certain aids on handling an Automatic in this manual. Have those aids duly registered?

We will assume that you have gulped down, more or less as entertainment, the things I have offered. I know that it would be unreasonable to expect the Reader to give all the little details their due importance, with one reading. That is why I think that a summation at this time would do good. Suppose we take as a basis a gun that, due to its peculiar construction, offers the most obstacles to the shooter, namely the .45 Automatic. Let us see whether we can't consolidate everything we know about the technique of successful shooting—

First off: We have to get busy on the equipment proper. We must try to make the gun fit us individually.

Then we go to work on ourselves.

The commercial model with well fitting parts is the one we pick out. We know that everything must work smoothly. There must be no binding of the slide. Wherever steel parts rub against each other, the path must be honed to perfection. That pertains particularly to the sear and hammer notches. We shall take great pains to get a fine trigger-action, possibly two pounds in the smooth Take-Up and two more pounds in the squeeze proper—in all four pounds. When we test the trigger, we feel at the end of the Take-Up, a distinct, although fine, Resistance point. From there on, the active path of the mechanism must be particularly smooth and crisp. We look at the extractor hook and, with the help of a shell, we find out whether it handles the shell properly.

We then get at the magazine. If its spring should have become weak, it should be replaced. The column of cartridges must be pushed up, decisively, by that spring. We fill the magazine and pump the slide, (Leave that trigger alone! !) and the cartridges should fly out fault-lessly. Of course, the handle-question offers a real prob-lem. We should have to experiment to find out whether the gun "hangs" to suit us. If not, (And it probably will not—) we doctor the handle. We may have to add to the lower portion of the back strap and, if possible, take some of the metal off the front strap, right where our middle finger rests—There isn't much that can be done there, but even a little might help. You may suc-ceed in contacting a clever gunsmith who might, through intelligent welding, succeed in changing the original angle so that it becomes more obtuse. The entire handle is too bulky for most hands. We will try to make it slimmer and lighter. If we thusly correct the bulk of the butt and also the angle between barrel-axis and handle, we have in mind, of course, to counterbalance a certain *desired* muzzle-heaviness. If such over-balance of muzzle should, after our corrective work, not exist, we *create* it by putting sufficient weight near the muzzle. Weighting the muzzle will cause the gun to "dip" and that is why we want to correct the angle of grip to frame, as outlined. You may well ask why it should be logical to cause the muzzle to dip, by adding weight to it, and then try to counteract this artificially created dip. Well, the .45 Automatic, as available, has too much butt-weight, facilitating "fluttering" and other inherent faults. This excess of butt-weight will have to be counter-balanced by weighting the muzzle and, of course, the resulting tendency of the muzzle to "dip" will have to be overcome by making the suggested angle-changes.

In short, we must balance the gun in bulk and weight.

Doing this might, at the same time, solve another problem, namely that of—err—"Longitudinal fulcrum"—Pheew! I prefer to stay rather vague on that topic—by force of necessity. On page 78 we found out something about the axial facility which the shooting position gives to our hand, that is: the hand turns the easier around its horizontal axis the more the gun is vertically and horizontally misbalanced. Let me explain: (Taking the elevation aspect of the gun). If one were able to stick a pin through it, the gun could teeter up and down with the muzzle (Vertical movement).

Inversely (Looking at the gun from above), if one were to stick a pin vertically through the frame, the gun could, with the pin as fulcrum, swing from left to right and back. (Horizontal movement.) If, however, we place the gun in our hand and roll the hand and wrist, we impart a third movement to the gun, which movement I like to call the "longitudinal movement." (For the reason that I cannot find a better expression—But, why quibble? You know what movement I mean!) All three movements influence the behaviour of the muzzle. (1) The vertical movement can be controlled by muzzle weighting and a correctly shaped handle. (2) The horizontal movement can be controlled through correct gripping. (3) The longitudinal movement is "terra nova" for us.

When shooting the uncorrected .45 Automatic, for instance, the longitudinal nuisance is very much apparent. Yet, I hesitate to recommend the application of a (mentally controlled) wrist-lock as it would tend to tighten the wrist—and handmuscles unduly—and we must avoid applying more than the "ripe banana" touch, advocated elsewhere.

If we do not control the first and second movements at all, I assert that not only these two but also the longitudinal movement will have to be reckoned with.

It may very well be that by applying the corrections as suggested above, the third movement may be sufficiently handicapped. A correct handle and a good muzzle-weight will take care of most everything.

If we hold our gun out, with full magazine, aiming at a target, it should "hang" so that the sights "hover" naturally under the bullseye or target, without quiver or canting and without too much of a physical effort. The all around balance of the gun must be right first, ere we wrestle with its ballistics.

We now take a look at our sights. While we must have perfect target sights, we also will want to use the gun for drawing from the holster. And, since we may assume that such "draw from the holster" is to be done quickly, the shape of our sights must be such as not to interfere. This interference of sights with a fast draw is often overemphasized. Still, we want to eliminate all chances of alibis and we pick sights that permit a smooth draw under most circumstances. We have roundly condemned the thin, military sights. We need a rather *thick* patridge post for the frontsight and a *wide* and *deep* rearsight slot, a slot whose vertical forward edges taper outward (Wider toward the muzzle). In a fast draw we cannot be bothered with trying to balance, with our eyes, a frontpost within a narrow and shallow rearsight-slot. The King frontsight with red bead and chromium mirror has no awkwardly projecting portions and will be ideal for Indoor-and Outdoor-Target and practical work. (See detail in Illustration No. 1.) The Whitex sight (Detail in Illustration No. 5), if used with the white side-pieces, is really unsurpassed for Outdoor-Target and fast work. Indoors, where the side-pieces must be taken off, the undercut frontsight-post, (Although an excellent target-post) would interfere with a fast draw, through its sharp edges.

Up to here, we have done nothing but attend to the mechanism and the balance and the appearance of our .45 Automatic.

Now, we have to concentrate on ourselves, the shooters.

Omitting a repetition of details such as stance, breathing, etc., we confine ourselves to overcoming the obstacles which we, ourselves, create, mainly mental obstacles.

It is no harder, physically, to balance the much heavier .45 Automatic than the .22 Woodsman. It is just as easy for us to work both triggers equally well. But, the moment the explosion takes place, we find a difference. Not that the recoil were so heavy that even a weaker person could not ride with it—(Unpleasant, no doubt, but sufferable)—We already discussed the peculiar "kick" of the heavy Automatic, caused by the apparent delay in the release of the chamber-pressures. Without further argument we may agree on the involuntary, apprehensive constriction of his bowels with which the beginner acknowledges the rude and ruthless effect that follows his innocent squeezing of some ol' trigger. An effect, by the way, that has, at the same time, the ring of some false overtone, namely the dull and hollow "slap" of the slide against the chamber end. We, somehow, seem to know how steel clashing against steel should sound, but this "slap" here seems to lack genuineness. Just as a bell made of lead would not give tonal resonance,

so does this delayed dead slap of the slide seem out of
tune with the otherwise healthy noise of the explosive
action. Yet, this same empty, leaden slurt transmits the
sensation of somebody slamming a heavy stick against the
chamber, trying to knock the shooting hand forward.
There is really nothing we can do about that feature, be
it then to endeavor to resign ourselves to it. It surely
is not a sales point for this clumsy gun.

But, let's get at the main attraction—the pièce de résis-
tance as it were, in the way of annoyance—Those infernal
blasts that unnerve—the "anticipation" of the fireworks
that causes the jitters—

Flinch?

I have always, resolutely, combated the existence of
"Flinch." My intention was to minimize a purely mental
handicap that has always been given an unreasonable
amount of importance. Once we acknowledge this ob-
stacle consciously, I argue, once it registers distinctly as
such, we will want to take steps to overcome it and most
shooters, not being schooled in things of a psychological
order, will get into an awful mire. With each unsuccessful attempt the thing piles up importance until we have
a real job on our hands. But, by treating the matter as
secondary, we can concentrate on other things such as
squeeze, hold, etc., etc.—and, by and by, the "anticipation"
falls by the wayside.

This, my attitude, still holds unreservedly. But, in
shooting the .45 Automatic a new element enters which
we cannot very well relegate into the background. It is
the forceful assault of irritated air-waves upon our nervous
system, waves which our slow senses categorically register
as "Sound."

Let me cite from my war experience. Suppose a 10.5
cm shell explodes quite close to us, say within 25 feet.
We lie flat on the ground and thus are outside the sphere
of the explosion-cone within which the white-hot, ragged

bits of steel scream upwards. We are safe, comparatively. Unfortunately a word like "explosion" does not convey the situation. Not wishing to complicate the matter unduly, we will disregard the thermal origin, the more or less incomplete combustion. Nor shall we talk of vacui created by used-up oxygen, etc. The picture will appear much clearer if we express ourselves in terms of "compression." You see, within an incredibly short time, the small fraction of a second, the once whole steel-shell blast to pieces under the terrific expansion of the gases generated within. These gases brutally hit the still air which we breathe close by and compress it to such an extent as to almost solidify it—This compressed body of air, this giant sledgehammer, smashes against every little nerve-end under the surface of our skin and makes it quiver in outrageous protest. Our whole system shrivels, so pronounced at times that, if there is no elasticity left after the equalization of the surrounding air-tension, the nerve-ends continue writhing, and healthy, sturdy men are reduced to nerve-shocked cripples, maybe for life. A war movie-film with soundtrack may be as realistic as possible; in fact, it may have been taken right at the worst spot of battle, yet it will never convey the full effect, because it is impossible to transmit that abrupt assault of the air to the spectators.

To a smaller extent, a very much smaller extent, similar things happen when firing a large caliber Automatic. The compressive action of the explosion stays within a small radius, to be sure, but within this small radius, its effect is noticeable—not so much with one shot or with ten shots. But, everytime a shot rings out, the tiny nerve-ends which lie closest to the gun (Namely those in the shooting hand, the arm and the more delicate ones in the head, the eyes and more noticeably, those in the ears) get more and more sensitized and on raw edge. Of course, we know perfectly well that nothing is going to happen to us—We are perfectly safe (In contrast to the battle scene)

—just the same, a reaction is felt, slight at first, but hammering away at the same nerve-ends—time and again. We try—We must try to minimize this effect—We stuff cotton in our ears (With large cannon, one opens the mouth to equalize the created pressures within the canals of the mouth, nose and ears) which helps a lot. We close our eyes, which is bad. We shrink away from this instrument of torture—and our shooting becomes worse as we go along. We cannot just ignore the situation. We must face it and do something purposely and actively, *cope* with it.

In shooting the .45 Automatic, we are therefore faced with a slightly larger task in that we have to combat this added nuisance of this augmented flinch. (Which we dismissed as trivial in Revolver shooting.) We could not afford to wrestle with this annoyance intelligently if, at the same time, we were forced to tackle all sorts of tricks which a wrongly designed Automatic might offer in the way of bad shape, bad trigger-pull, bad balance, bad sights, bad ammunition. We therefore try to perfect the mechanical, ballistical and architectural features of our gun *before* we go to work on ourselves in earnest. After we are sure that we have done all we could do, we will find that our remaining task is much easier.

We start shooting the .45 Automatic *outdoors* first and we stuff cotton in our ears. We don't fire more than ten shots during the early sessions and only increase the number of shots as we get better acquainted and as our scores warrant it. It takes a lot of patience, admittedly. But it is not the hopeless thing which it has appeared, up to now. By and by, we will come to exult at the positive, martial action—We actually look eagerly forward to feeling this purposeful, lashing thing in our hand—And our scores will mount—We are "licking" the .45 Automatic.

You may ask now, why we should go to so much

trouble if we need have much less with other, better guns. But, as I said in the introduction, we wanted to illuminate the hardest shooting gun. Naturally, if we succeed in licking that, the others will be mere child's play.

We mentioned the muzzle flash somewhere, a phenomena that increases as the barrel shortens. Outdoors, this flash annoys very little and, for that reason too, practicing outdoors at first offers a basical advantage. Indoors, alas, we are reminded of a fotoflash sometimes. That ball of fire, in the dark, harmless of course, attacks our retina with a disconcerting suddenness. However, it is surprising how easily one gets used to it. We need not waste much time on the flash.

In the "Technique" chapters, we have spoken about the proper hold, the squeeze and other things. If you were to reread these portions carefully, we need not repeat them here again. Just permit me to draw your special attention to the "banana" pressure (In holding) and to that old resistance-point (In squeezing). This resistance-point is your signal upon which you really "start" squeezing.

THE IDEAL AUTOMATIC

Should we not, after perusal of what we have gone into so far, have formed an approximate opinion of what we might consider "The Ideal Automatic", using available material and data?

Suppose we take a shot at it—

All right then:—We can conceive of a gun which weighs about 30 ounces. Its "Hang" is so balanced that, with a distinct muzzle-heaviness (So necessary for a steady hold) and a scientifically shaped grip, the gun neither dips its muzzle nor pokes it too high. A tightly screwed barrel rather than a floating one, of 6″ length has our preference. The receiver should have fast, non-jarring and non-jamming action. The lateral aspect should be one of slender proportions, withal the centre of "mass" should be well forward and not near the handle. The insertion of the magazine should not materially shift the weight so far back that the gun becomes butt-heavy and the weight distribution (The location of centre of weight as related to the lateral plane) must be made so carefully that a change in the weightload of the magazine (With each shot this load is diminished by the weight of a loaded cartridge) does not effect a shift of the metacentre.

Several causes for mis- or malfunctions etc. in our present models are directly traceable to the magazine. The Auto-magazine now, is more of an adjunct to the gun than an integral part of it. It is mostly stamped of sheet-steel, as casually as the clips for the Military Rifle Cartridges.

The mechanically correct design of the "magazine-lip" is indispensable for the smooth function of the action. We believe that the upper part of the magazine, the "LIP" part should be incorporated fixedly in the gun proper and the magazine should have no other function than to "hold" a number of cartridges, its spring pushing the cartridges into the "Lip-Section" of the action, as called for. The cartridge should lie horizontally within the magazine and travel upward in that position. Upon reaching the "Lip-Section" of the receiver, the cartridge should be in "ready" position. There, correctly and independently placed, its further movements are controlled within the receiver—thus that it glides smoothly and unerringly into the barrel chamber. This movement of the cartridge within the receiver should be tied in mechanically with the forward motion of the slide; by that I mean that there should be a mechanically dependent interrelation—Or, if that is not clear enough, let me state, how in contrast, it is being done in our present models. The slide, pushed forward by the recoil spring, "peels" off a cartridge with a little projection that catches the cartridge at its primer-end, if it sticks up far enough. But, sometimes the slide does not catch anything because the magazine spring did not push up well enough, or the "Lip-Section" of the magazine is faulty. There being no cartridge in position, the slide shuts on an empty chamber and there is no beloved blast or flash when the trigger is squeezed. If the gun had an integral pre-chamber or "ready"-position-bearing, properly and substantially constructed and this happened to be empty, then the mechanical tie-in should keep the slide open, same as it should happen when the magazine is empty, after the last shot. (A very desirable feature).

Intimately connected with the aforementioned "pre-seating" of the cartridge is the action of the extractor which has two functions: First, to "hook" into the cannelure of the case and to stay hooked with the case in the barrel chamber; secondly: with the withdrawal of the slide it is to pull out the empty case. The first function is generally fulfilled. When one looks at the actual extraction, however, a weak mechanical feature is exposed. The extractor, hooked into the cannelure, is being pulled backward with the slide and, perforce, the empty cartridge case has to follow. But, as the case is being extracted from the form-fitting chamber it is being pushed sideways by the spring-actuated extractor hook the more it protrudes. Since the extractor pulls on one spot of the cannelure periphery only we have a reason for a case not being properly expelled, despite some ejector-contrivance. It may be caught by the returning slide while still hanging diagonally and there is your jam. The whole present procedure is gambling on speed and luck. It is expected that the case will be "flipped" out somehow, helped by the recoil-gas-pressure. One trusts to chance that this flipping will be completed before the slide jams home. Now, if it were mechanically possible to devise an extractor mechanism that would grip the case at *two* points of its periphery, 180 degrees removed, the case could be withdrawn parallel to the barrel axis. As soon as the slide has receded a little more than the length of the empty case, one extractor hook should open, pushing an ejector bar against the primer-sector just freed from that one hook and the case is bound to fly out. With an arrangement as suggested, the careful balancing of springs would be of lesser importance.

It may be argued that some breech-block-faces have a recess, the approximate shape of the case diameter, holding the case there by the extractor hook pressure. Still, tumbling of the empty case must take place since "jams" do occur.

Let me resume: If studies were conducted, probing the advisability of "pre-placing" of the next cartridge, (divorced from the magazine), of the proper extraction and ejection, the delicacy of balancing springs and recoil pressures would lose importance and "jams" would be eliminated, once and for all. No matter how fast the slide travels, the empty case will be out of the way since every phase of the extractor and ejector functions would take place at geometrically fixed points.

All this is just theoretical talk. I am not an engineer, nor even a mechanic and I cannot, therefore, conduct practical experiments along the suggested lines.

However, if it *is* one of the weaknesses of Automatics to "jam", then, for Pete's sake, let's get rid of the causes and, maybe, my ramblings show one way.

But, let's proceed with our ideas about the ideal Automatic. Being primarily a "centre-fire" weapon, we should produce a .22 Rimfire conversion for the same gun. (Ah— I have landed right back on my pet subject). No kidding, in order to call our Automatic "ideal" it must permit us to practice with cheap ammunition. Of course, the use of the conversion should not entail arduous and intricate labour, but should allow us to shift from one calibre to the other in jig-time, without too many accessories.

How about a quickly exchangeable firing pin? Or a pin with a universal head, suitable for centre-*and* rim-fire cartridges? Further, how about the feature of an easily adjustable recoil-spring-pressure?

Well, well—there is food for thought—

Although I am not a mechanic, as said before, I claim that the subject is not a very difficult one. Have you ever seen a bottle-making machine? Or a cigaret-making machine? These things *are* truly the products of human genius. The task, *we* have before us in the matter of our ideal Automatic appears like child's play in comparison!

How about it?

Maybe, I am all at sea—But, let's start *thinking* about things! Let's begin *talking* about them! Let's tinker and experiment—You, who have mechanical minds and tools to work with! If we have to take the laboratory work away from the gun-manufacturers, let's do so! And, when we have found a workable solution, let's soak those bums, what? Just think of where the Radio-Industry would be today if it hadn't been for the Amateur-tinkerers—

Even, if we should not arrive at the proper thing in the near future, it will make the manufacturers prick their ears. They will *wake* up and get busy, durn their stringy hides. We have done a little. We have, f. i., the 7.65 Lueger and its conversion. But it is not ideal as yet. Come, come, me hearties! Put your shoulders to the wheel!

As for the ballistical functions, I aver that we should develop a progressive powder that burns completely in a short pistol barrel. With such a powder, the gasification can take place more gradually and with less of a shock-action. A powder which permits absolute combustion within the length of say a barrel of four inches. Ordinarily, such a short barrel causes a considerable loss of muzzle velocity since a part of the gases burn after the bullet has left the muzzle and, in consequence, the muzzle-blast and muzzle-flash are enhanced in the ratio in which the barrel length is shortened.

Of course, the ideal powder has to have a fixed relation to the twist, number and depth of grooves and lands. Too tight a bore, lands too wide, an unfavorable cone-entrance into the rifling, will increase gas pressure and will shift the point of maximum pressure in the direction of the chamber, influencing not only the muzzle velocity adversely but also the barrel vibrations and, indirectly, the point of impact. In this matter of barrel vibrations, I advocated tightly screwed barrels because of definite peculiar differences in the vibrations, which act more unfavourably in floating barrels.

We, apparently, need high muzzle velocity and a bullet design ballistically favourable so as to get a flat trajectory to allow us to hit small things within, say fifty yards, even if the sights were adjusted to pointblank at the latter maximum distance.

The painless dissipation of the necessarily higher (?) pressures may have to be found in a certain minimum "mass" of the frame or slide, unless, as hinted somewhere in this Manual, a sort of hydraulic shock-absorber device could be employed.

The moment when the bullet leaves the barrel, its destiny is analyzed by the oracle of "external ballistics" and we have to digest expressions such as penetration, explosive effect and splinter effect. (Just a few that I remember) Alright, let's get it over with:

Penetration: Is relatively strongest with a solid, non-mushrooming bullet of high impact velocity and rises the smaller the calibre and the higher its sectional load. This, of course, if the bullet has sufficient stability to resist tumbling.

Explosive effect: High impact velocity is transmitted to the bodily fluids and forces them apart with a socalled, hydro-dynamic effect. The body sections which contain the most fluids are influenced the most, naturally.

Splinter effect: With dis-integrating bullets, the splinter effect, if enhanced by centrifugal force, causes also a strong shock or a shattering of many nerve-strings and fluid vessels.

The humane bullet which I advocate so vigourously, should have sufficient penetration and, if possible, little explosive effect (Theoretically interdependent at present), but no splinter effect at all. Let's see if we cannot develop something along those lines.

I have to mention certain defensive anticipatory reflex actions (A drink please, Watson!) which cause whole groups of vessels, muscles or what have you, to dodge out of the path of a fast bullet. I wish that I might be a surgeon for a moment, so that I could explain this mysterious behaviour at greater length. Suffice it to say that if the antecedents of such cases were thoroughly analyzed, valuable ballistical data could be obtained. (Or, maybe, they have already studied this thing—But then: Where the hell is the ideal bullet—?)

As for impact on human bone, it is expected of our ideal bullet (And ballistics) that it drill a clean hole, with the least deflection, and continue its flight without mushrooming and tumbling. The angle at which a bone surface is hit, may be of great importance to the slow, heavy, lead-ball of large area, but should offer no problem to our fast and solid bullet.

Come to think of it, I haven't said anything as yet about bullet-energy. At the moment that the bullet leaves the muzzle, even with complete powder combustion, there remains a certain gas-tension in the barrel. The push of these liberated gases against the bottom of the bullet may influence the stability of it during flight, causing it to girate or tumble. A proper bullet will soon steady itself—

Oh—oh—fellow, cut it, will you? Isn't all this from the realm of pure ballistics? Taken from some of the sacred books? Sorry, boys, I am thoroughly ashamed— And I promise not to break out again. These things, of course, are known to the munition boys—Need I give more than my shy hints?

However, I shall say stubbornly that, according to my stunted conception of these holy things, we haven't hit the proper powders and primers as yet, nor is the co-relation of these to bullet shape, weight etc. satisfactorily solved—

BEAUTY AND THE BEAST

It seems to me that in many cases beauty of lines and utility depend upon each other. In the Automatic field I might say that a pistol which shows unharmonious outward appearance, will seldom please in a practical sense. If we, for instance, compare the 7.63 Mauser with the 7.65 Lueger or with the "Woodsman," my contention seems fully borne out. If there is anything more convincing, in the matter of lines, than the Lueger, for instance, I like to know about it. Its picture is one of competent efficiency withal beautiful. And one knows what the Lueger is capable of, as a matter of common agreement. Could one say equally nice things of the big Mauser? Despite its superior ballistics? Decidedly not. Does the .45 Government Automatic show pleasing design? As one looks at things from different angles, it cannot be avoided that repetitions creep up. The reader is, by now, sufficiently aware of my antipathy toward the .45 Automatic. It is deficient in almost every respect, even if my criticism should draw the suspicion that I am "looking" for things to squawk about. However, there are so few redeeming factors in the .45 Automatic that I feel quite safe in my sort of wholesale condemnation. This gun cannot change my viewpoint namely that beauty of lines and efficiency go hand in hand. Any gun, whether it be the .45 Automatic or others, which strikes one as lacking in beauty, will prove deficient in various respects and in the same ratio.

Of course, we know that tastes differ considerably. I, certainly, cannot see eye to eye with the important gentry that was instrumental in the adoption of the .45 Automatic. Maybe, my artistic sensibilities are finer—or something. But, whether or not: actual performance will bear witness.

And this, my contention, is shared by many, many

thousands. Can it be that the taste of the dissenters is normal? If so, we may take a look at any gun and judge its potential performance fairly safely by its outward lines.

Doodads and fancy trimmings, of course, are unimportant. The "outward appearance" of which we talked, must be of inate, genuine directness. The angle of grip to frame may often determine the usability of a gun. Proper distribution of weight will, inevitably, show in correct placement of groups. A clumsy looking, stubby gun will rarely prove satisfactory, no matter if it were to have pearl-handles and beautiful engravings. A certain slenderness appears as more conducive to effective beauty. Now, since one cannot make guns slimmer by slenderizing the frame and grip (Since a man's hand demands a certain fullness), the solution seems to lie in longer barrels and slides. This, combined with scientific (And therefore beautiful) angle of grip to frame would, automatically bar all the short, runty Automatic junk that one meets up with. Therefore, my comparatively short list of suitable Automatics. Our main object in having and handling an Automatic should be: satisfaction at efficient performance. We want to "hit" things and not just "brandish" Boudoir pieces or Engineering cripples.

So, my friend, if a gun appeals to your sense of beauty, you have part of a basis upon which the decision to acquire the gun may safely rest.

RAMBLINGS

In this chapter, I would like to throw all restraint aside and talk about things as if I were talking to myself. Irresponsibly, maybe. But just once, I want to ramble and not be called to task. I'd like this little concession from you: Don't reproach me if you don't like it—Just forget that you have read it.

Several months of intelligent work have passed—You are considered a fine shot now—Competitions do not occur so often that their event would fill all of the time that your ambition has set aside for you. You cast about for other fields of endeavour. You don't attempt to become an acrobat who throws a penny up in the air and hits it six times before it touches the ground. These darn coins are so aggravatingly small and they have the habit, when hit by mistake, to shoot off into space at a tangent, making further accidental hits almost impossible. If you should ever meet up with one of the ilk that claims to have done the trick, just control yourself and count up to "100" before you comment. Better yet, walk rapidly away and spare yourself a long stretch in the jug, for homicide. There are lots of strange things that people are supposed to have done, but, being a good shot yourself, you discount things! I shall therefore not impose upon you by recounting the thing that I did once: "Well Sir, I was standing at the edge of a forest and three hundred yards away"—Your smile, fellow, is anything but polite—All right, put that on every time these bohunks start bragging, what?

But, there *are* things that you really can do, beside shooting at paper targets. No one wants to eat caviar all the time. Being in a frivolous mood I might caricature the frowsy stuff I once read in a pedantically serious book on pistol shooting. I suggest that you get a steel plate big enough to cover and protect a person. Cut a slot in the plate, say 5″ long and 1″ wide. The idea is to have somebody step behind the plate and stick his finger through the slot. You then proceed to shoot at that finger. This exercise provides you with all the excitement of real hunting. It is not a stationary target because the finger is sure to twitch and wiggle, particularly if your victim is somewhat apprehensive. Of course, at first you will be wide of your mark. As you become proficient, you can ask the person to make it more interesting. Have him stick his finger out unexpectedly and withdraw it after a second. That way you are taught to be on the alert and your shooting will be speeded up. Ask your favorite neighbor to lend you a hand. If he should be busy with other things, you should have no trouble in hunting up some relative—They are better off behind a shield anyway.

William Tell's son took it without a protecting shield —and where is he now? But enough of that!

Don't at any time get cocky with your gun. Don't, for instance, shoot cigarettes out of a person's mouth, even in profile. A little unequality in the powder load of the cartridge and all your contrition cannot undo what might happen if you should miss the cigarette.

Being a sort of maniac on shooting at cigarettes, I curbed my homicidal proclivities by cutting two slots in the bulls-eye of a paper target and sticking the cigarette in the slot, vertically. Stand 60 feet away and try to pop the thing, with one shot. If that becomes too easy, fasten the cigarette horizontally and see what happens.

As a rule, I don't think much of "plinking." One is apt to become careless and sloppy. But, if you go at it in a more serious manner, it may be of value.

Let's see: Put up a tin can. Stand 25 feet away, look fixedly at the tin can—and go home! Shooting at that can would be too silly for words, yet many good shooters get a perverse delight out of popping at a decrepit tin can. Of course, we scientists claim that it illustrates the germ of the insatiable desire in every shooter to see things "happen", to sort of prove his handgun as an instrument of destruction. The very young and the very old ones visualize, palpitatingly, its "killing" propensities.

Writer believes that, once the handgun is taken out of the class of sportive equipment, it is being robbed of its gentlemanly nobleness and the grim, grey aspect of death is injected. Instead of exultation over a hit in the coveted ten-ring, the iris dilates at seeing a thing, full of vibrant life, suddenly stiffen into a cadavre, animal or human. Very seldom will the pistol be called upon to provide meat for the table and even cases, where self-defense could be cited as a supporting argument, are rare. Of course, in Police or Military work, the handgun becomes a tool of the trade and its more serious side is evident.

I realize that it would be like "swimming against the current" in being so set upon confining the handgun to sportive functions only. Well then: If we do any practicing along more realistic lines, let our practice be directed at something a little less silly than popping at a lone tin can. Let's visualize and simulate situations that fire the imagination.

Line up, say five tin cans, about a foot apart. At first stand 25 feet away and take a shot at each can. Start deliberately and take them in rotation. Then take the outer ones first and shoot toward the middle. The idea is to train yourself to hit the cans at will, increasing your speed and, later on, the distance. It sounds easy—and it will be easy with sufficient practice. The exercise teaches you to accelerate your responses. Of course, every shot must be a "hit" and the distance and the speed should not be increased unless one is fairly sure of hitting everytime. Nothing is quite as futile as a miss—There is enough anticipation in the game to force one to make an effort at organizing one's facilities. Once the pistol is up, the shot should follow immediately.

Now, suppose, you have become quite good at, say up to 45 feet. Your five cans are hit in quick succession, in predetermined rotation.

Then it is time to inject "Drawing from the holster." That should really be the final aim in this kind of practice: To start from the holster! Now, this "drawing" business is a thing all by itself. Before we go into that, I would like to get things down to earth again. I believe, nay I *know*, if one wants to become a dangerous hombre, it is only necessary to draw quickly and fire one telling shot; not five or six shots, just *one* shot. Rapid-fire in a serious encounter is nothing but "baloney." Never mind what the wrinkled crummies blow in your ears: It's totally silly to draw and bang out your magazine. Hell, one hit and your man shouldn't have to be shot deader five more times. If you don't get him with your first shot, you have played your most important card.

No! I say: Draw! Hit! and Hold the Drop! The tin can practice has taught you to be organized for every shot—If further shots in an encounter should be necessary, they should be released with some semblance of order. All this sounds very nice on paper, but of twenty-five men out of a group, there will be twenty-five different reactions to dangerous situations. All the wise dope given above presupposes a target, moving or stationary, that doesn't spit back. If your victim shows the slightest inclination toward restiveness, better tie your pants. Of course, you may be the exception—But, haven't I seen you blanch at the mention of your own mother-in-law's name?

I am not going to attempt to define "Bravery"—There ain't no sich animal. You are either desperate enough or dumb enough not to violently react to danger. I know that when I volunteered for dangerous patrols, as a youngster, it was vanity that drove me, vanity not yet dimmed by pain or fright. No matter how brave and fearless others may have thought me to be, I was just ignorant. I didn't know what the word "danger" could imply. Of course, life (or in this case: death) was a severe teacher and, after I saw the light, I ceased to be brave and courageous and vain. When I went, it was duty that made me go—And I was a better soldier for that.

Sometimes, I meet up with a vacuous soul parading his lightning draw and the paper hit. The smile that crooks around the corners of my mouth, I can't see—and I don't want to see it. These bozos give me a pain in the neck.

And yet, I shouldn't be too hard on them—In order to show their mettle in a serious fray, they should have to be masters of the technique and, if conditions should happen to be just right, they should be superior over their opponent. On that basis, practicing the theory of quick draw and a fast first hit, is entirely commendable, particularly for the Police and the Military. In fact, I will go so far as to say that each and every officer and man should practice along these lines.

Out of the many, many millions of rounds that blazed from .45 Automatics during the late war, there may have been three, or possibly four hits. From a humane point of view that was very gratifying but, of course, this performance did not tally with the original idea behind the thing. Now, I know that my above statement lacks what one might call: absolute accuracy. Nobody likes to admit having missed. Sometimes, fortunately, we are able to check up. A little while ago, a fire broke out in our little village—One side of the house was enveloped in flames.

Perilously close to that side stood a motorcar. The volunteers, brave people mind you, didn't like the idea of approaching since there was danger of an explosion of the gas tank. A former Army-man volunteered to get his .45 Automatic. Within a few minutes he returned and, taking careful aim from about twenty feet, he blazed seven shots into the tank. The extinguishing work was resumed and the fire brought under control. The roar that went up when it was found that none of the shots could be located, did not come from the gas-tank!

The moral that I would like to draw is: There should be no reason why men who have to carry a handgun habitually, in the pursuit of their calling, should be poor shots. Despite what I said against the .45 Automatic, it is an accurate gun nevertheless and it can be mastered. The present stinginess in the way of ammunition allotment is one of the main reasons why familiarity with the gun is not achieved. To lick the .45 Automatic, provided of course that the man started right, extensive and intelligent practice is necessary. As long as the man is confined to a few rounds per year, he might as well have no gun at all. Here is something for our American genii to work on: Invent a sub calibre attachment to the .45 Automatic that permits the use of cheap .22 Rimfire cartridges—Or, possibly, a *centre*fire shell of like calibre. A wide field— Why the hell don't you boys get busy?

I venture to say that, with enough practice in the sub-calibre, firing the larger shell should not meet with many difficulties.

Unless we get such a devise, let me again put a thought down that should find attention in the higher circles: 99 9/10th of all the .45 Automatics issued are not worth a damn, since the shooters can't hit with the darn things. Holding out on ammunition is the poorest policy imaginable. You Higher-Ups who are in a position to do something about this: What's holding you back? If nothing *is* done, then withdraw the .45 Automatic because it would only be an ornament—and not an overly pretty one at that.

It's a shame to see the scores that pass for qualifications. It is not for me to discuss the military value of the handgun. But, evidently, its importance has been acknowledged, because it was officially accepted. Would it not be logical to decide to get "shooters" behind the adopted gun? Sufficient ammunition and compulsory, intelligent practice as a part of the curriculum—

Oh no! I am not through yet!

Just giving a man a gun, enough ammunition, instruction and practice won't do the trick. Two more things will be necessary in order to get everything out of the combinations. The first thing is: to perfect the gun mechanically and, secondly, to "individualize" it!

"What ho——?" will the generals say, wrinkling their bushy eyebrows. I am not kidding, fellows! Let's see:

(a) The .45 Automatic should be equipped with sturdy, adjustable sights, with contrasting patridge posts 1/10″ wide. There is no sensible reason for the round, thin abominations that adorn the gun now. Some silly awss must have had a nightmare.

(b) The mechanism should be carefully fitted, same as is done in the commercial guns.

(c) The action should be honed and the trigger adjusted to four lbs.

(c) A better and more practical grip should be substituted.

What the hell: There is no war right now and, probably, won't be for years to come. Now is the time, then, to pay attention to detail. No need for rush-jobs.

As for the "individualizing" part, the men should be examined with sighting devices and classified. There will, possibly, be no more than five main groups, signifying the aberrations from "normal centre." Before a gun is issued, its sights are micrometered into one of the five adjustments, a matter of a few minutes. This gun should fit all men of a certain group. Now, in this sighting thing I am only guessing, of course. A certain percentage will triangle left/high, another right/high—or left/low—or right/low—It doesn't matter which way it is done, as long as a certain uniformity within the system is maintained. A class "B" man with a "B" sight-setting on his gun should do fairly well.

It may be argued that such fine adjustment is not necessary. But, when one realizes that there are sometimes sighting differences of 5 inches and more at fifty feet between men of otherwise normal eyesight, my idea shouldn't sound so very ridiculous.

I know what I say here, will be just so much water under the bridge. One need, however, only look at the performances during the world-war and one wonders whether it is wise to continue an obviously silly situation. Nineteen years have gone over the land and "training" and "equipment" have practically not changed—

What a rut!

HOLSTERS

The proper place for an Automatic is in a suitable holster. The flat shape of the gun is eminently adapted to being worn or concealed about the body. There is no bulkiness to contend with or to make it's presence conspicuous.

These advantages do not only extend to it's overall flatness, but also to it's overall length. The revolver has three functional sections, lined up behind each other, namely, the barrel, the cylinder and the action. (With the handle under it, extending some more.) The Automatic, given the same length of barrel, is so much shorter for the reason that there is no cylinder. The cartridges are contained in the handle, located directly under the slide. (With the exception of the big Mauser which is more of a hand-carbine than anything else).

The very adaptability of the Automatic for being carried in a holster, was one of the reasons that caused the Military to discard the Revolver. And that brings us to the matter of holsters. There are an endless variety of holsters in the market. Principally, they can be divided into two categories: The shoulder-holster and the belt-holster. The shoulder-holster, if made properly and with an open front, has much to recommend it. The name is, possibly, derived from the fact that the weight of the assembly is carried by the shoulder. The location of the holster is really under the arm, between the arm-pit and the hip-bone. The automatic is easily accessible and can

be drawn with speed.   However, there are certain disadvantages.   This holster, to permit perfect draw, should
be quite securely fastened.   This necessitates quite a lot of
harness which one has to strap on.   Another point is that,
even with an open front shoulder-holster, the movements
necessary for the draw carry the gun out of a smooth
swing.   The gun hand, for it's swoop, has to start rather
high.   It has to be brought upward, takes hold of the gun
from above (An awkward manipulation), pulls the gun
out across the chest and swings toward the target.   And,
although I dare say that one could become quite dexterous
with sufficient practice, the fact of the long, angular travel
will always make a shoulder-holster a poor second to the
belt-holster.

Never mind the phony stuff one sees in the Gangster-
and- G-Men Screen-melodramas.

Let's look at the belt-holster now: One can keep the
belt-holster on the gun-arm side.   (On the right side of
the belt for right-handers.)   This could be called the
"direct" belt-draw.   There are holsters to be had with an
open front and, although I don't personally favour this
draw, quite fast draws are possible nevertheless.   If one
wears a jacket, however, this direct belt-draw is awkward,
indeed.   My experience and that of many others has shown
that a "cross-draw" holster offers the least disadvantages.
In this affair, the belt-holster is located on the left side of
the belt (For right-handers) and vice versa.   In drawing,
the hand need be brought up to the height of the belt only
and swoops down upon the gun handle, pulls it shortly
across the body and forward toward the target.   In order
to offer the least impediment, the cross-draw holster is
fixed at a certain angle, say about 30° from the vertical.
In this position, the gun-hand does not have to pull the
gun straight up and out, but takes the slanted gun partly
across the body and forward, in one smooth, fast swing.
Even with a coat, matters are not materially delayed.

Coats, as a rule, are buttoned to the right and the gun hand can swiftly reach under. (Left handers would have to button their coats to the left) Or, better yet, the opposite, non-shooting hand can easily pull the coat open and aside, giving free access to the gun. The cross-draw holster, theoretically and practically, permits of the fastest draw, since the motions need only be short, without awkward and retarding angular deviations.

I hate, like the dickens, to take a peremptory attitude but, for the sake of brevity, so necessary in a Manual, I shall now make the decision to favour the cross-draw for you Readers.

The holster shape depends upon the gun used. This is obvious, yet one sees sometimes holsters that fit like the "hand-me-downs" in a Ready-to-wear-emporium. The holster must fit the gun like a tailor-made suit, that is: it mustn't be too large for the sake of maintaining a fixed position of the gun, nor must it be too tight. The gun must be withdrawable with ease. The leather of the holster should be "moulded" over the gun so that there is no idle space within the holster which might permit shifting of the gun. You see, when we draw, we don't look at the holster or the gun. Practice has taught our brain a great amount of familiarity with the position of the holster and upon releasing our mental command to "Draw," this command is relayed with lightning speed to the muscles in question and these will, unerringly, contract and expand to a sufficient degree so as to bring our fingers over the gun in the shortest and fastest way. And our muscles will follow through by taking hold of the gun too, if the thing hasn't changed its position within the holster. Everything will happen automatically and instinctively and we must see to it that there is no switch in muscle-commands by changes in the position of holster, holster-angle and gun. This being so downright logical, we shall not dispute it any further, what?

I spoke about an angle of 30°. The more horizontally the gun lies, the easier will be the draw, of course. That would indicate an angle of almost 90° from the vertical. In that position, however, the gun would simply drop out of the holster by itself. It wouldn't be a practical holster anymore. An angle of 30° still permits the gun to stay in the holster by its own weight. We assume that we employ no straps, springs or catches to achieve this artificially. These kinds of things are handicaps. We don't want them! No, let the gun stay in the holster by its weight alone. The better fitted the holster is, the better it will do that and still permit a favorable angle.

Another holster detail is: to see that the trigger guard is instantly accessible. That is, when darting the gun-hand to the holster, the trigger-finger should flit right into its final position, or into the trigger guard, in front of the trigger. We leave the trigger guard uncovered therefore and cut the curve in the leather so that it just covers the forward steel curve of the trigger guard.

Having gotten this far, we have to amend our statement of a few sentences back, namely: that the trigger finger in the draw should fly into its "final" position. To do that, we should have to cut away the leather on the underside too. The trigger finger could then poke right through and be in position ere the gun leaves the holster. I have tried both ways but have found that it is almost impossible to secure the gun sufficiently if one were to cut away too much of the holster. We have therefore compromised by thrusting our trigger finger into the trigger-guard until it touches the backpart of the holster and, while our other fingers encircle the stock (Which, of course, is accessible all around) and pull the gun out, our trigger-finger slips in further until, by the time that the gun is ready to cross the body, the finger is "home." Let's resume: A modeled, formfitting, leather holster without straps or springs, sufficiently cut away as to leave the handle free and which doesn't cover the outward part of the trigger-guard; the assembly held securely at an angle of 30°, with the gun handle leaning in the direction of the navel, is the ideal outfit.

I went a step further. In order not to be compelled to have to "thread" the belt through the holster loop all the time, I had a loop sewed on the underside of the holster, with a flap going over the belt, then through this loop on the back of the holster to a click button. The flap and loop are shaped and re-enforced thus that a holster position of 30° is maintained at all times. With my idea which I have adapted to various models, the motion of gun draw is reduced to instinctive reaction, the way it should be. No fumbling. No fussing. It is as easy as finding the tip of your nose which motion, acknowledgedly, is easy and unerringly to do with your hand. Just try to reach the tip of your nose with your right hand and you must admit that it can be done fast and—you will never miss. If you should have trouble in that connection, something is seriously wrong with you. But, if it is only compunction at using your nose, try the lobe of your right ear.

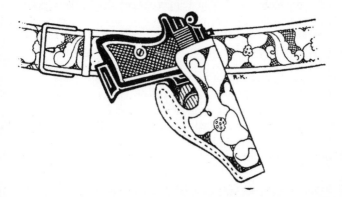

THE "DRAW"

In dealing with this matter of going in for practical
shooting, I assume that the shooter, most of the time, is
by his lone self. It is easy when in congenial company,
to devise clever little games that help to develop one's
skill in practical shooting.

Now, let me ask: What is the object of "practical"
shooting? I suppose, all of us have a little bit of a barbaric
vein in us. We don't go out of our way, to be sure,
but if opportunity should arise, we want to kill us somebody, say a badman or an enemy soldier or even a lil' bit
of a lion or so. "Practical Shooting." Damn it, that's
what the gun was invented for. Well—maybe you are
right! I have a lot to say on the subject of "practical"
shooting. Does it convey anything but killing and maiming? It is "practical" to "kill and cripple?" Of course
we shall not deny situations where—But, I withdraw my
question. We will just assume that we want to practice
"practical" shooting because it is the thing to do.

We may define it briefly as "the ability to draw our
gun quickly, align it with speed and discharge it, without pulling, at the target."

Upholding what we had learned about the fundamentals
of Slow Fire, we have gone through Time-and Rapid-
Firing. But we still have to admit that we have done no
"practical" shooting yet. Slow—Time—and Rapid Fire
are forms of competition. They sort of represent the

foundation from which we may go on now. And right here, we must first agree on one thing: Not the ability to slambang a number of shots, but our perfection in getting out *one* shot, the *first* shot, fast and accurately, is what constitutes practical shooting. From the moment, the impulse is given, all our fibres must be organized to such unified cooperation that the shot must register a good hit within the shortest time possible.

Not deviating in the slightest from what we have learned, we must acquire "speed." Drawing from the holster, stance, cocking, bringing the gun up and forward, sighting and squeezing stay principally the same. If formerly our pedantic movements could be compared to a "Slow Motion Film," because we had lots of time, we must now accelerate the wheels to within our capability. And you will be surprised to learn how fast human beings are considered, even with a "one second draw." I must admit, the learning of fast draw is a slow process. Not because we do not wish to storm forward, but because we have to restrain ourselves—Don't smile—This is no contradiction! Yes, we have to hold back! We must not go too fast!

Let me explain: Assuming that we have the right holster, at the right angle, permitting of unhampered, smooth draw and a gun that we are thoroughly familiar with. We must not try to stand before a mirror and get the gun out with lightning speed! A fumble is sure to follow. No! We go at the thing leisurely. We stand before a full size mirror, let's say. The fellow in the mirror is our enemy. That's the one we want to give a headache to. We take a stance which we think feels natural. Then we stand relaxed and study the expression of the apparition. We tell him that we don't, somehow, fancy his face. However, we don't work ourselves into a frenzy, you know. We are going to count up to "3" and then let him have it, sort of casual, without rancor, what? All right! Here

goes! "One"—breath—"Two"—another breath—"Three!"
Our hand goes down to the gun—(Not fast, mind you,
just natural), takes it out of the holster, cocks and carries it
to arm length. The bead is at the nose of our adversary.
We squeeze the trigger!—The whole action may take
us fully three seconds. That's fast enough for the beginning. The thing is to see that the action is carried
smoothly. There should be no yanking or pulling or jerk-
ing. It must be one beautiful, perfectly rounded swoop-
ing motion, even if done slowly. S-l-o-w, but smooth!
We practice this slow but smooth draw. We have ample
chances now to *study* ourselves. We find, for instance, that
the gun does not withdraw easily from the holster or that
the holster moves part way with the gun or that the motion
of extending the arm was faster than the draw itself. We
can now *correct* ourselves. We can attend to technical
things such as the shape of the holster, its angle. We find
that by holding our open fingers in a certain way, we
facilitate matters. We do not look at our hand, but
keep our eyes steadily in those of our enemy. In short,
we must be able to draw the gun comfortably and unerringly and carry it forward, without getting any part of
the procedure faster than the other. No matter how long
it takes for the action. Rhythm! Rhythm! From the
moment we murmur "Three" up to the time of the finished
squeeze, there should be one deliberate, clean motion.
Once we can do that, the rest is easy. If the action should
take fully three seconds, it takes three seconds and during
the short time of your first practice session, all your draws
should take three seconds, no longer, no shorter.

The ideal perfection of this basical draw, although slow,
provides you with work for the next few weeks. Remember: three seconds from command to finished squeeze.
Curb that darn impatience of yours! There is no short cut!
Start *right* by starting with the *slow* draw! Practice and
practice! Slow draw! We have lots of time! We have made

up our minds that this is going to be a long-drawn out affair and we will not spoil things by losing our patience. We are looking for smoothness, not for speed! If your will power is well developed, no hasty speeding will corrupt the foundation you are building. We step before the mirror for a few minutes every day and do this slow stunt for, say three weeks. Oh-Oh—here we have practiced for three weeks already and I have not even warned you to see that your gun be empty! Heck, my friends will never forgive me! And use a .22 calibre gun. It's easier on yourself now and, later, on your pocket book. Now, we have mastered that! The rest is less hard. We will set aside the following three weeks for practice on the "Two Second Draw." In a month and a half after starting from scratch we are able to execute a beautiful and faultless "Two Second Draw."

What next?—Right, my infallible Watson! Three more weeks devoted to the "One Second-Draw," what?—And so on—!

Well, speaking for myself, I consider a draw executed within $\frac{1}{2}$ second a damn fast draw. But, there are people who never get enough. Still, I would say that 1/100th of a second for a draw would be putting matters a little too fine. Let's agree, for the sake of getting peace in the family, that a "one second draw" is sufficiently fast for rough, every day work. It possibly took us from six to nine weeks. Not so bad, considering that things were a bit hard on our patience. But here it is! And now a word of wisdom. Our bright, shiny "second" draw is ours, but it won't stay ours, if we stop practicing every day. It's one of those fool things. Stop practicing and the thing gets rusty. It's a neverending drudge, but who started this anyway? Who wanted to be the speed-marvel? Who wanted to—Ah, never mind! We are all Nuts, one way or the other, what?

We are "second" draw artists now! But we do not

know what to do with this treasure—All right, things become serious now. We go to an outdoor range or some place outdoors where there is enough room around us so that we can work, unhampered by corpses of fool passers-by that get bumped off by flying bullets. A hillside or a beach with a wide expanse of water as background (With no craft on it, of course), or a stone-quarry are ideal. Prop up a mansize target on a few boards, say 6 feet long and 2½ feet wide, when put side by side. Use your own ingenuity. Put up something that offers the area of a fullgrown man. Stand five feet away. Take your favorable stance, load your pistol and put it in the holster, with hammer down. Having practiced drawing for nine weeks, you should feel quite confident. Here goes! One—Two—Three—Out comes your pistol, the hammer is cocked on the way and—there goes the shot! Hell, you missed that big target—at five feet! Well—well —Go slower then! Start with the "Two Second Draw" and stay with it until you score a hit everytime. Then speed up your draw! Maybe, you get to pare it down to the old "One second" draw, by and by! But, whatever you do, make it your business *never to miss* your target! Oh yes, my friend, it's a long drawn out affair, as we agreed in the beginning. And all the while we have to exercise the usual care when playing around with loaded fire-arms.—It's a lot of fun, though.

We started with five feet, because we wanted to make it easy to register hits with every shot. Nothing is to stop us, when mastering this distance, to walk back ten feet. The fun grows, let me tell you. By Golly, you are quite the dangerous Shot now. Don't overdo your practicing! Never fire more than, say 50 shots a day. Some day, you will find yourself hitting at twenty—thirty —or even forty feet, with unerring, uncanny accuracy. Ah—Your confidence is a beautiful thing—I believe, you are actually swaggering—but—(Dash those old "buts"—)

You are no more dangerous than a Policeman *would* be if he were practicing too. Your ambition must be higher than that. How about using a five inch bullseye? Instead of the foolishly big target? All right! Go back to the five feet distance. Mind you, a "second" draw and a hit *every time*—or no go! Boy, oh Boy, are we having fun— Oh, I could go on, ad infinitum! But, for the sake of preventing sleepless nights, I might say that, if you get to the point where you can hit the large five inch bull at 25 feet with a one-second draw, you are a deadly shot and no fooling! I would hate to have an argument with you! I myself occasionally miss the bull and my draw never became faster than a full second. But then, I had other things to do than practicing for the world championship in fast drawing. When my shot is out, I always *keep* the pistol lined up at the target, ready for another shot. After the elapse of a few seconds I take it down and repeat the draw. Once you are fairly fast and show steady hits, you can invent changes in your practice schedule that are better adapted to whatever work you wish to specialize in. You see, so far we have only shot at immobile targets. Hitting a squirrel on the move at 25 feet, drawing from the holster, requires a high amount of organized fibre-co-operation and, luckily for the squirrel (Who has never offended anyone willingly), not many shooters can do it! I mean, with any certainty.

Although grudgingly, I must say that the speedy draw-and hit-business changes your whole appearance and behaviour. Without mentioning your achievements, you seem manlier, somehow. A quiet, yet purposeful assurance exudes from you which makes people want to meet you and listen to you. And what is more pleasant than have people listen to you, what? Yes, it's a great thing, this "practical" shooting, were it not for the many innocent little victims like the squirrel mentioned. But perhaps, you can pick on rats or other vermin—

PREPARING FOR THE FRAY

During that dismal period of 1914-1918 when my pistol-shooting was, perforce, of the "practical" variety, I was still too dumb and unsettled to methodically register my impressions and reactions. When I shot—I just shot —and to hell with how important any possible notes might be for the benefit of posterity. I was in jams— that's all that counted—And I didn't want to die—

The phases of the melees rolled thunderously over me and bogged me down and my only thoughts were: to try to help terminate proceedings, somehow. Since advancing, in most cases, was no more dangerous than retreating, it didn't matter much which way we were going. We just followed orders—But each little jam, I mean each *personal* jam, presented a major catastrophe to me, a ponderous threat of which I was the centre—Would I jot down technical or psychological data? Like hell! I just shot! And shot!

And, after the thing was over, I was too damn worn and too apathetic to care much about what wisdom I might have preserved, for the sporting fraternity twenty years hence. Give me sleep—something to eat—and leave me alone!

Of course, certain impressions stayed engraved upon my mind and, with maturity, I should be able to condense the chaos into an orderly picture. Alas! Now it is my abhorrence at things seen, terrible things that tend to close my lips.

Friends, too often and too lightly do we talk of using the pistol on a human target. Of how we would plug him in the belly or any old place as long as he gets knocked over. Discussions ensue as to what calibre, powder load, bullet shape, velocity will do the job best and most thoroughly. But, most of those that revel in that kind of talk are either inexperienced or fairly sure of not being called upon to perform.

It is a sad fact that our opponent is equally as thoughtless as we and he also wants to plug away at bellies—our bellies—and that side of the picture is less pleasant to contemplate than we first thought. Orders are orders! In another major debacle—Heaven forbid—we will be drafted once more and again: Orders will be orders—and we follow them and we shoot—and are shot at. Oh, how we hate to get our intestines violently disarranged. How we hate to want to stay hungry, before battle, just because with empty bowels the sawbones will find less of a mess—And again it will become a question of who is more accurate and faster—and, incidentally, who the Guardian Angel's pet is. That is why we practice in peacetime. We practice, not to impress stupid people with the idea of how smart we are or how dangerous we *would* be if, alas, we didn't have that lil' heart trouble that will force us to stay home while others, the lucky stiffs, are grabbing the honours of saving the country.

No, we practice, without fanfares, because we know that it is a deadly serious thing, this thing of war, of maiming, of killing.

And, we go at the thing seriously, with some method. Before we form definite throughts about suitable melee-shooting-ranges, we try to collect some salient points which we came across when we were living the actual thing. A melee, let us understand, is not a peacetime target session—We shooters will have left the realm of sport and we are then bearers and receivers of destruction.

If we have been good target shots before, it will help us in a melee, *but we are not target-shooting anymore.* The deliberation which we loved, the careful adjudication of situation and circumstance, the exultance over difficult achievement, have no place in the scheme of battle or skirmish—There is violent upheavel—furious riot—fearful, murderous detonations rattle our nervous system—There is the reek of sulphur, of gases and powder and burning flesh and things—There are the moans and screams of suffering humanity—There are twisting, twisted bodies ground into ugly caricatures—all around us and we are the *centre* of everything—Every man that crumbles is a human like us—Every missile is meant for us—and in another second we, ourselves, will be just another one of those scores of squirming, screaming worms—that will stiffen into something shapeless, only to be shoveled later into the big maw—where lime and dirt and weeds, as if in commiseration, make posterity forget that here, under our very feet, at one time, the greatest tragedy that can befall man, was enacted—and so what?

Do you think that we had time for cogitation, for careful weighing of circumstances? No!—The deliberation of the target sport was not here—No scopes to check the exact location of impact—This here was wild and reckless and—shockingly real! And, our harrassed eyes were hunting for the splashes of our *misses,* so that we might hurriedly correct our next aim—We did not expect hits with our first shots. We could never hope to estimate the everchanging distances—We shot! To see *how far* we missed and then we held over or under, left or right.

Ah yes! That is one of the things we learned, we who went through it and survived: this watching for the splash of our misses, this finding of our range by hasty trial. And, as we lost some of our greenness and turned into seasoned Oldtimers, we learned to avoid long-range shooting with pistols and we didn't bang away anymore just to empty our magazine—We shot at a target (we kept reminding us) that came fast and kept coming, a target that spat death and wounds and we tried to lay it low (If our fevered mind did register the location of our misses) with our second or third shot. And when it went down, through design or hit, our sights went on another—and miss—splash—miss—splash—hit—down—another—

And, then it was over—and we cleaned our tools and oiled them—we who were able—and then, maybe, we slept, dreamless, like the many others who could never rise.

It behooved the great Spirit that we should come through —a little battered—a little crippled—but, here we are to tell our young ones.

May it behoove Him, too, that they need never go through the same thing.

However, we puny cogs do not shape history—we do not change destiny—But, we can try to profit by experience—and prepare, in times of peace, leisurely—deliberately.

We target-shooters therefore endeavour to "approach" melee-conditions by selecting a sort of universal "battle" range, similar to the one of which a friend of mine writes: "On my farm I had a small 'hollow' or valley, surrounded by high hills on three sides. It faced North-East, almost ideal for shooting at any time of the day. Up in the end of the valley I set up a range with the targets on three sides—in fact, they were strung around the bottom of the hills in a circle, taking in three full quarters of the compass. These targets were of all kinds, built-up backstops which were situated at standard distances and used in straight target shooting—then swinging targets, tin-can-stands, sticks stuck up with a big tin-can hung on them—and rotten stumps, large rocks, etc., etc. It would have taken a full box of 50 cartridges to have gone around the entire range and shoot twice at every available target. The firing point was situated, not in the middle of all these targets, but to one side, giving a distance of 25 yards to one hill, 50 yards to the opposite hill and 100 yards to the hill in front. In fact, I had a complete small-bore range with targets up to 200 yards. But, for pistol practice, I moved up into the valley."

Such a range will, by force of circumstance, teach the shooter to watch for the bullet splashes if he wants to be able to correct his sighting shots at all. There should be no scopes or binoculars to assist him—He *will* have to shoot with both eyes open or he is licked right from the start. How can one, I ask you, observe impact-splashes by squinting "one-eyed" through sights? One has a larger field with binoculars than with monoculars—And, one needs to see more than just the target and the impact-splashes. It may very well be, having noticed that your first shot missed 4 inches to the left and high, that by holding low and right with your second shot, you bring down the target. But, bringing down the target is not, in itself, sufficient. You see, we are working on the precept of melee-conditions and, in a melee, alas, there is generally more than one, shall we call him "miscreant"?

You have been taught in this Manual not to lower your gun after a shot, but to "hold the drop" after your opponent goes down—just in case. That is all right if there is only one. But, in our picture, you are supposed to take care of several. So, immediately, as you register a "hit," swing your gun at the next target and it is a good idea (Since in real warfare, your playmates do not come at you all bunched together, but are spread out in a long skirmish line) not to pick a target too close to the last one. It should be, at least, 20 to 25 feet to the right or left, even though it may be located 10 to 20 or even 50 feet further away—and regardless of whether the sun is in your face or not. That gives you a new, unknown range and new light—and different wind conditions—And, unless you are a wizard at guessing distances, you will miss your new target. That, however, is what we must learn to expect: namely to *miss* with the first shots because then we are on the lookout for the tell-tale splashes in the dirt or against a rock—The best and the simplest range-finders in the world, these splashes.

Your magazine will, probably, be empty after your first or second hit—Good work, ol' boy! It won't do now, although having brought down your man, to reach for the bottle every time, in order to celebrate—Sure, you proved yourself a good, effective shot—But, there is more work ahead of you—If, instead of slamming in your second loaded magazine and getting to work on your next man, you look into the bottle too often, that skirmish line will tend to grow in numbers and even attain a sort of pinkish hue—And pinkish things are hard to hit, as I found out when I went after elephants in India.

If you want to add finesse to your practice, lie on your belly, say 200 feet from where you want to start shooting. Jump up and run as fast as you can, 30 or 40 feet forward and plump down again—full length, the face snuggled close to Mother Earth. Count "30" and then jump and run and flop down again. That will give you four or five good, healthy runs up to the front-line and if, once there, you carefully lift your face to pick out your first target and you jump up and aim and shoot and expect a "hit," you are just on the verge of being optimistic. No, you look for a close "miss" and the good ol' impact-splash. Hold your "bead" up and correct it quickly and squeeze again. Don't, for the sake of everything that is holy to you, bang out your magazine recklessly. Aim and squeeze, correct your aim and squeeze—correct again and the target will come down. Then swing, immediately, over to any other one—It doesn't make any difference if it's 50 or 75 feet away from the first one—*All* you do is: to *splash at* it and you will know at once where your shots go—You are not wild.

Ah—good practice—this—and healthy—and absolutely harmless. (You don't want to infuse real danger and detonations—and hunger and horror—That would put too fine an edge on things.)

The lonely lads, deep in the country, have the advantage over us city slickers, in that Mother Nature often will assist them in picking a suitable melee-range, right on their farm.

This practice is really a "one-man-affair." Too dangerous otherwise! There can be no back-seat-admonitions from friend Mother-In-Law—Of course, if she *insists*— Why begrudge her the fun? And, pray, let her start with you: 200 feet away from the firing line—four to five good, vigorous sprints—There is subtle satisfaction hidden in that kind of game.

Unless you have the eyes of a falcon, I am afraid that .22's would not make effective splashes. Ideally suited would be the .45 cartridge as it will dig up a "shovel full." However, the .38 Super and the .30 Lueger are not so bad either.

Will you believe me now, when I insisted all along upon *ample* and contrasting sights? Why did I advocate a thick patridge post, either of the red-King or the black/ white "Whitex" variety? Why did I preach about a wide and deep rear-sight-slot?

Simply because there will be no time for micrometric monkey-business. That thick front-post just has to slip comfortably into an ample rear-slot, or you will never make the grade. Battle-sights, I call them!

I explained, somewhere else, that in an honest to goodness melee, the cool and deliberate actor just "isn't." There will be a certain looseness in his intestinal region as 10.5's and 15's and trench-bombs and hand-grenades recklessly traverse the air around him, without seeming justification or semblance of order, but, somehow, all coming his way—He suddenly finds himself in an atmosphere so rude and unspeakably shocking that he tends to become somewhat ruffled—Ha—if only I could actually transpose our reader into the middle of such an affair, just for five minutes, he would take for gospel everything I have told him, among others: That he shouldn't expect to win the war with close hits, but rather (much rather) with close "misses."

And he will, from then on, join me in smirking at those blustering, bragging "Firelikehell" theoretical belly-busters who work for effects on a dumb gallery.

And he will, further, agree that the "melee-range and practice" as outlined will come as close to the ideal as is humanly possible, without losing sight of absolute, all-round safety.

Practice like that will unloosen those reflexes which we expounded in "Sixguns and Bullseyes." We encourage and facilitate instinctive releases and reactions. We will be enabled, through "practice" to form the "habit" of doing the right thing at the right time. We do not have to make quick decisions consciously, but we come to rely on "reflexes" to give the necessary orders to our muscular and nervous system. In short, we do certain things through selective habit and I aver that, if a man were fortified by habit, he would make a much more effective antagonist than the best, deliberate target-shot.

But, here is a seeming anomaly: In order to do this "melee practice" successfully, one must, alas, be a fair target shot first.

Concluding you might ask: Is this "Melee practice" worth the candle? The criterion will always be the actual melee—and, may the gods prevent them—but then: It never hurts to know more than one did before— (Military and Police: Please take note!) In fact, our melee-practice offers a fascination all its own—Our life will be that much richer—through achievement.

And Life, in its funny and unpredictable ways, *may* ask us to deliver.

BALLISTICAL BLOTTO

Although, in this chapter, we shall talk about ornithology and corpses, all in one breath, there will be little confusion other than in the ranks of the ballistic sharps. And since I have always had a weakness for torturing bedbugs and cooties, my ramblings must be laid at the door of—ah—nevermind!

How can we start effectively? I mean, I have to think of my reputation—I want to appear as if I had a concise mind—I don't care to divulge any possible ignorance on my part—

Corpses—That's it! We need corpses—Not any old corpses, but corpses that have been made what they are with the help of "sectional density"—There's that scientist again—No stopping me now! Brace yourself, brother. Here I come!

Let's invade that intimate circle of ballistic sorcerers—Let's be rude to them——

Their talk about "sectional area of bullet" etc., sounds very impressive. But, if a handgun is to be used for combat, that is against human targets, then psychological factors certainly enter which experimental shooting at cattle, cadavres, etc., cannot ever bring out.

I believe that the .38 Super Automatic shell is fully as effective on homo sapiens as its larger .45-brother. They are indeed rare cases, possibly those transgressing the borders of sanity on the part of the recipient, where a second bullet is necessary. It is essential that the shooter "master" his gun sufficiently well so as to enable him to *aim* and *hit* at vital places. If the shooter is a poor one and only then, of course, an excuse for the existence of the large .45 calibre may be found. *Where*ever that shot impacts, damage will result.

But that, in my opinion, fortifies the position of the smaller .38 Super. If the .38 bullet hits a vital spot, the target is finished. Without doubt! Hitting a non-vital place, however, there may be a chance of patching the poor fellow up. After all, in warfare, our adversary bears no personal grudge. He was drafted, against his will possibly, to commit murder. He may be a nice chap for all we know. If we happen to kill him, c'èst la guerre. But, why make a permanent cripple out of him? He might have escaped like the rest of us, but inscrutable fate decreed against him. He did not deserve it anymore than we—Long after the madness, we lucky ones follow the tranquil life of the smug bourgois, but this poor devil is supposed to pay and pay the terrible debt which he didn't incur, his soul seared with shame and repulsion——

If the idea were to produce the most terribly crippling, shattering, tearing havoc, why not the "dum dum bullet"? Why make any effort at all to preserve the apparent decency of the so-called "humane" bullet? No. No! The "destructive" power of the .45 calibre is a cruel argument. It is thought that the dumb soldiers can't hit anything anyway, but if they should "contact" then it might as well be bones completely shattered and the viscera sprinkled over the landscape.

Hell, those coldblooded "Stay-behind-the-lines" give me a pain. I wish I could observe them, gobbling up knowledge in places like the Somme of unhappy memory for just one week, or at Chateau Thierry, or hell of hells: Duaumont.

Experimental shooting at cattle and cadavres—Give me a drink, someone!

Why, if we know that our tiny .22 Long Rifle bullet can kill at half a mile, (about as far as anyone would care to shoot at human beings), why then all this "BIG ARTILLERY"—stuff? Of course, I don't advocate the .22 calibre as an effective medium in combat, because I don't like to have the whole Army and Police on my neck. About the only further arguments I could marshal for the .22 calibre is that it would cut down the noise of battle considerably and that the men could carry a great many more rounds with them to play around with.

There is another category of blood-thirsty demons though: The surgeons. They claim that the small calibre bullets are sometimes hard to find when they are buried in the tissue, the victim might have internal hemorrhages etc. etc. and, therefore, my plea for a less destructive bullet would defeat itself. I don't blame the sawbones if they like to have their work laid out nicely—Nobody cares to dig around in bodies looking for a tiny bullet. But, haven't I tooted the horn for the .30 Lueger and the .38 Super? No, I don't particularly clamour for the .22 calibre on human beings. I just want a "humane" bullet. (To tell the truth: I don't want any bullet at all, at all. I am all right the way I am, thank you.) A humane bullet —One that has *penetration* rather than expansion, one that does not tumble easily, cuts a clean path; ballistics in general that facilitate good marksmanship through moderated recoil and blast. A .38 Super bullet is about the ceiling.

I know—I know darn well that, in messing around with things of this sort, I shall get into hot water—To be consistent and in order to evade the odium of denseness, I should now lecture on bullet-shape, weight, powder, primer, breech-pressures, barrel-lengths, twist, one and twostep and my favorite Dunhill—But, I am too canny for that! See those vultures with their ballistic textbooks perched greedily on the rocks nearby, ready to pounce upon the half-wit? SHOOOOO, you birds! Or better: Stick around. Here's where you come in! Open up your books and spit out those ol' formulae—Tell the good folks about what's in the books, what? Oh—oh—Just as I expected! One at a time! Please! Please! There, there—They are at each others throats—Look at those feathers fly—Listen to those raucous screeches—Nice company—Here's where I leave—

Me—? I am not discussing ballistics—I mislaid my books. I know damn well that, in order to discuss ballistics intelligently, one has to be a real scientist and not just some half-baked emulator of book-data. I am merely championing here the cause of us poor fellows at the *receiving* end, in combat. We want to be dead, if we have to. We want to be wounded, if it cannot be helped—But, we *don't* want to be crippled! I am championing the cause of us men who have to *shoot* the guns that are given us. We want to be able to fire the damn things without falling over backwards everytime we jerk that trigger. We want to be able to *place* our shots, if possible and not just bang out "Lead" indiscriminately, thoughtlessly. In short, we don't want to be flinching from that damn overgrown recoil that spoils our aim.

I am championing—Hell, I need another drink!

Say—Don't buzzards and cadavres go together though?

HOMO SAPIENS AND OTHER GAME

I should not want to be so impolite as to ever interrupt a heated controversy about the ballistic requirements for various purposes, with a cold "What the hell are you talking about?" Particularly not, if the debaters were of the friendly clan who can wax hot over anything that they don't agree with. There is another cotery which argues just to be opposite, but we do have people who do talk thoughtlessly and, I believe it was Nietzsche who professed downright scorn for the unintelligent. All this is to lead up to something, you bet. (I'm still greatly inspired by the foregoing "Ballistical Blotto". One of the favorite topics in shooting circles is ballistics and, of course, "the killing effect" of bullets. Learnedly or stubbornly, they will haggle back and forth, and dammit, sometimes I feel just a little sick of listening. Why can't this question be sensibly settled by my statement: If game is hit in a vital spot, it will not run away?

Normally no organism, I mean mammal organism, is able to continue it's biological functions if a vital center is paralized. (And it should be the sworn duty of the sportsman to forego shooting rather than to place any but *vital* shots.) It makes me boil to hear people harangue others and split hairs over bullet-weight, initial velocity, penetration and that other bunk. These things are nothing but stilts for the punk shooters. A buck can be brought down instantly with a .22 long rifle, say within 200 feet or even more. An elephant has a thick skin and a lot of meat and large bone. Naturally, one would go higher than a .22. But whether woodchuck or rhino, the vital spots are the brain and the spinal column. (When including "heart" shots, the matter does become a little more complicated and the discussion of the proper ballistics might be justified. The heart of game, depending upon the location and angle of impact, may be protected by more or less powerful bones, such as shoulder blades, etc.)

All other shots into non-vital areas are unsportsmanlike. I don't care a damn that the shooter might have lost his game, if he had not risked one of those punk shots, relying on ballistics to carry him through.

There may be situations, I dare say there *are* situations, where a victim, crazed by pain caused by a non-vital shot, will run straight at the shooter. It may not know what it is doing; it may have no other intention than to get away from the sudden and mysterious, outrageous onslaught, get away somewhere, anywhere—

Here, Nimrod rises to the occasion if he is not too craven and runs, and (What do the books say?) cooly pumps bullets into his ferocious attacker.

When J. K. Jerome, in his column, advised a wistful old lady that the best way to cure her cat of fits, would be to take the animal between her knees, and with a pair of scissors snip just the tip of her pet's tail off, he omitted to say that the lady should not do it in the kitchen where she keeps her porcelain, and he had a lawsuit on his hands. The cat simply didn't give a rap how high the walls were and how many dishes she brought down. Just a dumb beast. I say that if the shooter is not sure that he can hit a vital spot, he should either try to stalk closer until he *is* sure, or give up the shot. And I don't care whether anybody likes this or not. It sounds like sense to me.

I grant that to the average Nimrod who goes hunting once in a blue moon, there is nothing quite as humiliating

than to entirely miss his game. If only he were to hit the
buck just somewhere, he mumbles, that would be satisfaction of a sort. Even if it were somewhere in the haunches.
The hunter may be too excited or too inexperienced to
place a vital shot. Instead of lying down now and to wait
docilely so that he could be scalped at leisure, the damn
buck tries to escape. The "corpus delicti" disappears. The
huntsman, thoroughly mad, blames his gun, the ballistics—
he blames everything but his own lousy shooting ability.
If he had a cartridge, he vows, a cartridge that would lay
the critter low, no matter *where* the bullet connects, that's
the cartridge he wants—and he crabs and clamours for
explosive bullets and such rot.

The dumb buck does not stop to reason that, maybe,
he had better lie down, and cauterize his wound by licking
it. It does not enter the poor animal's mind that by chasing
madly over the landscape he might aggrevate the serious
mess in his shattered stifle. He just runs and stumbles
until he is exhausted, blind, unreasoning fear driving him
on, until he *has* to bed down—His feverish eyes will stare
uncomprehendingly around—Only a short while ago he
was grazing contentedly—and then something struck him
cruelly—it seemed to knock his leg right from under him
as he lunged into mad flight—The wound hurts terribly—
he retches—and the red life fluid oozes steadily. From
time to time, a shudder goes through him as gangrene
ravages his frame—he suffers in silence—until the last—
and then he stiffens—The curtain goes down on drama
—while, miles away, his irate slayer, filled with wounded
pride, keeps on railing at insufficient ballistics—the very
kind of creature that is responsible for all that "destructive
ballistics"—stuff.

Up to now I have held myself in—I am still amiable
and amenable to a forgiving drink. But don't these
geezers go ahead and project the topic into higher game?
There are people who have no compunction to talk about

the effect of ballistics upon the highest developed mammal, Homo Sapiens. That is the time when I generally leave the room. It's sickening. Well, I can't evade the issue here and I have had in mind to talk about it anyway. Alright then: Let's establish right at the outset the vital difference between "human" and "animal" game. Animal lives mostly by instinct, not by reasoning. An animal's prime emotion is fear. It can't reason that an iron tube, 200 feet away, can cause violent, excruciating pain. It's fear of the man-smell which causes it to run. But take man: He has reason—He knows damn well what a rifle will do to him if he gets hit. While fear does play a great role in his life, some of his other emotions may momentarily be equally powerful. How were it otherwise possible that he could walk right into enemy fire? There's "hope" that he may escape without a scratch, there's "patriotism" (Oh yes, there is such a thing) and, through reason, even "fear" will be driving him on. He may know that if he stays where he is, he will die. If he were flanked by fire from two machine guns and also had fire from the front, he would surely be safer after he succeeded in taking the machine gun to one side. He would prefer to take a chance on that rather than choose certain death.

If a company of infantry advances toward the enemy— the impulse may be by command or example—the momentum is sustained by mass psychology, by the fact that there are a number of men together, all intent upon doing the same thing. One man rises suddenly, runs forward and flops himself to the ground—the others follow, singly or in groups, some never rise, but a number will advance. The thing works the other way around, too. One man starts to run home, a few follow and the whole remainder may retreat. There may have been an act of reasoning first, convincing the man that the task to advance is hopeless. There may have been fear or other emotions. Mass psychology is a fickle thing.

What can we deduct from the above? Can we form a picture of what the behavior of man will be when he gets hit by a bullet? We can try.

As a basis, we shall have to take the more or less seasoned soldier. The very fresh or green ones don't know what danger, wounds, pain, hunger, death mean. Their education proceeds fast though. The man is not concerned so much with high patriotic ideas as with his own life. He knows not whether he will be alive tomorrow—but he *hopes* to be. The worst that he expects to happen to him, is some wound which will send him to a hospital, not so severe, mind you, as to cripple him. Well, at a certain time tonight there's going to be an attack by his outfit. He fidgets around, not showing it too much—but the time gets nearer—finally the command to "Go over"! Over they go! Forward—down—up—forward—Zing!—The man is hit! Instinctively he drops to the ground—Filled with wild panic—He is ignorant as yet of the extent of his wound—Everything seems magnified with the shock that he "got his." Will he fight on when he is even slightly wounded by a fast, small calibre "humane" bullet? Don't make me laugh. He has other things on his mind. He knows about "loss of blood," about "gangrene," about "cauterization," about "rest and care"—Through reason, he knows that "life" is the most precious thing to him, he knows that "aggrevation" through further exertion will threaten to sap his life or will cripple him. He wants to save what's left of him. He doesn't want to bleed to death. He doesn't want to die. The affairs around him—the affairs of a Nation or the World—have lost their importance—they are overshadowed by the tragedy that has befallen him—He is "hors de combat"—definitely! He will crawl away from further danger which is all around him—back to the lines—back to where there are doctors and help and rest. Is it necessary to "tear" him apart?—To cripple him beyond repair, with cunningly

devised ballistics? So long as he is put "hors de combat?"
No! It is *not* necessary! Because, I repeat, man has
reason! He would consider himself a damn fool if he
were not to try to save what's left of him. In our example, he has received a non-vital, not too serious wound,
let's say a flesh wound through his thigh. If the wound
is more serious, but not vital, say that he can't walk back,
he will stay where he is. In either case, he is "hors de combat," there being no vital shot. The chances are one in
ten thousand that a man will *not* act the way I described.
From this premise we can go on and see what sectional
density, penetration, etc. may be required of a bullet—It
makes one sick to hear the bolony about the slow ball of
.45 calibre and its "killing" power. When the big wags
at the Hague Conference, before the war, talked of a
"humane" bullet, they condemned the expanding dum-
dum bullet. If I remember rightly, a bullet which the
Russians had then, was condemned, because its shortness
or some other thing caused it to tumble too easily, thus
tearing too much meat. I will not swear to that. I am
merely arguing for the "humane" bullet (although that
name in itself is a travesty). By that I mean a bullet
which travels cleanly through tissue and bone and doesn't
expand too much. If a good shooter behind the gun
makes a connection with a vital spot, it's too bad, the case
is over. If, however, the victim is hit in a non-vital spot,
he may recover and not stay a cripple for life. This principle should also be applied to animal game with the modi-
fication that, if we are not sure of hitting a vital spot, we
don't shoot. In war times, alas, we have no choice.

And all you old crummies who wag about a .38 Automatic bullet having less shocking power, less killing power
than the .45, you've never seen actual warfare and never
will if you can help it. Get your bed-pans out and warm
your feet, damn your meddling souls.

ALLEGRETTO

A tale of the infant that got into a rut—although its start in life was ambitious enough—A matter of too many In-laws. After we slashed our path through the jungle of junk and through the maze of the vines of tradition, we hope that we laid bare the essential. Out of a legion of good and bad models, we selected a few with merit—But, although we found much to criticize, we leave the scene with the feeling that things are going to hum— Fertile minds will start to mull and probe and experiment —And we are filled with expectant hope.

The Automatic, mechanically and ballistically perfected, appears within our vision, a beautiful, sleek tool withal powerful and accurate and dependable. A gun of effective calibre yet permitting practice with the economical .22 L. R. cartridge through the aid of a clever conversion assembly.

Modern—in step with the times! The tool with which to train men. Doesn't one read of enormous sums being appropriated for armaments, all the world over? These are troublous times and, indeed, remote seem the chances for eternal peace. We hear of big battleships, of fortifications, of artillery, of tanks—But, the essence of it all is "MARKSMANSHIP." Take that away and the armaments defeat their own ends. The nation which is not expert in marksmanship, is just supporting war-material-makers, is spending its appropriations foolishly. What

better tool could there be for the acquisition of marksmanship than the modern, easyshooting Automatic? Let a
man be expert with an Automatic and he will fit into most
branches of the Military, without much additional training.

A Nation of Handgun-Shooters is well prepared for
emergencies.

A Nation of Handgun-Sportsmen will have efficient
units to draw upon. Are we not also safe in assuming
that such a Nation would, at the same time, be better
equipped to cope with crime? Crime which, we hear,
extorts incredible values yearly, materially and morally?

One should think that all this sounds logical, sane, good
horse-sense. Alas, our American system being infested,
sick, with crooked politics, our future hopes, our sportsmen
bend under the weight of Pistol Laws. The very thing
that Mephisto himself would choose if he had set out
to weaken us: He would let us spend fabulous sums for
armaments, but he would prevent us, by hook or crook,
from acquiring marksmanship, without which all the
equipment would be useless.

When will we wake up? Isn't all this gun legislation
so very obvious? Who are the devilish forces that work
the strings, that order the Legislator-puppets around? Is
there a Cotery of insidious moles that is mocking us?

Why don't we drag that swarthy mob out of it's lair?
Why don't we step on them? Are there not 125,000,000
sane people within our borders? Have all these then become so dumb that they even gloat over being so docile?

There is no chauvinistic tendency in our little Manual—
But, Hell, let's become alert! If we believe in preparad-
ness, if we agree to the vast expenditures for armaments,
nay, if we demand such armaments, then let us learn what
to do with them! That's common sense! Therefore, cast
a suspicious eye on all those shyster representatives that
put their pudgy fingers in Gun-Legislation! There will be
a foul odor somewhere!

Summing up the picture in perspective, we advocate:

(1) Preparedness
(2) Intelligent training (Based on pistol-mastery)
(3) Modernization of gun-legislation
(4) Careful choice of basic weapons
(5) Intense laboration in the field of ballistics as it applies to the Automatic
(6) Making the Individual "automatic-conscious"

The cycle, when enumerating the six points backwards, will be complete. From the individual marksman to preparedness. If preparedness is the best remedy against war, is then our plea for it in any way chauvinistic, aggressive? The sooner we drop the mantle of indifference, the better it will be for humanity in general.

Taken independently, our handgun-sport affords us untold pleasure, recreation in peaceful years, makes us renew sane patriotism and furnishes a wider and more tolerant outlook on life in general. We, of the happy Clan: We welcome you!

FINALE

We have reached the back-cover—Are we appeased? Heck no!

How can we be, in this era of transition?

We are acutely conscious of the fact that, if we want our share in the matter of progress, we must drop our indifference and *demand* things, *do* things—get active!

We learn from others. There was a period of utter stagnation in the Rifle-Shooting game, prior to 1920. Up to that time, the shooters used whatever material the factories were pleased to put on the market. With much grumbling, yet loyally, the rifle-shooters plodded along until some impatient ingrates had the audacity to think for themselves. These renegades went to their gunsmiths and, shyly at first, hatched improvements—Their experience told them that they should have better stocks, better sights, better actions, better ballistics. True pioneers that they were, they refused to continue their former loyalty to the staid fossils that, their betters told them, were the ultimate and would ever be.

Soon, performances improved, as they could not otherwise, and the independents ventured further—They had tasted blood!

Others followed—and, in the course of a few years, matters stood reversed. The Die-hards began to hide their "old trusties" behind their backs—Everybody that amounted to something had custom-built guns that fitted him and with which he could really do something!

The makers viewed with alarm this revolt against sacred, if somewhat mossy, tradition and, relunctantly at first, then later quite enthusiastically (When sales improved over night), they adjusted themselves to the new trend. With the result that what they offer today is greatly improved and modern—And the shooters' ideas carry now quite some weight!

Do you get the picture?

We, with our Automatic Handguns, stand today where the rifle-shooters started off almost a generation ago!

Today, we must meekly take what the High Lords dictate we should have.

My friends! If we shooters want better hand-guns, we have to take the initiative. Are we not just as intelligent as the riflemen years ago? Is not our number quite imposing?

That is the real purpose behind this Manual:

We want the shooters to realize that better guns *can* be made.

We want to find out what we *want* to make the guns better.

We want to fill you with impatience and eager anticipation!

Dammit! If better guns are a possibility, then we *want* better guns—and, we want them now!

Things will have to move! It's about time!

To get the full benefit out of this Manual, you will have to consult *Sixguns and Bullseyes,* somehow. This present book is only a sequence to *Sixguns and Bullseyes,* as you can readily see. Topics like *Technique* have just been touched—Others, like *Time and Rapid-Firing—Competition—Sights—Handles* and others have been left out here —The reason is the very back-cover that stares us in the face. But, I hope that your outlook on handguns has been widened now and that your attitude toward the Automatic has received a healthy impulse. I enjoyed, hugely, the many comments on *Sixguns and Bullseyes* with which many reader-friends bombarded me—From some of them I learned a whole lot and I am a nut about hearing other people's views—Have no hesitation, therefore, to unburden yourself. Where possible, I shall be glad to answer— After all, we want to see more and better Automatics in coming matches.

We want to put the Automatic over, by excelling the Revolver scores.

It *can* be done and it *will* be done if, all of us, pull together!

In the very near future—(Alas, the printer is stamping his foot——)

All right, fellows: Let's go!

Here's to the AUTOMATIC!

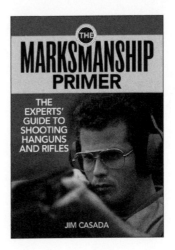

Shoot
Your Guide to Shooting and Competition
by Julie Golob

Whether you're a firearms enthusiast, an experienced shooter, or someone who has never even held a gun, *Shoot: Your Guide to Shooting and Competition* will help you explore different types of firearms, understand crucial safety rules, and learn fundamental shooting skills. This book provides an introduction to a wide variety of shooting sports through detailed descriptions that relate each type of competition to everyday activities and interests. High-quality photography from actual competitions and step-by-step instructional images augment the clearly written descriptions of both basic and advanced shooting skills.

Throughout the book, Julie shares beneficial tips, explains sport-specific lingo, and stresses vital safety concerns. Going beyond just a skill-building manual for those new to firearms and shooting, *Shoot* addresses competition stress, goal setting, logging, and beneficial practice techniques to help all shooters, from novices to champions, excel and take their skills to the next level.

$16.95 Paperback

Shooter's Bible Guide to Firearms Assembly, Disassembly, and Cleaning

by Robert A. Sadowski

Shooter's Bible, the most trusted source on firearms, is here to bring you a new guide with expert knowledge and advice on gun care. Double-page spreads filled with photos and illustrations provide manufacturer specifications on each featured model and guide you through disassembly and assembly for rifles, shotguns, handguns, and muzzleloaders. Step-by-step instructions for cleaning help you to care for your firearms safely. Never have a doubt about proper gun maintenance when you own *Shooter's Bible Guide to Firearms Assembly, Disassembly, and Cleaning*, a great companion to the original *Shooter's Bible*.

Along with assembly, disassembly, and cleaning instructions, each featured firearm is accompanied by a brief description and list of important specs, including manufacturer, model, similar models, action, calibers/gauge, capacity, overall length, and weight. With these helpful gun maintenance tips, up-to-date specifications, detailed exploded view line drawings, and multiple photographs for each firearm, *Shooter's Bible Guide to Firearms Assembly, Disassembly, and Cleaning* is a great resource for all firearm owners.

$19.95 Paperback